The Music Lover's Literary Companion

The Music Lover's Literary Companion

compiled by
Dannie and Joan Abse

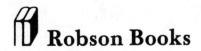 Robson Books

**FIRST PUBLISHED IN GREAT BRITAIN IN 1988
BY ROBSON BOOKS LTD, BOLSOVER HOUSE,
5-6 CLIPSTONE STREET, LONDON W1P 7EB.
THIS ROBSON PAPERBACK EDITION FIRST
PUBLISHED 1990**

This collection copyright © 1988 Dannie and Joan Abse

British Library Cataloguing in Publication Data

The music lover's literary companion.
  1. Literature. Special subjects. Music – anthologies
  I. Abse, Dannie *1923*–   II. Abse, Joan *1926*–
  808.80357

  ISBN 0 86051 525 7 HB
  ISBN 0 86051 654 7 PB

Printed in Finland

For Milein Cosman and in memory of Hans Keller

Contents

Introduction

Many of the world's most revered writers and thinkers have borne witness to their experience of music and attempted to define its power. Some would claim, rhetorically, that it reaches the harbour of the soul as naturally as rivers flow into the sea and the stars wheel about the poles of heaven, referring, of course, to music as majestic, say, as Bach's St Matthew Passion or his B Minor Mass rather than to 'Three Blind Mice' or 'I'm Dreaming of a White Christmas'.

John Milton, in his thoughts about music, touched on the notion that in a true dialogue with God we would speak with the tongues of music as perhaps we once did when first the morning stars sang together over Eden, before the banishment of Adam and Eve. Like others before him, he was willing to believe music to be the language of our lost Paradise and of any Paradise possibly to come. That human beings have a proclivity to conceive of music as possessing a celestial origin can perhaps be illustrated by a charming anecdote related by Leigh Hunt in his *Autobiography:* 'I have heard that when Dr Franklin invented the Harmonica he concealed it from his wife till the instrument was fit to play; and then woke her one night, when she took it for the music of the angels.'

Some writers have tried to define music. Rilke called it 'the breathing of statues'; George Bernard Shaw, 'the brandy of the damned' – echoing the Talmud where we can learn how Solomon, the wisest of men, was misled into worshipping idols by the music of a thousand instruments brought to him by the daughters of Pharaoh. While music makes one man prance before idols, another caper nimbly in a lady's chamber to the lascivious pleasing of a lute (or nowadays to an electronic blare), and yet another to bear arms to the accompaniment of inflaming drum, bagpipe and trumpet, most are soothed by it, uplifted by music's more chaste beneficence. Indeed, even in this transistor age, despite ubiquitous Muzak, it is still perhaps held to be a kind of holy anodyne as it was once when David played on his harp for the pathologically depressed King Saul. The Greeks, too, considered music to be a spiritual unguent. Pythagoras was but one who believed in 'musical medicine'. Iamblichus writing his *Life of Pythagoras*, in the fourth century A.D., tells us of a lovesick youth of Taurominium, insane with jealousy and about to burn down his rival's house. Pythagoras apparently happened to be star-gazing when he was informed of the impending tragic conflagration. At once he ordered a flute player to sound a Phrygian melody with a spondaic rhythm. This, Iamblichus relates, restored the raving young man to quietude and sanity.

Is it any wonder then that poets have paid homage over and over again to the patron saint of music?

> Blessed Cecilia, appear in visions
> To all musicians, appear and inspire:
> Translated Daughter, come down and startle
> Composing mortals with immortal fire

wrote W.H.Auden. Coleridge more drily remarked that: 'St Nepomuc was installed the guardian of bridges, because he had fallen over one, and sunk out of sight. Thus, too, St Cecilia is said to have been first propitiated by musicians, because, having failed in her attempts, she had taken a dislike to the art and all its successful professors.'

Many are those who have expressed similar negative opinions without, however, questioning St Cecilia's credentials. Segovia groaned: 'There are two million guitar students in Japan alone'; Max Beerbohm, more cheerfully, that 'Wagner has done undeniable good in humbling the singers.' And that notable antagonist of musical instruments, Ambrose Gwinett Bierce, has opined that there are two instruments worse than a clarinet – two clarinets; that a bassoon is a brazen instrument into which a fool blows out his brains; that an accordion is an instrument in harmony with the sentiments of an assassin; that a fiddle's music is simply the friction of a horse's tail on the entrails of a cat.

Music has its undeniable potency even to those of us who are not musically literate. It can exert its malice and its benediction when it reminds us of things past, inducing feelings of regret and loss. Sören Kierkegaard confessed: 'In Stralsund I almost went mad hearing a young girl playing the pianoforte, among other things Weber's last waltz over and over again. The last time I was in Berlin it was the first piece I heard in the Thiergarten, played by a blind man on the harp. It seems as though everything was intended to remind me of the past.'

How memorable is that story of a Chinese general defending a city long besieged by the Mongols and who, no food left, climbed desperately on to the battlements one moonlit night. The Mongols were all encamped around the city. The general could see them from the high walls. There was silence. There were the tents, above them the moon and stars flung high, and the general played on his pipe, played the most lonely, the most forlorn and desolate melodies of the steppes. The enemy soldiers heard the music and were moved. By dawn they had become utterly homesick and departed.

Given the variety and richness of available texts, especially from the last two centuries, it is perhaps surprising that there have been relatively few significant compilations of creative prose and attention-commanding poems about music. Of course there are notable novels about music and musicians, among them *Gambara* by Balzac, *Jean Christophe* by Romain Rolland and *Dr Faustus* by Thomas Mann, but we have been unable to make satisfactory excerpts from them as we have done from a few others. Short stories, of course, as well as autobiographical comments, are another matter.

Jacques Barzun edited one substantial anthology of literature about music in 1952 but excluded poetry altogether, justifying this omission by declaring that the eulogies of poets about music seemed lame in comparison with prose pieces! He wrote: 'It would be easy to fill several volumes with verses in praise of music but barring a few brief lines they would, if put side by side with the right piece of prose, fail to carry conviction.' We trust that this compilation devastatingly disproves Mr Barzun's pronouncement about poetry concerning music though not about prose. Poets have written serious and enjoyable poems expressing their experience of music with increasing frequency this century as well as lighter verses, witty and pointed. Besides, there is no competition between prose and poetry. We hope all the pieces here, whatever their form and prosodic strategy, however ordered, will touch the reader into welcome acknowledgements as music itself can do to attentive auditors.

The Nature of Music

William Shakespeare

From *The Merchant of Venice*

> For do but note a wild and wanton herd,
> Or race of youthful and unhandled colts,
> Fetching mad bounds, bellowing and neighing loud,
> Which is the hot condition of their blood;
> If they but hear perchance a trumpet sound,
> Or any air of music touch their ears,
> You shall perceive them make a mutual stand,
> Their savage eyes turn'd to a modest gaze
> By the sweet power of music: therefore the poet
> Did feign that Orpheus drew trees, stones, and floods;
> Since nought so stockish, hard, and full of rage,
> But music for the time doth change his nature.
> The man that hath no music in himself,
> Nor is not mov'd with concord of sweet sounds,
> Is fit for treasons, stratagems, and spoils;
> The motions of his spirit are dull as night,
> And his affections dark as Erebus:
> Let no such man be trusted. Mark the music.

Rainer Maria Rilke

To Music

Music. Breathing of statues, perhaps.
Stillness in pictures. You language
where language ends. You time
poised to soar in the direction
of ineffable vanishings.

Feelings for what? Oh, you transformation
of feelings into audible...landscape!
You stranger! Music! Space that's outgrown us,
soul-space. Inscape, that transcending our limits,
surges away beyond us –
holiest parting –
where what is within surrounds us
as practised horizon, as other
side of the air,
pure,
gigantic,
no longer lived in.

Adapted by Elwyn Jones

John Milton

At a Solemn Musick

Blest pair of Syrens, pledges of Heaven's joy
Sphere-born harmonious sisters, Voice and Verse,
Wed your divine sounds, and mix'd power employ
Dead things with inbreath'd sense able to pierce;
And to our high-rais'd phantasy present
That undisturbed song of pure concent,
Aye sung before the sapphire-colour'd throne
To Him that sits thereon,
With saintly shout, and solemn jubilee;
Where the bright Seraphim, in burning row,
Their loud up-lifted angel trumpets blow;
And the Cherubick host, in thousand quires,
Touch their immortal harps of golden wires,
With those just Spirits that wear victorious palms,
Hymns devout and holy psalms
Singing everlastingly:
That we on earth, with undiscording voice,
May rightly answer that melodious noise;
As once we did, till disproportion'd sin
Jarr'd against Nature's chime, and with harsh din
Broke the fair musick that all creatures made
To their great Lord, whose love their motion sway'd
In perfect diapason, whilst they stood
In first obedience, and their state of good.
O may we soon again renew that song,
And keep in tune with Heaven, till God ere long
To his celestial consort us unite,
To live with Him, and sing in endless morn of light!

Peter Porter

From *Three Poems for Music*

Though this is not in Hesiod,
Music was stolen from a God:

Not fire but notes the primal giver
Paid for with helpings of his liver

And virtuosi of the earth
Outsang the Gods who gave them birth.

When Orpheus plays we meet Apollo,
When there's theology to swallow

We set it to music, our greatest art,
One that's both intellect and heart,

There war and peace alike depict us
(Drums and trumpets in the Benedictus) –

It sang beneath the Grecian boat,
It kept Pythagoras afloat,

It suffered poets, critics, chat
And will no doubt survive Darmstadt;

This brandy of the damned of course
To some is just a bottled sauce,

Its treasons, spoils and stratagems
Aleatory as women's hems

Yet beauty who indulged the swan
At death completes her with a song

And Paradise till we are there
Is in these measured lengths of air.

Wallace Stevens

Mozart, 1935

Poet, be seated at the piano.
Play the present, its hoo-hoo-hoo,
Its shoo-shoo-shoo, its ric-a-nic,
Its envious cachinnation.

If they throw stones upon the roof
While you practise arpeggios,
It is because they carry down the stairs
A body in rags.
Be seated at the piano.

That lucid souvenir of the past,
The divertimento;
That airy dream of the future,
The unclouded concerto ...
The snow is falling.
Strike the piercing chord.

Be thou the voice,
Not you. Be thou, be thou
The voice of angry fear,
The voice of this besieging pain.

Be thou that wintry sound
As of the great wind howling,
By which sorrow is released,
Dismissed, absolved
In a starry placating.

We may return to Mozart.
He was young, and we, we are old.
The snow is falling
And the streets are full of cries.
Be seated, thou.

Speaking Personally

George Bernard Shaw

How I Became a Music Critic

From *London Music in 1888-89 as heard by Corno di Bassetto*

When my maiden novel, called Immaturity, was printed fifty years after it was written, I prefaced it with some account of the unhappy-go-lucky way in which I was brought up, ending with the nine years of shabby genteel destitution during which my attempts to gain a footing in literature were a complete and apparently hopeless failure.

I was rescued from this condition by William Archer, who transferred some of his book reviewing work to me, and pushed me into a post as picture critic which had been pushed on him, and for which he considered himself unqualified, as in fact he was. So, as reviewer for the old Pall Mall Gazette and picture critic for Edmund Yates's then fashionable weekly, The World, I carried on until I found an opening which I can explain only by describing the musical side of my childhood, to which I made only a passing allusion in my Immaturity preface, but which was of cardinal importance in my education.

In 1888, I being then 32 and already a noted critic and political agitator, the Star newspaper was founded under the editorship of the late T. P. O'Connor (nicknamed Tay Pay by Yates), who had for his very much more competent assistant the late H. W. Massingham. Tay Pay survived until 1936; but his mind never advanced beyond the year 1865, though his Fenian sympathies and his hearty detestation of the English nation disguised that defect from him. Massingham induced him to invite me to join the political staff of his paper; but as I had already, fourteen years before Lenin, read Karl Marx, and was preaching Socialism at every street corner or other available forum in London and the provinces, the effect of my articles on Tay Pay may be imagined. He refused to print them, and told me that, man alive, it would be five hundred years before such stuff would become practical political journalism. He was too goodnatured to sack me; and I did not want to throw away my job; so I got him out of his difficulty by asking him to let me have two columns a week for a feuilleton on music. He was glad to get rid of my politics on these terms; but he stipulated that – musical criticism being known to him only as unreadable and unintelligible jargon – I should, for God's sake, not write about Bach in B Minor. I was quite alive to that danger: in fact I had made my proposal because I believed I could make musical criticism readable even by the deaf. Besides, my terms were moderate: two guineas a week.

I was strong on the need for signed criticism written in the first person instead of the journalistic 'we'; but as I then had no name worth signing, and G. B. S. meant nothing to the public, I had to invent a fantastic personality with something like a foreign title. I thought of Count di Luna (a character in Verdi's Trovatore), but finally changed it for Corno di Bassetto, as it sounded like a foreign title, and nobody knew what a corno di bassetto was.

As a matter of fact the corno di bassetto is not a foreigner with a title but a musical instrument called in English the basset horn. It is a wretched instrument, now completely snuffed out for general use by the bass clarinet. It would be forgotten and unplayed if it were not that Mozart had scored for it in his Requiem, evidently because its peculiar watery melancholy, and the total absence of any richness or passion in its tone, is just the thing for a funeral. Mendelssohn wrote some chamber music for it, presumably to oblige somebody who played it; and it is kept alive by these works and by our Mr Whall. If I had ever heard a note of it in 1888 I should not have selected it for a character which I intended to be sparkling. The devil himself could not make a basset horn sparkle.

For two years I sparkled every week in The Star under this ridiculous name, and in a manner so absolutely unlike the conventional musical criticism of the time that all the journalists believed that the affair was a huge joke, the point of which was that I knew nothing whatever about music. How it had come about that I was one of the few critics of that time who really knew their business I can explain only by picking up the thread of autobiography which I dropped in my scrappy prefix to Immaturity. For the sake of those who have not read the Immaturity preface, or have forgotten it, I shall have to repeat here some of my father's history, but only so far as is necessary to explain the situation of my mother . . .

My father was past forty, and no doubt had sanguine illusions as to the future of his newly acquired business when he fell in love with my mother and was emboldened by her expectations and his business hopes to propose to her just at the moment when marriage seemed her only way of escape from an angry father and a stepmother. Immediately all her relatives, who had tolerated this middle-aged gentleman as a perfectly safe acquaintance with an agreeable vein of humor, denounced him as a notorious drunkard. My mother, suspicious of this sudden change of front, put the question directly to my father. His eloquence and sincerity convinced her that he was, as he claimed to be, and as he was in principle, a bigoted teetotaller. She married him; and her disappointed and infuriated aunt disinherited her, not foreseeing that the consequences of the marriage would include so remarkable a phenomenon as myself.

When my mother was disillusioned, and found out what living on a few hundreds a year with three children meant, even in a country where a general servant could be obtained for eight pounds a year, her condition must have been about as unhappy and her prospects as apparently hopeless as her aunt could have desired even in her most vindictive moments.

But there was one trump in her hand. She was fond of music, and had a mezzo-soprano voice of remarkable purity of tone. In the next street to ours, Harrington-street, where the houses were bigger and more fashionable than in our little by-street, there was a teacher of singing, lamed by an accident in childhood which had left one of his legs shorter than the other, but a man of mesmeric vitality and force. He was a bachelor living with his brother, whom he supported and adored, and a terrible old woman who was his servant of all work. His name was George John Vandeleur Lee, known in Dublin as Mr G. J. Lee. Singing lessons were cheap in Dublin; and my mother went to Lee to learn how to sing properly. He trained her voice to such purpose that she became indispensable to him as an amateur *prima donna*. For he was a most magnetic conductor and an indefatigable organizer of concerts, and later on of operas, with such amateur talent, vocal and orchestral, as he could discover and train in Dublin, which, as far as public professional music was concerned, was, outside the churches, practically a vacuum.

Lee soon found his way into our house, first by giving my mother lessons there, and then by using our drawing room for rehearsals. I can only guess that the inadequacies of old Ellen in the Harrington-street house, and perhaps the incompatibilities of the brother, outweighed the comparative smallness of our house in Synge-street. My mother soon became not only *prima donna* and chorus leader but general musical factotum in the whirlpool of Lee's activity. Her grounding in Logier's Thoroughbass enabled her to take boundless liberties with composers. When authentic band parts were missing she thought nothing of making up an orchestral accompaniment of her own from the pianoforte score. Lee, as far as I know, had never seen a full orchestral score in his life: he conducted from a first violin part or from the vocal score, and had not, I think, any decided notion of orchestration as an idiosyncratic and characteristic part of a composer's work. He had no scholarship according to modern ideas; but he could do what Wagner said is the whole duty of a conductor: he could give the right time to the band; and he could pull it out of its amateur difficulties in emergencies by sheer mesmerism. Though he could not, or at any rate within my hearing never did, sing a note, his taste in singing was classically perfect. In his search for the secret of *bel canto* he had gone to all the teachers within his reach. They told him that there was a voice in the head, a voice in the throat, and a voice in the chest. He dissected birds, and, with the connivance of medical friends, human subjects, in his search for these three organs. He then told the teachers authoritatively that the three voices were fabulous, and that the voice was produced by a single instrument called the larynx. They replied that musical art had nothing to do with anatomy, and that for a musician to practise dissection was unheard of and disgusting. But as, tested by results, their efforts to teach their pupils to screech like locomotive whistles not only outraged his ear but wrecked the voices and often the health of their victims, their practice was as unacceptable to him as their theory.

Thus Lee became the enemy of every teacher of singing in Dublin; and they reciprocated heartily. In this negative attitude he was left until, at the opera, he heard an Italian baritone named Badiali, who at the age of 80, when he first discovered these islands, had a perfectly preserved voice, and, to Lee's taste, a perfectly produced one. Lee, thanks to his dissections, listened with a clear knowledge of what a larynx is really like. The other vocal organs and their action were obvious and conscious. Guided by this knowledge, and by his fine ear, his fastidious taste, and his instinct, he found out what Badiali was doing when he was singing. The other teachers were interested in Badiali only because one of his accomplishments was to drink a glass of wine and sing a sustained note at the same time. Finally Lee equipped himself with a teaching method which became a religion for him: the only religion, I may add, he ever professed. And my mother, as his pupil, learnt and embraced this musical faith, and rejected all other creeds as uninteresting superstitions. And it did not fail her; for she lived to be Badiali's age and kept her voice without a scrape on it until the end.

I have to dwell on The Method, as we called it in the family, because my mother's association with Lee, and the *ménage à trois* in which it resulted, would be unpleasantly misunderstood without this clue to it. For after the death of Lee's brother, which affected him to the verge of suicide, we left our respective houses and went to live in the same house, number one Hatch-street, which was half in Lower Leeson-street. The arrangement was economical; for we could not afford to live in a fashionable house, and Lee could not afford to give lessons in an unfashionable one, though, being a bachelor, he needed only a music room and a bedroom. We also shared a cottage in Dalkey, high up on Torca Hill, with all Dublin Bay from Dalkey Island to Howth visible from the garden, and all Killiney Bay with the Wicklow mountains in the background from the hall door. Lee bought this cottage and presented it to my mother, though she never had any legal claim to it and did not benefit by its sale later on. It was not conveniently situated for rehearsals or lessons; but there were musical neighbors who allowed me to some extent to run in and out of their houses when there was music going on.

The *ménage à trois*, alternating between Hatch-st. and Dalkey, worked in its ramshackle way quite smoothly until I was fifteen or thereabouts, when Lee went to London and our family broke up into fragments that never got pieced together again.

At the end of my schooling I knew nothing of what the school professed to teach; but I was a highly educated boy all the same. I could sing and whistle from end to end leading works by Handel, Haydn, Mozart, Beethoven, Rossini, Bellini, Donizetti and Verdi. I was saturated with English literature, from Shakespear and Bunyan to Byron and Dickens. And I was so susceptible to natural beauty that, having had some glimpse of the Dalkey scenery on an excursion, I still remember the moment when my mother told me that we were going to live there as the happiest of my life.

And all this I owed to the meteoric impact of Lee, with his music, his method, his impetuous enterprise and his magnetism, upon the little Shaw household where a thoroughly disgusted and disillusioned woman was suffering from a hopelessly disappointing husband and three uninteresting children grown too old to be petted like the animals and birds she was so fond of, to say nothing of the humiliating inadequacy of my father's income. We never felt any affection for Lee; for he was too excessively unlike us, too completely a phenomenon, to rouse any primitive human feeling in us. When my mother introduced him to me, he played with me for the first and last time; but as his notion of play was to decorate my face with moustaches and whiskers in burnt cork in spite of the most furious resistance I could put up, our encounter was not a success; and the defensive attitude in which it left me lasted, though without the least bitterness, until the decay of his energies and the growth of mine put us on more than equal terms. He never read anything except Tyndall on Sound, which he kept in his bedroom for years. He complained that an edition of Shakespear which I lent him was incomplete because it did not contain The School for Scandal, which for some reason he wanted to read; and when I talked of Carlyle he understood me to mean the Viceroy of that name who had graciously attended his concerts in the Antient Concert Rooms. Although he supplanted my father as the dominant factor in the household, and appropriated all the activity and interest of my mother, he was so completely absorbed in his musical affairs that there was no friction and hardly any intimate personal contacts between the two men: certainly no unpleasantness. At first his ideas astonished us. He said that people should sleep with their windows open. The daring of this appealed to me; and I have done so ever since. He ate brown bread instead of white: a startling eccentricity. He had no faith in doctors, and when my mother had a serious illness took her case in hand unhesitatingly and at the end of a week or so gave my trembling father leave to call in a leading Dublin doctor, who simply said 'My work is done' and took his hat. As to the apothecary and his squills, he could not exist in Lee's atmosphere; and I was never attended by a doctor again until I caught the smallpox in the epidemic of 1881. He took no interest in pictures or in any art but his own; and even in music his interest was limited to vocal music: I did not know that such things as string quartets or symphonies existed until I began, at sixteen, to investigate music for myself. Beethoven's sonatas and the classical operatic overtures were all I knew of what Wagner called absolute music. I should be tempted to say that none of us knew of the existence of Bach were it not that my mother sang My Heart Ever Faithful, the banjo-like *obbligato* of which amused me very irreverently.

Lee was like all artists whose knowledge is solely a working knowledge: there were holes in his culture which I had to fill up for myself. Fortunately his richer pupils sometimes presented him with expensive illustrated books. He never opened them; but I did. He was so destitute of any literary bent that when he published a book entitled The Voice, it was written for him by a scamp of a derelict doctor whom he entertained for that purpose, just as in later years his prospectuses and press articles were written by me. He never visited the Dublin National Gallery, one of the finest collections of its size in Europe, with the usual full set of casts from what was called the antique, meaning ancient Greek sculpture. It was by prowling in this gallery that I learnt to recognize the work of the old masters at sight. I learnt French history from the novels of Dumas *père*, and English history from Shakespear and Walter Scott. Good boys were meanwhile learning lessons out of schoolbooks and receiving marks at examinations: a process which left them pious barbarians whilst I was acquiring an equipment which enabled me not only to pose as Corno di Bassetto when the chance arrived, but to add the criticism of pictures to the various strings I had to my bow as a feuilletonist.

Meanwhile nobody ever dreamt of teaching me anything. At fifteen, when the family broke up, I could neither play nor read a note of music. Whether you choose to put it that I was condemned to be a critic or saved from being an executant, the fact remains that when the house became musicless, I was forced to teach myself how to play written music on the piano from a book with a diagram of the keyboard in it or else be starved of music.

Not that I wanted to be a professional musician. My ambition was to be a great painter like Michael Angelo (one of my heroes); but my attempts to obtain instruction in his art at the School of Design presided over by the South Kensington Department of Science and Art only prevented me from learning anything except how to earn five shilling grants for the masters (payment by results) by filling up ridiculous examination papers in practical geometry and what they called freehand drawing.

With competent instruction I daresay I could have become a painter and draughtsman of sorts; but the School of Design convinced me that I was a hopeless failure in that direction on no better ground than that I found I could not draw like Michael Angelo or paint like Titian at the first attempt without knowing how. But teaching, of art and everything else, was and still is so little understood by our professional instructors (mostly themselves failures) that only the readymade geniuses make good; and even they are as often as not the worse for their academic contacts.

As an alternative to being a Michael Angelo I had dreams of being a Badiali. (Note, by the way, that of literature I had no dreams at all, any more than a duck has of swimming.) What that led to was not fully explained until Matthias Alexander, in search, like Lee, of a sound vocal method, invented his technique of self-control.

I had sung like a bird all through my childhood; but when my voice broke I at once fell into the error unmasked by Alexander of trying to gain my end before I had studied the means. In my attempts to reproduce the frenzies of the Count di Luna, the sardonic accents of Gounod's Mephistopheles, the noble charm of Don Giovanni, and the supernatural menace of the Commendatore, not to mention all the women's parts and the tenor parts as well (for all parts, high or low, male or female, had to be sung or shrieked or whistled or growled somehow) I thought of nothing but the dramatic characters; and in attacking them I set my jaws and my glottis as if I had to crack walnuts with them. I might have ruined my voice if I had not imitated good singers instead of bad ones; but even so the results were wretched. When I rejoined my mother in London and she found that I had taught myself to play accompaniments and to amuse myself with operas and oratorios as other youths read novels and smoke cigarets, she warned me that my voice would be spoiled if I went on like that. Thereupon I insisted on being shewn the proper way to sing. The instructive result was that when, following my mother's directions, I left my jaw completely loose, and my tongue flat instead of convulsively rolling it up; when I operated my diaphragm so as to breathe instead of 'blowing'; when I tried to round up my pharynx and soft palate and found it like trying to wag my ears, I found that for the first time in my life I could not produce an audible note. It seemed that I had no voice. But I believed in Lee's plan and knew that my own was wrong. I insisted on being taught how to use my voice as if I had one; and in the end the unused and involuntary pharyngeal muscles became active and voluntary, and I developed an uninteresting baritone voice of no exceptional range which I have ever since used for my private satisfaction and exercise without damaging either it or myself in the process.

Here I must digress for a moment to point a moral. Years after I learnt how to sing without spoiling my voice and wrecking my general health, a musician-reciter (Matthias Alexander aforesaid) found himself disabled by the complaint known as clergyman's sore throat. Having the true scientific spirit and industry, he set himself to discover what it was that he was really doing to disable himself in this fashion by his efforts to produce the opposite result. In the end he found this out, and a great deal more as well. He established not only the beginnings of a far reaching science of the apparently involuntary movements we call reflexes, but a technique of correction and self-control which forms a substantial addition to our very slender resources in personal education.

Meanwhile a Russian doctor named Pavlov devoted himself to the investigation of the same subject by practising the horrible voodoo into which professional medical research had lapsed in the XIX century. For quarter of a century he tormented and mutilated dogs most abominably, and finally wrote a ponderous treatise on reflexes in which he claimed to have established on a scientific basis the fact that a dog's mouth will water at the sound of a dinner bell when it is trained to associate that sound with a meal, and that dogs, if tormented, thwarted, baffled, and incommoded continuously, will suffer nervous breakdown and be miserably ruined for the rest of their lives. He was also able to describe what happens to a dog when half its brains are cut out.

I should add that there is no reason to suppose that Pavlov was by nature a bad man. He bore a strong external resemblance to myself, and was wellmeaning, intelligent, and devoted to science. It was his academic environment that corrupted, stultified, and sterilized him. If only he had been taught to sing by my mother no dog need ever have collapsed in terror at his approach; and he might have shared the laurels of Alexander.

And now I must return to my story. Lee's end was more tragic than Pavlov's. I do not know at what moment he began to deteriorate. He was a sober and moderate liver in all respects; and he was never ill until he treated himself to a tour in Italy and caught malaria there. He fought through it without a doctor on cold water, and returned apparently well; but whenever he worked too hard it came back and prostrated him for a day or two. Finally his ambition undid him. Dublin in those days seemed a hopeless place for an artist; for no success counted except a London success. The summit of a provincial conductor's destiny was to preside at a local music festival modeled on the Three Choirs or Handel Festivals. Lee declared that he would organize and conduct a Dublin Festival with his own chorus and with all the famous leading singers from the Italian opera in London. This he did in connexion with an Exhibition in Dublin. My mother, of course, led the chorus. At a rehearsal the contralto, Madame Demeric Lablache, took exception to something and refused to sing. Lee shrugged his shoulders and asked my mother to carry on, which she did to such purpose that Madame Lablache took care not to give her another such chance.

At the Festivals Lee reached the Dublin limit of eminence. Nothing remained but London. He was assured that London meant a very modest beginning all over again, and perhaps something of an established position after fifteen years or so. Lee said that he would take a house in Park Lane, then the most exclusive and expensive thoroughfare in the West End, sacred to peers and millionaires, and — stupendous on the scale of Irish finance — make his pupils pay him a guinea a lesson. And this he actually did with a success that held out quite brilliantly for several seasons and then destroyed him. For whereas he had succeeded in Dublin by the sheer superiority of his method and talent and character, training his pupils honestly for a couple of years to sing beautifully and classically, he found that the London ladies who took him up so gushingly would have none of his beauty and classicism, and would listen to nothing less than a promise to make them sing "like Patti" in twelve lessons. It was that or starve.

He submitted perforce; but he was no longer the same man, the man to whom all circumstances seemed to give way, and who made his own musical world and reigned in it. He had even to change his name and his aspect. G. J. Lee, with the black whiskers and the clean shaven resolute lip and chin, became Vandeleur Lee, whiskerless, but with a waxed and pointed moustache and an obsequious attitude. It suddenly became evident that he was an elderly man, and, to those who had known him in Dublin, a humbug. Performances of Marchetti's Ruy Blas with my sister as the Queen of Spain, and later on of Sullivan's Patience and scraps of Faust and Il Trovatore were achieved; but musical society in London at last got tired of the damaged Svengali who could manufacture Pattis for twelve guineas; and the guineas ceased to come in. Still, as there were no night clubs in those days, it was possible to let a house in Park Lane for the night to groups of merrymakers; and Lee was holding out there without pupils when he asked me to draft a circular for him announcing that he could cure clergyman's sore throat. He was still at Park Lane when he dropped dead in the act of undressing himself, dying as he had lived, without a doctor. The postmortem and inquest revealed the fact that his brain was diseased and had been so for a long time. I was glad to learn that his decay was pathological as well as ecological, and that the old efficient and honest Lee had been real after all. But I took to heart the lesson in the value on London fashionable successes. To this day I look to the provincial and the amateur for honesty and genuine fecundity in art.

Meanwhile, what had happened to the *ménage à trois*? and how did I turn up in Park Lane playing accompaniments and getting glimpses of that artstruck side of fashionable society which takes refuge in music from the routine of politics and sport which occupies the main Philistine body?

Well, when Lee got his foot in at a country house in Shropshire whither he had been invited to conduct some private performances, he sold the Dalkey cottage and concluded his tenancy of Hatch-street. This left us in a house which we could afford less than ever; for my father's moribund business was by now considerably deader than it had been at the date of my birth. My younger sister was dying of consumption caught from reckless contacts at a time when neither consumption nor pneumonia was regarded as catching. All that could be done was to recommend a change of climate. My elder sister had a beautiful voice. In the last of Lee's Dublin adventures in amateur opera she had appeared as Amina in Bellini's La Sonnambula, on which occasion the tenor lost his place and his head, and Lucy obligingly sang most of his part as well as her own. Unfortunately her musical endowment was so complete that it cost her no effort to sing or play anything she had once heard, or to read any music at sight. She simply could not associate the idea of real work with music; and as in any case she had never received any sort of training, her very facility prevented her from becoming a serious artist, though, as she could sing difficult music without breaking her voice, she got through a considerable share of public singing in her time.

Now neither my mother nor any of us knew how much more is needed for an opera singer than a voice and natural musicianship. It seemed to us that as, after a rehearsal or two, she could walk on to the stage, wave her arms about in the absurd manner then in vogue in opera, and sing not only her own part but everybody else's as well, she was quite qualified to take the place of Christine Nilsson or Adelina Patti if only she could get a proper introduction. And clearly Lee, now in the first flush of his success in Park Lane, would easily be able to secure this for her.

There was another resource. My now elderly mother believed that she could renounce her amateur status and make a living in London by teaching singing. Had she not the infallible Method to impart? So she realized a little of the scrap of settled property of which her long deceased aunt had not been able to deprive her; sold the Hatch-street furniture; settled my father and myself in comfortable lodgings at 61 Harcourt-st; and took my sisters to the Isle of Wight, where the younger one died. She then took a semi-detached villa in a *cul-de-sac* off the Fulham Road, and waited there for Lucy's plans and her own to materialize.

The result was almost a worse disillusion than her marriage. That had been cured by Lee's music: besides, my father had at last realized his dream of being a practising teetotaller, and was now as inoffensive an old gentleman as any elderly wife could desire. It was characteristic of the Shavian drink neurosis to vanish suddenly in this way. But that Lee should be unfaithful! unfaithful to The Method! that he, the one genuine teacher among so many quacks, should now stoop to outquack them all and become a moustachioed charlatan with all the virtue gone out of him: this was the end of all things; and she never forgave it. She was not unkind: she tolerated Lee the Charlatan as she had tolerated Shaw the dipsomaniac because, as I guess, her early motherless privation of affection and her many disappointments in other people had thrown her back on her own considerable internal resources and developed her self-sufficiency and power of solitude to an extent which kept her up under circumstances that would have crushed or embitttered any woman who was the least bit of a clinger. She dropped Lee very gently: at first he came and went at Victoria Grove, Fulham Road; and she went and came at 13 Park Lane, helping with the music there at his At Homes, and even singing the part of Donna Anna for him (elderly *prima donnas* were then tolerated as matters of course) at an amateur performance of Don Giovanni. But my sister, who had quarreled with him as a child when he tried to give her piano lessons, and had never liked him, could not bear him at all in his new phase, and, when she found that he could not really advance her prospects of becoming a *prima donna*, broke with him completely and made it difficult for him to continue his visits. When he died we had not seen him for some years; and my mother did not display the slightest emotion at the news. He had been dead for her ever since he had ceased to be an honest teacher of singing and a mesmeric conductor.

Her plans for herself came almost to nothing for several years. She found that Englishwomen do not wish to be made to sing beautifully and classically; they want to sing erotically; and this my mother thought not only horrible but unladylike. Her love songs were those of Virginia Gabriel and Arthur Sullivan, all about bereaved lovers and ending with a hope for reunion in the next world. She could sing with perfect purity of tone and touching expression

> Oh, Ruby, my darling, the small white hand
> Which gathered the harebell was never my own.

But if you had been able to anticipate the grand march of human progress and poetic feeling by fifty years, and asked her to sing

> You made me love you.
> I didnt want to do it.
> I didnt want to do it,

she would have asked a policeman to remove you to a third-class carriage.

Besides, though my mother was not consciously a snob, the divinity which hedged an Irish lady of her period was not acceptable to the British suburban parents, all snobs, who were within her reach. They liked to be treated with deference; and it never occurred to my mother that such people could entertain a pretension so monstrous in her case. Her practice with private pupils was negligible until she was asked to become musical instructress at the North London College. Her success was immediate; for not only did her classes leave the other schools nowhere musically, but the divinity aforesaid exactly suited her new *rôle* as schoolmistress. Other schools soon sought her services; and she remained in request until she insisted on retiring on the ground that her age made her public appearances ridiculous. By that time all the old money troubles were over and forgotten, as my financial position enabled me to make her perfectly comfortable in that respect.

And now, what about myself, the incipient Corno di Bassetto?

Well, when my mother sold the Hatch-street furniture, it never occurred to her to sell our piano, though I could not play it, nor could my father. We did not realize, nor did she, that she was never coming back, and that, except for a few days when my father, taking a little holiday for the first time in his life within my experience, came to see us in London, she would never meet him again. Family revolutions would seldom be faced if they did not present themselves at first as temporary makeshifts. Accordingly, having lived since my childhood in a house full of music, I suddenly found myself in a house where there was no music, and could be none unless I made it myself. I have recorded elsewhere how, having purchased one of Weale's Handbooks which contained a diagram of the keyboard and an explanation of musical notation, I began my self-tuition, not with Czerny's five finger exercises, but with the overture to Don Giovanni, thinking rightly that I had better start with something I knew well enough to hear whether my fingers were on the right notes or not. There were plenty of vocal scores of operas and oratorios in our lodging; and although I never acquired any technical skill as a pianist, and cannot to this day play a scale with any certainty of not foozling it, I acquired what I wanted: the power to take a vocal score and learn its contents as if I had heard it rehearsed by my mother and her colleagues. I could manage arrangements of orchestral music much better than piano music proper. At last I could play the old rum-tum accompaniments of those days well enough (knowing how they *should* be played) to be more agreeable to singers than many really competent pianists. I bought more scores, among them one of Lohengrin, through which I made the revolutionary discovery of Wagner. I bought arrangements of Beethoven's symphonies, and discovered the musical regions that lie outside opera and oratorio. Later on, I was forced to learn to play the classical symphonies and overtures in strict time by hammering the bass in piano duets with my sister in London. I played Bach's Inventions and his Art of Fugue. I studied academic textbooks, and actually worked out exercises in harmony and counterpoint under supervision by an organist friend named Crament, avoiding consecutive fifths and octaves, and having not the faintest notion of what the result would sound like. I read pseudo-scientific treatises about the roots of chords which candidates for the degree of Mus. Doc. at the universities had to swallow, and learnt that Stainer's commonsense views would get you plucked at Oxford, and Ouseley's pedantries at Cambridge. I read Mozart's Succinct Thoroughbass (a scrap of paper with some helpful tips on it which he scrawled for his pupil Sussmaier); and this, many years later, Edward Elgar told me was the only document in existence of the smallest use to a student composer. It was, I grieve to say, of no use to me; but then I was not a young composer. It ended in my knowing much more about music than any of the great composers, an easy achievement for any critic, however barren

Ralph Ellison
From *Living with Music*

In those days it was either live with music or die with noise, and we chose rather desperately to live. In the process our apartment – what with its booby-trappings of audio equipment, wires, discs and tapes – came to resemble the Collier mansion, but that was later. First there was the neighborhood, assorted drunks and a singer.

We were living at the time in a tiny ground-floor-rear apartment in which I was also trying to write. I say 'trying' advisedly. To our right, separated by a thin wall, was a small restaurant with a juke box the size of the Roxy. To our left, a night-employed swing enthusiast who took his lullaby music so loud that every morning promptly at nine Basie's brasses started blasting my typewriter off its stand. Our living room looked out across a small back yard to a rough stone wall to an apartment building which, towering above, caught every passing thoroughfare sound and rifled it straight down to me. There were also howling cats and barking dogs, none capable of music worth living with, so we'll pass them by . . .

At the top of our pyramid of noise there was a singer who lived directly above us; you might say we had a singer in our ceiling. Now, I had learned from the jazz musicians I had known as a boy in Oklahoma City something of the discipline and devotion to his art required of the artist. Hence I knew something of what the singer faced. These jazzmen, many of them world-famous, lived for and with music intensely. Their driving motivation was neither money nor fame, but the will to achieve the most eloquent expression of idea-emotions through the technical mastery of their instruments (which, incidentally, some of them wore as a priest wears the cross) and the give and take, the subtle rhythmical shaping and blending of idea, tone and imagination demanded of group improvisation. The delicate balance struck between strong individual personality and the group during those early jam sessions was a marvel of social organization. I had learned too that the end of all this discipline and technical mastery was the desire to express an affirmative way of life through its musical tradition and that this tradition insisted that each artist achieve his creativity within its frame. He must learn the best of the past, and add to it his personal vision. Life could be harsh, loud and wrong if it wished, but they lived it fully, and when they expressed their attitude toward the world it was with a fluid style that reduced the chaos of living to form.

The objectives of these jazzmen were not at all those of the singer on our ceiling, but though a purist committed to the mastery of the *bel canto* style, German *lieder*, modern French art songs and a few American slave songs sung as if *bel canto*, she was intensely devoted to her art. From morning to night she vocalized, regardless of the condition of her voice, the weather or my screaming nerves. There were times when her notes, sifting through her floor and my ceiling, bounding down the wall and ricocheting off the building in the rear, whistled like tenpenny nails, buzzed like a saw, wheezed like the asthma of a Hercules, trumpeted like an enraged African elephant – and the squeaky pedal of her piano rested plumb center above my typing chair. After a year of non-co-operation from the neighbor on my left I became desperate enough to cool down the hot blast of his phonograph by calling the cops, but the singer presented a serious ethical problem: Could I, an aspiring artist, complain against the hard work and devotion to craft of another aspiring artist?

Then there was my sense of guilt. Each time I prepared to shatter the ceiling in protest I was restrained by the knowledge that I, too, during my boyhood, had tried to master a musical instrument and to the great distress of my neighbors – perhaps even greater than that which I now suffered. For while our singer was concerned basically with a single tradition and style, I had been caught actively between two: that of the Negro folk music, both sacred and profane, slave song and jazz, and that of Western classical music. It was most confusing; the folk tradition demanded that I play what I heard and felt around me, while those who were seeking to teach the classical tradition in the schools insisted that I play strictly according to the book and express that which I was *supposed* to feel. This sometimes led to heated clashes of wills. Once during a third-grade music appreciation class a friend of mine insisted that it was a large green snake he saw swimming down a quiet brook instead of the snowy bird the teacher felt that Saint-Saëns' *Carnival of the Animals* should evoke. The rest of us sat there and lied like little black, brown and yellow Trojans about that swan, but our stalwart classmate held firm to his snake. In the end he got himself spanked and reduced the teacher to tears, but truth, reality and our environment were redeemed. For we were all familiar with snakes, while a swan was simply something the Ugly Duckling of the story grew up to be. Fortunately some of us grew up with genuine appreciation of classical music *despite* such teaching methods. But as an inspiring trumpeter I was to wallow in sin for years before being awakened to guilt by our singer.

Caught mid-rage between my two traditions, where one attitude often clashed with the other and one technique of playing was by the other opposed. I caused whole blocks of people to suffer.

Indeed, I terrorized a good part of an entire city section. During summer vacation I blew sustained tones out of the window for hours, usually starting – especially on Sunday mornings – before breakfast. I sputtered whole days through M. Arban's (he's the great authority on the instrument) double- and triple-tonguing exercises – with an effect like that of a jackass hiccupping off a big meal of briars. During school-term mornings I practiced a truly exhibitionist 'Reveille' before leaving for school, and in the evening I generously gave the ever-listening world a long, slow version of 'Taps,' ineptly played but throbbing with what I in my adolescent vagueness felt was a romantic sadness. For it was farewell to day and a love song to life and a peace-be-with-you to all the dead and dying.

On hot summer afternoons I tormented the ears of all not blessedly deaf with imitations of the latest hot solos of Hot Lips Paige (then a local hero), the leaping right hand of Earl 'Fatha' Hines, or the rowdy poetic flights of Louis Armstong. Naturally I rehearsed also such school-band standbys as the *Light Cavalry* Overture, Sousa's 'Stars and Stripes Forever', the *William Tell* Overture, and 'Tiger Rag'. (Not even an after-school job as office boy to a dentist could stop my efforts. Frequently, by way of encouraging my development in the proper cultural direction, the dentist asked me proudly to render Schubert's *Serenade* for some poor devil with his jaw propped open in the dental chair. When the drill got going, or the forceps bit deep, I blew real strong.)

Sometimes, inspired by the even then considerable virtuosity of the late Charlie Christian (who during our school days played marvelous riffs on a cigar box banjo), I'd give whole summer afternoons and the evening hours after heavy suppers of black-eyed peas and turnip greens, cracklin' bread and buttermilk, lemonade and sweet potato cobbler, to practicing hard-driving blues. Such food oversupplied me with bursting energy, and from listening to Ma Rainey, Ida Cox and Clara Smith, who made regular appearances in our town, I knew exactly how I wanted my horn to sound. But in the effort to make it do so (I was no embryo Joe Smith or Tricky Sam Nanton) I sustained the curses of both Christian and infidel – along with the encouragement of those more sympathetic citizens who understood the profound satisfaction to be found in expressing oneself in the blues.

Despite those who complained and cried to heaven for Gabriel to blow a chorus so heavenly sweet and so hellishly hot that I'd forever put down my horn, there were more tolerant ones who were willing to pay in present pain for future pride.

For who knew what skinny kid with his chops wrapped around a trumpet mouthpiece and a faraway look in his eyes might become the next Armstrong? Yes, and send you, at some big dance a few years hence, into an ecstasy of rhythm and memory and brassy affirmation of the goodness of being alive and part of the community? Someone had to; for it was part of the group tradition – though that was not how they said it.

'Let that boy blow,' they'd say to the protesting ones. 'He's got to talk baby talk on that thing before he can preach on it. Next thing you know he's liable to be up there with Duke Ellington. Sure, plenty Oklahoma boys are up there with the big bands. Son, let's hear you try those "Trouble in Mind Blues". Now try and make it sound like ole Ida Cox sings it.'

And I'd draw in my breath and do Miss Cox great violence.

Thus the crimes and aspirations of my youth. It had been years since I had played the trumpet or irritated a single ear with other than the spoken or written word, but as far as my singing neighbor was concerned I had to hold my peace. I was forced to listen, and in listening I soon became involved to the point of identification. If she sang badly I'd hear my own futility in the windy sound; if well, I'd stare at my typewriter and despair that I should ever make my prose so sing. She left me neither night nor day, this singer on our ceiling, and as my writing languished I became more and more upset. Thus one desperate morning I decided that since I seemed doomed to live within a shrieking chaos I might as well contribute my share; perhaps if I fought noise with noise I'd attain some small peace. Then a miracle: I turned on my radio (an old Philco AM set connected to a small Pilot FM tuner) and I heard the words

> Art thou troubled?
> Music will calm thee . . .

I stopped as though struck by the voice of an angel. It was Kathleen Ferrier, that loveliest of singers, giving voice to the aria from Handel's *Rodelinda*. The voice was so completely expressive of words and music that I accepted it without question – what lover of the vocal art could resist her?

Yet it was ironic, for after giving up my trumpet for the typewriter I had avoided too close a contact with the very art which she recommended as balm. For I had started music early and lived with it daily, and when I broke I tried to break clean. Now in this magical moment all the old love, the old fascination with music superbly rendered, flooded back. When she finished I realized that with such music in my own apartment, the chaotic sounds from without and above had sunk, if not into silence, then well below the level where they mattered. Here was a way out. If I was to live and write in that apartment, it would be only through the grace of music. I had tuned in a Ferrier recital, and when it ended I rushed out for several of her records, certain that now deliverance was mine.

But not yet. Between the hi-fi record and the ear, I learned there was a new electronic world. In that realization our apartment was well on its way towards becoming an audio booby trap. It was 1949 and I rushed to the Audio Fair. I have, I confess, as much gadget-resistance as the next American of my age, weight and slight income; but little did I dream of the test to which it would be put. I had hardly entered the fair before I heard David Sarser's and Mel Sprinkle's Musician's Amplifier, took a look at its schematic and, recalling a boyhood acquaintance with such matters, decided that I could build one. I did, several times before it measured within specifications. And still our system was lacking. Fortunately my wife shared my passion for music, so we went on to buy, piece by piece, a fine speaker system, a first-rate AM-FM tuner, a transcription turntable and a speaker cabinet. I built half a dozen or more preamplifiers and record compensators before finding a commercial one that satisfied my ear, and, finally, we acquired an arm, a magnetic cartridge and – glory of the house – a tape recorder. All this plunge into electronics, mind you, had as its simple end the enjoyment of recorded music as it was intended to be heard. I was obsessed with the idea of reproducing sound with such fidelity that even when using music as a defense behind which I could write, it would reach unconscious levels of the mind with the least distortion. And it didn't come easily. There were wires and pieces of equipment all over the tiny apartment (I became a compulsive experimenter) and it was worth your life to move about without first taking careful bearings. Once we were almost crushed in our sleep by the tape machine, for which there was space only on a shelf at the head of our bed. But it was worth it.

For now when we played a recording on our system even the drunks on the wall could recognize its quality. I'm ashamed to admit, however, that I did not always restrict its use to the demands of pleasure or defense. Indeed, with such marvels of science at my control I lost my humility. My ethical consideration for the singer up above shriveled like a plant in too much sunlight. For instead of soothing, music seemed to release the beast in me. Now when jarred from my writer's reveries by some especially enthusiastic flourish of our singer, I'd rush to my music system with blood in my eyes and burst a few decibels in her direction. If she defied me with a few more pounds of pressure against her diaphragm, then a war of decibels was declared.

If, let us say, she were singing *Depuis le Jour* from *Louise*, I'd put on a tape of Bidu Sayão performing the same aria, and let the rafters ring. If it was some song by Mahler, I'd match her spitefully with Marian Anderson or Kathleen Ferrier; if she offended with something from *Der Rosenkavalier*, I'd attack her flank with Lotte Lehmann. If she brought me up from my desk with art songs by Ravel or Rachmaninoff, I'd defend myself with Maggie Teyte or Jennie Tourel. If she polished a spiritual to a meaningless artiness I'd play Bessie Smith to remind her of the earth out of which we came. Once in a while I'd forget completely that I was supposed to be a gentleman and blast her with Strauss' *Zarathustra*, Bartok's *Concerto for Orchestra*, Ellington's 'Flaming Sword,' the famous crescendo from the *Pines of Rome*, or Satchmo scatting, 'I'll be Glad When You're Dead' (you rascal you!). Oh, I was living with music with a sweet vengeance.

One might think that all this would have made me her most hated enemy, but not at all. When I met her on the stoop a few weeks after my rebellion, expecting her fully to slap my face, she astonished me by complimenting our music system. She even questioned me concerning the artists I had used against her. After that, on days when the acoustics were right, she'd stop singing until the piece was finished and then applaud – not always, I guessed, without a justifiable touch of sarcasm. And although I was not getting on with my writing, the unfairness of this business bore in upon me. Aware that I could not have withstood a similar comparison with literary artists of like caliber, I grew remorseful. I also came to admire the singer's courage and control, for she was neither intimidated into silence nor goaded into undisciplined screaming; she persevered, she marked the phrasing of the great singers I sent her way, she improved her style.

Better still, she vocalized more softly, and I, in turn, used music less and less as a weapon and more for its magic with mood and memory. After a while a simple twirl of the volume control up a few decibels and down again would bring a live-and-let-live reduction of her volume. We have long since moved from that apartment and that most interesting neighborhood and now the floors and walls of our present apartment are adequately thick and there is even a closet large enough to house the audio system; the only wire visible is that leading from the closet to the corner speaker system. Still we are indebted to the singer and the old environment for forcing us to discover one of the most deeply satisfying aspects of our living. Perhaps the enjoyment of music is always suffused with past experience; for me, at least, this is true.

It seems a long way and a long time from the glorious days of Oklahoma jazz dances, the jam sessions at Halley Richardson's place on Deep Second, from the phonographs shouting the blues in the back alleys I knew as a delivery boy, and from the days when watermelon men with voices like mellow bugles shouted their wares in time with the rhythm of their horses' hoofs and farther still from the washerwomen singing slave songs as they stirred sooty tubs in sunny yards; and a long time, too, from those intense, conflicting days when the school music program of Oklahoma City was tuning our earthy young ears to classical accents – with music appreciation classes and free musical instruments and basic instruction for any child who cared to learn and uniforms for all who made the band. There was a mistaken notion on the part of the some of the teachers that classical music had nothing to do with the rhythms, relaxed or hectic, of daily living, and that one should crook the little finger when listening to such refined strains. And the blues and the spirituals – jazz – ? they would have destroyed them and scattered the pieces. Nevertheless, we learned some of it all, for in the United States when traditions are juxtaposed they tend, regardless of what we do to prevent it, irresistibly to merge. Thus musically at least each child in our town was an heir of all ages. One learns by moving from the familiar to the unfamiliar, and while it might sound incongruous at first, the step from the spirituality of the spirituals to that of the Beethoven of the symphonies or the Bach of the chorales is not as vast as it seems. Nor is the romanticism of a Brahms or Chopin completely unrelated to that of Louis Armstrong. Those who know their native culture and love it unchauvinistically are never lost when encountering the unfamiliar.

Living with music today we find Mozart and Ellington, Kirsten Flagstad and Chippie Hill, William L. Dawson and Carl Orff all forming part of our regular fare. For all exalt life in rhythm and melody; all add to its significance. Perhaps in the swift change of American society in which the meanings of one's origin are so quickly lost, one of the chief values of living with music lies in its power to give us an orientation in time. In doing so, it gives significance to all those indefinable aspects of experience which nevertheless help to make us what we are. In the swift whirl of time music is a constant, reminding us of what we were and of that toward which we aspired. Art thou troubled? Music will not only calm, it will ennoble thee.

Philip Larkin

From *The Pleasure of Jazz*

Few things have give me more pleasure in life than listening to jazz. I don't claim to be original in this: for the generations that came to adolescence between the wars jazz was that unique private excitement that youth seems to demand. In another age it might have been drink or drugs, religion or poetry. Whatever it happens to be, parents are suspicious of it and it has a bad reputation. I can tell adolescents don't feel like this about jazz today. For one thing, there are so many kinds that to talk about jazz as such would leave them puzzled as well as cold. Then again, it has become respectable: there are scholarly books on it, and adult education courses; it's the kind of interest that might well be mentioned on a university entrance form. And there's so much of it: records, wireless, television, all dispense it regularly. In the Thirties it was a fugitive minority interest, a record heard by chance from a foreign station, a chorus between two vocals, one man in an otherwise dull band. No one you knew liked it.

Nevertheless, it had established itself in my life several years before I consciously heard anything that could properly be called real jazz. This happened by way of the dance band, a now vanished phenomenon of twelve or fourteen players (usually identically uniformed) that was employed by a hotel or restaurant so that its patrons could dance. Their leaders were national celebrities, and had regular time on the radio: five-fifteen to six in the afternoon, for instance, and half-past ten to midnight. They were in almost no sense 'jazz' bands, but about every sixth piece they made a 'hot' number, in which the one or two men in the band who could play jazz would be heard. The classic 'hot number' was 'Tiger Rag': It had that kind of national-anthem status that 'When the Saints Go Marching In' had in the Fifties. Harry Roy had a band-within-a-band called the Tiger Ragamuffins. Nat Gonella's stage show had a toy tiger lying on the grand piano. Trombonists and tuba players became adept at producing the traditional tiger growl. I found these hot numbers so exciting that I would listen to hours of dance music in order to catch them when they came, in this way unconsciously learning many now forgotten lyrics. Those hot numbers! When the bands began to visit the local Hippodrome, I was able actually to see them played, the different sections suddenly rising to play four bars then sitting sharply down again; the shouts of 'Yeah man', the slapped bass, the drum breaks. It was the drummer I concentrated on, sitting as he did on a raised platform behind a battery of cowbells, temple blocks, cymbals, tom-toms and (usually) a Chinese gong, his drums picked out in flashing crimson or ultramarine brilliants. Even the resident Hippodrome drummer, a stolid man with horn-rimmed glasses, excited me enough for me to insist that our tickets were for his side of the house, so that I could see what he was doing. I wanted to be a drummer. My parents bought me an elementary drum kit and a set of tuition records by Max Abrams (that will date the anecdote), and I battered away contentedly, spending less time on the rudiments than in improvising an accompaniment to records.

I recount this simply to show that I was, in essence, hooked on jazz even before I heard any, and that what got me was the rhythm. That simple trick of the suspended beat, that had made the slaves shuffle in Congo Square on Saturday nights, was something that never palled. My transition to jazz was slow. The first jazz record by an *American* band I ever owned was Ray Noble's 'Tiger Rag' (it had a drum break). The second, rather surprisingly, was the Washboard Rhythm Kings' 'I'm Gonna Play Down by the Ohio'. The third was Louis Armstrong's 'Ain't Misbehavin'. After that they came thick and fast. Sitting with a friend in his bedroom that overlooked the family tennis-court, I watched leaves drift down through long Sunday afternoons as we took it in turn to wind the portable HMV, and those white and coloured Americans, Bubber Miley, Frank Teschmacher, J. C. Higginbotham, spoke immediately to our understanding. Their rips, slurs and distortions were something we understood perfectly. This was something we had found for ourselves, that wasn't taught at school (what a prequisite that is of nearly everything worthwhile!), and having found it, we made it bear all the enthusiasm usually directed at more established arts. There was nothing odd about this. It was happening to boys all over Europe and America. It just didn't get into the papers. It was years before I found any music as commanding as Jimmy Noone's 'The Blues Jumped a Rabbit,' Armstrong's 'Knocking' a Jug' or 'Squeeze Me', Bessie Smith's 'Backwater Blues', or the Chicago Rhythm Kings' 'I Found a New Baby'.

At Oxford my education grew. I met people who knew more about jazz than I did, and had more records, and who could even parallel my ecstasies with their own. The shops, too, were full of unreturned deletions, some of which have never been reissued to this day (the Sharkey Bonano Vocalions, for instance, or Louis Prima's' 'Chasin' Shadows'). I wish I could say that we could recite Black Swan matrixT numbers, or knew what was available on Argentine HMV, or played instruments and formed a band, or at least had enough musical knowledge to discuss the records we played intelligently. Only one of our circle could read music: he played the saxophone, but his taste didn't really accord with mine: he was too fond of phrases such as 'not musically interesting' or 'mere rhythmic excitement'. True, our response to Fats Waller's 'Dream Man' or Rosetta Howard's 'If You're a Viper' was a grinning, jigging wordlessness, interspersed with a grunt or two at specially good bits. For us, jazz became part of the private joke of existence, rather than a public expertise: expressions such as 'combined pimp and lover' and 'eating the cheaper cuts of pork' (both from a glossary on 'Yellow Dog Blues') flecked our conversations cryptically; for some reason, Kaminsky's plaintive little introduction to 'Home Cooking' became a common signal, and any of us entering the steam-filled college bath-house would whistle it to see if it was taken up from behind any of the bolted partition doors.

Felix Mendelssohn

Mendelssohn at Buckingham Palace

GRAHL SAYS THAT the only friendly English house, the house that is really comfortable and where one feels at ease, is Buckingham Palace. I know several others but on the whole I agree with him. Joking apart, Prince Albert asked me to go to him on Saturday at two o'clock so that I may try his organ. I found him all alone but as we were talking away the Queen came in wearing a house-dress. She said she was obliged to leave for Claremont in an hour. Catching sight of the music pages strewn all over the floor by the wind, 'Goodness,' she said, 'how dreadful' and began to pick up the music. Prince Albert helped and I was not idle. Then Prince Albert began to explain the organs stops to me and while he was doing it the Queen remarked that she would put everything straight again.

I begged the Prince to play something so that, I said, 'I might boast about it in Germany'. Thereupon he played me a chorale by heart, with pedals, so charmingly and clearly and correctly that many an organist could have learnt something and the Queen (who had finished her tidying up) sat beside him and listened very pleased. Then I had to play and I began my chorus from *St Paul*: 'How lovely are the messengers'. Before I got to the end of the first verse they both began to sing the chorus very well and all the time Prince Albert managed the stops for me so expertly – first a flute, then full at the forte, the whole register at D major and then making such an excellent diminuendo (all by heart) that I was heartily pleased. Then the Crown Prince of Gotha came in and there was more conversation, the Queen asking me whether I had composed any new songs. 'You should sing one to him,' said Prince Albert, and after a little begging she said she would try my 'Frühlingslied' in B flat if 'it is still here as all my music is packed up for Claremont'. Prince Albert went to look for it but came back saying that it had been packed. 'Perhaps it could be unpacked' said I. 'We must send for Lady——' (I didn't catch the name). The bell was rung and the servants went to look but came back embarrassed. Then the Queen went herself and while she was away Prince Albert said to me: 'She begs you to accept this present as a souvenir', and gave me a case with a beautiful ring on which was engraved 'V.R. 1842'.

When the Queen came back she said: 'Lady——has left and has taken all my things with her. It is most unseemly.' (I cannot tell you how that amused me.) I then begged that I might not be made to suffer for the accident and expressed the hope that she might sing another song. After consultation with her husband he said: 'She will sing something of Gluck's.' Then we five proceeded through the long corridors to the Queen's sitting-room where, next to the piano, stood an enormous fat rocking horse with two great birdcages and pictures on the walls; beautifully bound books were on the table and music on the piano. The Duchess of Kent came in too, and while they were all talking I rummaged a little amongst the music and found my first set of songs. So naturally I begged the Queen to choose one of those rather than a song of Gluck's to which she consented. What do you think she chose? 'Schöner und schöner' and sang it beautifully in tune, in strict time and with very nice expression. Only where, after 'Der Prosa Last und Mühe' (where it goes down to D and then comes up by semitones) she sang D sharp each time. The first and second time I gave her the D natural, but the last time (when it should be D sharp) she sang D natural. Except for this mistake it was very charming and on the long G at the end I have never heard better or purer tone from any amateur. I felt obliged to confess that the song had really been written by Fanny (I found it difficult; but pride must have a fall) and begged the Queen to sing one of my own. She said she would if I gave her some help and sang 'Lass dich nur nichts dauern' without a mistake and with charming feeling and expression. I thought that one must not pay too many compliments on an occasion of this sort so I merely thanked her very much, but she said: 'If only I hadn't been so nervous; I have really a long breath.' Then I praised her heartily and with a clear conscience as she had sung the last part with the long C so well, taking the C and the next three notes in the same breath as is seldom done.

After this Prince Albert sang 'Er ist ein Schnitter' and then he said I must play (improvise?) something before I went and gave me as themes the chorale which he had played on the organ and the song he had just sung. If everything had happened as usual I should have improvised very badly for that is what happens to me when I am specially anxious to do well. But I have rarely improvised as well. I was in the mood for it and played a long time and enjoyed myself. Of course I also brought in the songs the Queen had sung but it worked in so naturally that I would have been glad to go on for ever. They followed me with so much intelligence and attention that I felt more at ease than I ever did in improvising before an audience. Then the Queen said: 'I hope you will come and visit us soon again in England.' I took my leave and down below I saw the beautiful carriages waiting with their scarlet outriders and in a quarter of an hour the flag was lowered and the papers said 'Her Majesty left the Palace at 30 minutes past three'. It was a delightful day! I must add that I asked permission to dedicate my A minor symphony to the Queen, that having really been the reason of my visit to England and because the English name would be doubly suited to the Scottish piece. Just as the Queen was going to sing she said: 'The parrot must be taken out or he will scream louder than I can sing', upon which Prince Albert rang the bell and the Prince of Gotha said: 'I will carry him out,' but I said 'Allow me' and lifted the cage and carried it out to the astonished servants.

This long description will make Dirichlet put me down as an aristocrat but tell him that I swear I am more of a radical than ever.

Niccolò Paganini
Letter to the *Revue Musicale*

The French public has given me so many proofs of kindness and appreciation that I must conclude that my performances have not been below my standard. To entertain any doubt on the subject is impossible in view of the pains artists have taken to reproduce my features in the portraits with which the walls of Paris have been plastered. And it is not merely portraits; these gentlemen have gone much further. Yesterday walking along the Boulevard des Italiens, I saw in the window of a print shop a lithograph representing 'Paganini in prison'. 'Good,' I said, 'here are honest men trying to make capital out of the slander that has followed me for fifteen years.' I was examining with amusement the careful drawing of details the artist's fancy had suggested, when I noticed a group of people standing by and, no doubt, comparing the lithograph with the original, noticing how much I had changed since the days of my alleged detention. I realized then how gullible people were taken in, repaying the artist for his labour. It came into my head to suggest that, as the world must live, I should myself provide artists with anecdotes similar to that which is the subject of that jest. I beg you therefore to publish this letter in your *Revue Musicale*.

These gentlemen have shown me as a prisoner. They don't know why I was sent to prison. They know as little about it as I know myself or the men who started the story. Now there are many tales to provide artists with attractive subjects. It has been said, for instance, that finding a rival in my mistress's apartment I jealously stabbed him in the back when he could not defend himself. Others have asserted that jealousy led me to attack my mistress herself. They do not agree as to the manner in which I killed her. Some say I used a dagger; others assert that I poisoned her and laughed at her sufferings. They do as they please and there is no reason why artists should not enjoy the same freedom.

I now speak of what actually happened to me in Padua fifteen years ago. I had given a concert which had been fairly successful, and the day after I went to the ordinary. Arriving late, I was not noticed. One of the guests was discussing my playing; his neighbour, while praising my performance, added that there was really nothing unusual in the playing of Paganini since he had practised assiduously for eight years in a prison cell where his violin comforted his captivity. 'He had been condemned to a long term of imprisonment for the cowardly murder of one of the speaker's friends who had been Paganini's rival in love.' All the guests were horrified at the enormity of my crime. I then joined the conversation asking the speaker to tell me where it had happened. All eyes turned towards me; they were face to face with the principal actor of that tragic tale. The man who had told the story became terribly embarrassed. It was no longer a friend of his who had been murdered . . . he had heard people say . . . he had thought . . . he did not believe they could have lied . . . it was possible that he had made a mistake. That, sir, is the way in which the reputation of an artist is besmirched by lazy people who cannot believe that one can work as hard at liberty as under lock and key.

A still more ridiculous story, current in Vienna, tested the credulity of the enthusiast. I had just played my variations entitled *The Witches*, and had been applauded. A gentleman, described as pale, sad, with glowing eye, asserted that he found nothing remarkable in my playing since he had clearly seen the devil guiding the bow across the strings. A resemblance between myself and the demon proved a common bond; he was dressed in red, had a tail and horns. You will understand that after so detailed a description it was impossible to doubt the truth of the story and many were persuaded that they had learned the secret of my *tours de force*.

These rumours worried me for some time. I tried to show how absurd it all was. I pointed out that since I was fourteen years old I had been giving concerts and constantly before the public; that I had been orchestral leader and court musician for sixteen years, and that if I had been condemned to prison for killing a rival it must have happened when I was seven years old. In Vienna I appealed to the ambassador of my country to bear witness to my respectability, which he did, and for a time the slander was silenced. But something always remains, and I am not surprised to hear the old story again here. What can I do? I am resigned. But before closing this letter, I will add one more anecdote which has been the origin of these tales.

A violinist whose name ended in 'i' plotted with two villains to murder a village priest who was said to be rich. At the last moment one of the assassins lost courage and denounced his accomplices. They were arrested and condemned to twenty years' imprisonment. But General Menou, then Governor of Milan, set the violinist at liberty after he had served two years of his sentence. It is on this that my slanderers rely. The violinist's name ended in 'i' – hence it must have been Paganini; the victim, instead of a country priest, was either my mistress or my rival. I was imprisoned but, fortunately, my arms were free and I could use the bow. I thus discovered a new system. They insist in spite of all I can say. What can I do but accept the inevitable?

One hope remains, and it is that when I am dead my libellers will quit the game and those who make me pay so dearly for my success will leave my ashes in peace.

Hector Berlioz

Paganini and I

From *Mémoires*

And now for my opera and its deadly failure.

The strange career of Benvenuto Cellini had made such an impression on me that I stupidly concluded that it would be both dramatic and interesting to other people. I therefore asked Léon de Wailly and Auguste Barbier to write me a libretto on it. I must own that even our friends thought it had not the elements essential to success, but it pleased me, and even now I cannot see that it is inferior to many others that are played daily.

In order to please the management of the *Débats*, Duponchel, manager of the Opera – who looked upon me as a species of lunatic – read the libretto and agreed to take my opera. After which he went about saying that he was going to put it on, not on account of the music, which was ridiculous, but of the book, which was charming.

Never shall I forget the misery of those three months' rehearsals. The indifference of the actors, riding for a fall, Habeneck's bad temper, the vague rumours I had heard on all sides, all betrayed a general hostility against which I was powerless. It was worse when we came to the orchestra. The executants, seeing Habeneck's surly manner, were cold and reserved with me. Still they did their duty, which he did not. He never could manage the quick *tempo* of the saltarello; the dancers, unable to dance to his dragging measure, complained to me. I cried:

'Faster! Faster! Wake up!'

Habeneck, in a rage, hit his desk and broke his bow.

After several exhibitions of temper of this sort I said, calmly:

'My good sir, breaking fifty bows will not prevent your time being twice as slow as it ought to be. This is a saltarello.'

He turned to the orchestra.

'Since it is impossible to please M. Berlioz,' said he, 'we will stop for to-day. You may go.'

If only I could have conducted myself! But in France authors are not allowed to direct their own works in theatres.

Years later I conducted my *Carnaval Romain*, where that very saltarello comes in, without the wind instruments having any rehearsal at all; and Habeneck, certain that I should come to grief, was present. I rushed the allegro at the proper time and everything went perfectly.

The audience cried 'encore' and the second time was even better than the first. I met Habeneck as we went out, and threw four words at him over my shoulder.

'That's how it goes.' He did not reply.

I never felt so happy conducting as I did that day; the thought of the torments Habeneck had made me suffer increased my pleasure.

But to return to *Benvenuto*.

Gradually the larger part of the orchestra came over to my side, and several declared that this was the most original score they had ever played. Duponchel heard them and said:

'Was ever such a right-about face? Now they think Berlioz' music charming, and the idiots are praising it up to the skies.'

Still some malcontents remained, and two were found one night playing *J'ai du bon tabac* instead of their parts.

It was just the same on the stage. The dancers pinched their partners, who, by their shrieks, upset the chorus. When, in despair, I sent for Duponchel he was never to be found; attending rehearsal was beneath his dignity.

The opera came on at last. The overture made a furore, the rest was unmercifully hissed. However it was played three times.

It is fourteen years (I write in 1850) since I was thus pilloried at the opera, and I have just read over my poor score, carefully and impartially. I cannot help thinking that it shows an originality, a raciness and a brilliancy that I shall, probably, never have again and which deserve a better fate.

Benvenuto took me a long time to write and would never have been ready – tied as I was by my bread-earning journalistic work – had it not been for the help of a friend.

It was heart-breaking, and I had almost given up the opera in despair when Ernest Legouvé came to me, asking:

'Is your opera done?'

'First act not even ready yet. I have no time to compose.'

'But supposing you had time – '

'I would write from dawn till dark.'

'How much would make you independent?'

'Two thousand francs.'

'And suppose someone – If someone – Come, do help me out!'

'With what? What do you mean?'

'Why, suppose a friend lent it to you?'

'What friend could I ask for such a sum?'

'You needn't ask when I offer it – '

Think of my relief! In real truth, next day Legouvé lent me two thousand francs, and I finished *Benvenuto*. His noble heart – writer and artist as he was – guessed my trouble and feared to wound me by his offer! I have been fortunate in having many staunch friends.

Paganini was back in Paris when *Benvenuto* was slaughtered; he felt for me deeply and said:

'If I were a manager I would commission that young man to write me three operas. He should be paid in advance, and I should make a splendid thing by it.'

Mortification and the suppressed rage in which I had lived during those everlasting rehearsals, brought on a bad attack of bronchitis that kept me in bed, unable to work.

But we had to live, and I determined to give two concerts at the Conservatoire. The first barely paid its expenses so, as an attraction, I advertised the *Fantastique* and *Harold* together for the 16th December 1838.

Now Paganini, although it was written at his desire, had never heard *Harold*, and, after the concert, as I waited – trembling, exhausted, bathed in perspiration – he, with his little son, Achille, appeared at the orchestra door, gesticulating violently. Consumption of the throat, of which he afterwards died, prevented his speaking audibly and Achille alone could interpret his wishes.

He signed to the child, who climbed on a chair and put his ear close to his father's mouth, then turning to me he said:

'Monsieur, my father orders me to tell you that never has he been so struck by music. He wishes to kneel and thank you.'

Confused and embarrassed, I could not speak, but Paganini seized my arm, hoarsely ejaculating, 'Yes! Yes!' dragged me into the theatre where several of my players still lingered – and there knelt and kissed my hand.

Coming away in a fever from this strange scene, I met Armand Bertin; stopping to speak to him in that intense cold sent me home to bed worse than ever. Next day, as I lay, ill and alone, little Achille came in.

'My father will be very sorry you are ill,' he said, 'if he had not been ill himself he would have come to see you. He told me to give you this letter.'

As I began to open it, the child stopped me:

'He said you must read it alone. There is no answer.' And he hurried out.

I supposed it just a letter of congratulation; but here it is:

Dear Friend, – Only Berlioz can recall Beethoven, and I, who have heard that divine work – so worthy of your genius – beg you to accept the enclosed 20,000 francs, as a tribute of respect. – Believe me ever, your affectionate friend,

NICCOLO PAGANINI

PARIS, 18th Dec. 1838.

I knew enough Italian to make out the letter, but it surprised me so greatly that my head swam, and, without thinking of what I was doing, I opened the little note which was enclosed and addressed to M. de Rothschild. It was in French and ran:

Monsieur le Baron, – Would you be so good as to hand over the 20,000 francs that I deposited yesterday to M. Berlioz.

Paganini

Then I understood.

My wife, coming in, thought that some new trouble had fallen upon us.

'What is it now?' she cried. 'Be brave! we have borne so much already.'

'No, no – not that – '

'What then?'

'Paganini – has sent me – 20,000 francs!'

'Louis! Louis!' cried Henriette, rushing for her boy, 'come here to your mother and thank God.'

And together they knelt by my bed – grateful mother and wondering child. Oh Paganini! why could you not be there to see?

Naturally, my first thought was to thank him. My letter seemed so poor, so inadequate, that I am ashamed to give it here. There are feelings beyond words.

His munificent kindness was soon noised abroad and my room besieged by friends anxious to know the facts. All rejoiced and some were jealous – not of me, but of Paganini, who was rich enough to do such deeds. Then began the comments, fury and lies of my opponents, followed by the congratulatory letter of Janin and his eloquent article in the *Débats*.

For a week I lay in bed, burning with impatience to see and thank my benefactor. Then I hurried to his house and found him in the billiard-room. We embraced in silence then, as I poured forth broken thanks, he spoke and – thanks to the silence of the room – I was able to make out his words.

'Not a word! It is so little and has given me the greatest pleasure of my life. You cannot tell how much your music moves me. Ah!' he cried, with a blow of his fist on the table, 'now your enemies will be silenced for they know I understand and am not easily satisfied.'

But great as was his name it was not great enough to silence the dogs of Paris; in a few weeks they were again baying at my heels.

My earnest wish, now that all debts were paid and a handsome sum remained in hand, was to write a masterpiece, grand, impassioned, original, worthy of dedication to the master to whom I owed so much.

But Paganini, growing worse, had left for Nice, whence alas! he returned no more. I consulted him as to a suitable theme, but he replied:

'I cannot advise you. You best know what suits you best.'

After much wavering I fixed on a choral symphony on Shakespeare's *Romeo and Juliet*, and wrote the prose words for the choral portion, which Emile Deschamps, with his usual kindness and extraordinary versatility, put into poetry for me.

Ah! the joy of no more newspaper articles! – or at least hardly any. Paganini had given me money to make music, and I made it. For seven months, with only a few days' intermission, did I work at my symphony.

And, during those months, what a burning, exhilarating life I led!...I felt within me the god-like strength to win my way to that blessed hidden isle, where the temple of pure art raises its soaring columns to the sky.

To others must I leave it to say whether I ever truly looked upon its glories.

Such as it was, my symphony was performed three times running, and each time appeared to be a great success. To my sorrow, Paganini never heard it nor read it. I hoped to see him again in Paris; then to send him the printed score; but he died at Nice leaving to me the poignant sorrow that he would never judge whether the work, undertaken to please him and to justify his faith in its author, was worthy of his great trust.

He, too, seemed sorry not to have known it, and in his letter of the 7th January 1840, he wrote:

'Now it is well done; jealousy can but be silent.'

Dear, noble friend! He never saw the ribald nonsense written about my work; how one called my *Queen Mab* music a badly-oiled squirt, how another – speaking of the *Love-Scene*, which musicians place in the forefront of my work – said I *did not understand Shakespeare*!

Empty-headed toad, bursting with stupid self-importance! If you could prove that . . .

Never was I more deeply hurt by criticism, and yet none of these high priests of art deigned to point out the faults, which I thankfully corrected, when told of them.

For instance, Ernst's secretary, M. Frankoski, wrote from Vienna saying that the end of *Queen Mab* was too abrupt; I therefore wrote the present coda and destroyed the original one.

The criticisms of M. d'Ortigue I also appreciated. The rest of the alterations were my own.

But the symphony is enormously difficult for the executants, both in form and style, and needs most careful, conscientious practice and perfect conducting – which means that none but first-rate artists in each department could possibly do it.

For this reason it will never be given in London. They do not give enough time to rehearsals. The musicians there have no time for music.

Ludwig van Beethoven

The Heiligenstadt Testament

For my brothers Karl and (Johann) Beethoven.

O, you men who believe or declare that I am malevolent, stubborn or misanthropic, how greatly you wrong me! You do not know the secret cause behind the appearance. From childhood onwards my heart and mind have tended towards a gentle benevolence. I have always been disposed even to accomplish great deeds. Yet only consider that for six years I have been suffering an incurable affliction, aggravated by imprudent physicians. Year after year deceived by the hope of an improvement, finally forced to contemplate the prospect of a lasting illness, whose cure may take years or may even be impossible, born with a fiery, impulsive temperament, sensible, even, to the distractions of social life, I was yet compelled early in my life to isolate myself, to spend my life in solitude. Even if at times I wished to overcome all this, oh, how harshly I was driven back by the doubly grievous experience of my bad hearing, and yet I could not prevail upon myself to say to men: speak louder, shout, for I am deaf. Oh, how could I possibly admit to being defective in the very sense which should have been more highly developed in me than in other men, a sense which once I possessed in its most perfect form, a form as perfect as few in my profession, surely, know or have known in the past. Oh, I cannot do it. Therefore you must forgive me if you should see me draw back when I would gladly mingle with you. My affliction is all the more painful to me because it leads to such misinterpretations of my conduct. Recreation in human society, refined conversation, mutual effusions of thought are denied to me. Almost quite alone, I may commit myself to social life only as far as the most urgent needs demand. I must live like an exile. When I do venture near some social gathering, I am seized with a burning terror, the fear that I may be placed in the dangerous position of having to reveal my condition. So, too, it has been with me during the past half-year, which I spent in the country. When my reasonable physician ordered me to spare my hearing as much as possible, he almost accorded with my natural disposition, although sometimes, overpowered by the urge to seek society, I disobeyed his orders. But what an humiliation when someone standing next to me heard a flute in the distance and I heard nothing, or when someone heard the shepherd sing and, again, I heard nothing. Such occurrences brought me to the verge of despair. I might easily have put an end to my life. Only one thing, Art, held me back. Oh, it seemed impossible to me to leave this world before I had produced all that I felt capable of producing, and so I prolonged this wretched existence – truly wretched, (because I am cursed with) a body so irritable that a somewhat sudden change can plunge me from the best into the worst of states. Patience – so I am told, it is patience that I must now choose to be my guide: I have patience enough. My determination to hold out until it pleases the inexorable Fates to cut the thread shall be a lasting one, I sincerely hope. Perhaps there will be an improvement, perhaps not: I am prepared. Already in my 28th year I have been compelled to become a philosopher; this is no easy matter, more difficult for an artist than for anyone else. Divine one, thou canst see into my inmost thoughts, thou knowest them; thou knowest that love of my fellow men and the desire to do good are harboured there. O, men, when one day you read these words, reflect that you did me wrong; and let the unhappy man take comfort in his meeting with one of his kind; one who, despite all his natural disabilities yet did everything in his power to be admitted into the ranks of worthy artists and men. You, my brothers Karl and (Johann) as soon as I am dead (if) Professor Schmidt is still alive, ask him in my name to describe my illness, and add this document to his account, so that, as far as possible, the world may be reconciled with me after my death. At the same time I declare you both to be the heirs to my small fortune (if one can call it such). Divide it fairly, bear with and help each other. The evil you have done me, as you know yourselves, has long been forgiven you. To you, brother Karl, I give special thanks for the devotion shown to me in these recent times. It is my wish that you may lead lives better and more free from cares than my own. Recommend virtue to your children: for virtue alone, not money, can grant us happiness; I speak from experience. It was virtue that raised me up even in my misery; it is owing to virtue, and to my art, that I did not end my life by suicide. Farewell and love each other! I give thanks to all my friends, but especially to Prince Lichnowsky and to Professor Schmidt. I desire that the instruments given to me by Prince Lichnowsky be preserved by one of you; yet let no quarrel arise among you on this account. However, as soon as they can be of more use to you in this way, by all means sell them. How glad I am at the thought that even in the grave I may render you some service!

Now it is done. It is with joy that I hasten to meet my death. Should death come before I have had time to develop all my artistic faculties, then, in spite of my cruel fate, it will come too soon and I would wish that its coming might be delayed. Yet even then I shall be content: does not death liberate me from a state of endless suffering? Come whenever it pleases thee to come: bravely I shall come out to meet thee. Farewell and do not quite forget me when I am dead. I have

deserved this of you, for often in my lifetime I thought of you, wondering how I could make you happy; be so!
Heiligenstadt, October 6th, 1802

Ludwig van Beethoven

Heiligenstadt, October 10th

So I must bid you farewell – though sadly. Yes, the cherished hope – which I brought with me when I came here, of being healed at least to a certain degree, must now abandon me entirely. As the leaves of autumn fall and are withered, so, too – my hope has dried up. Almost as I was when I came here, I leave again – even the courage – which often inspired me on lovely summer days – is vanished. O Providence – let a single day of untroubled joy be granted to me! For so long already the resonance of true joy has been unknown to me. O when – O when, Divine one – may I feel it once more in the temple of Nature and of mankind? Never? – no – that would be too hard!

Translated by Michael Hamburger

Composers

Michael Hamburger

At fifty-five

Country dances
Bird calls
The breathing of leaves after thunder –
And now fugues.
Modulations 'impolite'
Syncopations 'unnatural'.
No more clapping of hands
When moonshine had opened their tear-ducts
Or fanfares clenched
Heroic nerves –
But a shaking of heads:
Can't help it, our decomposer,
Can't hear his own blundering discords.

As if one needed ears
For anything but chit-chat about the weather,
Exchange of solicitude, malice –
And birdsong, true, the grosser, the bouncing rhythms.
Uncommunicative? Yes. Unable
'Like beginners to learn from nightingales'.
Unwilling, too, for that matter –
To perform, to rehearse, to repeat,
To take in, to give back.

In time out of time, in the concert no longer concerted.
But the music all there, what music,
Where from –
Water that wells from gravel washed clean by water.
All there – inaudible thrushes
Outsinging the nightingales, peasants
Dancing weightless, without their shoes
Where from, by what virtue? None.
By what grace but still being here, growing older?
The water cleansed by gravel washed clean by water.

Fugue, ever itself –
And ever growing,
Gathering up – itself,
Plunging – into itself,
Rising – out of itself,
Fathoming – only itself
To end, not to end its flowing –
No longer itself –
In a stillness that never was.

Richard Wagner

A Pilgrimage to Beethoven

Want-and-care, thou patron-goddess of the German musician, unless he happens to be Kapellmeister to a Court-theatre or the like, – Want-and-care, thine be the name first lauded even in this reminiscence from my life! Ay, let me sing of thee, thou staunch companion of my life-time! Faithful hast thou been to me, and never left me; the smiles of Inconstance thou hast ever warded off, and shielded me from Fortune's scorching rays! In deepest shadow hast thou ever cloaked from me the empty baubles of this earth : have thanks for thy unwearying attachment! Yet, might it so be, prithee some day seek another favourite; for, purely out of curiosity, I fain would learn for once how life might fare *without* thee. At least, I beg thee, plague especially our political dreamers, the madmen who are breathless to unite our Germany beneath *one* sceptre: – think on't, there then would be but one Court-theatre, one solitary Kapell-meister's post! What would become of my prospects, my only hopes; which, even as it is, but hover dim and shadowy before me – e'en now when German royal theatres exist in plenty? – But I perceive I am turning blasphemous. Forgive, my patron-goddess, the dastard wish just uttered! Thou know'st my heart, and how entirely I am thine, and shall remain thine, were there a thousand royal theatres in Germany. Amen!

Without this daily prayer of mine I begin nothing, and therefore not the story of my pilgrimage to Beethoven!

In case this weighty document should get published after my death, however, I further deem needful to say who I am; without which information much therein might not be understood. Know then, world and testament-executor!

A middle-sized town of middle Germany is my birthplace. I'm not quite certain what I really was intended for; I only remember that one night I for the first time heard a symphony of Beethoven's performed, that it set me in a fever, I fell ill, and on my recovery had become a musician. This circumstance may haply account for the fact that, though in time I also made acquaintance with other beautiful music, I yet have loved, have honoured, worshipped Beethoven before all else. Henceforth I knew no other pleasure, than to plunge so deep into his genius that at last I fancied myself become a portion thereof; and as this tiniest portion, I began to respect myself, to come by higher thoughts and views – in brief, to develop into what sober people call an idiot. My madness, however, was of very good-humoured sort, and did no harm to any man; the bread I ate, in this condition, was very dry, and the liquid that I drank most watery; for lesson-giving yields but poor returns, with us, O honoured world and testament-executor!

Thus I lived for some time in my garret, till it occurred to me one day that the man whose creations I reverenced above all else was still *alive*. It passed my understanding, how I had never thought of that before. It had never struck me that Beethoven could exist, could be eating bread and breathing air, like one of us; but this Beethoven was living in Vienna for all that, and he too was a poor German musician!

My peace of mind was gone. My every thought became one wish: *to see Beethoven*! No Mussulman more devoutly longed to journey to the grave of his Prophet, than I to the lodging where Beethoven dwelt.

But how to set about the execution of my project? To Vienna was a long, long journey, and needed money; whilst I, poor devil, scarce earned enough to stave off hunger! So I must think of some exceptional means of finding the needful travelling-money. A few pianoforte sonatas, which I had composed on the master's model, I carried to the publisher; in a word or two the man made clear to me that I was a fool with my sonatas. He gave me the advice, however, that if I wanted to some day earn a dollar or so by my compositions, I should begin by making myself a little renommée by galops and pot-pourris. – I shuddered; but my yearnings to see Beethoven gained the victory; I composed galops and pot-pourris, but for very shame I could never bring myself to cast one glance on Beethoven in all that time, for fear it should defile him.

To my misfortune, however, these earliest sacrifices of my innocence did not even bring me pay, for my publisher explained that I first must earn myself a little name. I shuddered again, and fell into despair. That despair brought forth some capital galops. I actually touched money for them, and at last believed I had amassed enough to be able to execute my plan. But two years had elapsed, and all the time I feared that Beethoven might die before I had made my name by galops and pot-pourris. Thank God! he had survived the glitter of my name! – Saint Beethoven, forgive me that renommée; 'twas earned that I might see thee!

Joy! my goal was in sight. Who happier than I? I might strap my bundle and set out for Beethoven at once. A holy awe possessed me when I passed outside the gate and turned my footsteps southwards. Gladly would I have taken a seat in the diligence, not because I feared footsoreness – (what hardships would I not have cheerfully endured for such a goal!) – but since I should thus have reached Beethoven sooner. I had done too little for my fame as galop-composer, however, to be able to pay carriage-fare. So I bore all toils, and thought myself lucky to have got so far that they could take me to my goal. O what I pictured, what I dreamed! No lover, after years of separation, could be more happy at returning to his youthful love.

And so I came to fair Bohemia, the land of harpists and wayside singers. In a little town I found a troop of strolling musicians; they formed a tiny orchestra, composed of a 'cello, two violins, two horns, a clarinet and a flute; moreover there was a woman who played the harp, and two with lovely voices. They played dances and sang songs; folk gave them money and they journeyed on. In a beautiful shady place beside the highway I found them again; they had camped on the grass, and were taking their meal. I introduced myself by saying that I too was a travelling musician, and we soon became friends. As they played dance-music, I bashfully asked if they knew my galops also? God bless them! they had never heard of my galops. O what good news for me!

I inquired whether they played any other music than dances.

'To be sure,' they answered, 'but only for ourselves; not for gentlefolk.'

They unpacked their sheets, and I caught sight of the grand Septuor of Beethoven; astonished, I asked if they played that too?

'Why not? – replied the eldest, – 'Joseph has hurt his hand, and can't play the second violin to-day, or we'd be delighted to give it at once.'

Beside myself, I snatched up Joseph's violin, promised to do my best to replace him, and we began the Septuor.

O rapture! Here on the slope of a Bohemian highway, in open air, Beethoven's Septuor played by dance-musicians with a purity, a precision, and a depth of feeling too seldom found among the highest virtuosi! – Great Beethoven, we brought thee a worthy offering.

We had just got to the Finale, when – the road bending up at this spot toward the hills – an elegant travelling carriage drew slowly and noiselessly near, and stopped at last close by us. A marvellously tall and marvellously blond young man lay stretched full-length in the carriage; he listened to our music with tolerable attention, drew out a pocket-book, and made a few notes. Then he let drop a gold coin from the carriage, and drove away with a few words of English to his lackey; whence it dawned on me that he must be an Englishman.

This incident quite put us out; luckily we had finished our performance of the Septuor. I embraced my friends, and wanted to accompany them; but they told me they must leave the high road here and strike across the fields, to get home to their native village for a while. Had it not been Beethoven himself who was awaiting me, I

certainly would have kept them company. As it was, we bade each a
tender good-bye, and parted. Later it occurred to me that no one had
picked up the Englishman's coin. –

Upon entering the nearest inn, to fortify my body, I found the
Englishman seated at an ample meal. He eyed me up and down, and
at last addressed me in passable German.

'Where are your colleagues?' he asked.

'Gone home,' I replied.

'Just take out your violin, and play me something more,' he
continued, 'here's money.'

That annoyed me; I told him I neither played for money, nor had I
any violin, and briefly explained how I had fallen in with those
musicians.

'They were good musicians,' put in the Englishman, 'and the
Symphony of Beethoven was very good, too.'

Struck by this remark, I asked him if he practised music?

'*Yes*,' he answered, 'twice a week I play the flute, on Thursdays the
French horn, and of a Sunday I compose.'

That was a good deal, enough to astound me. In all my life I had
never heard tell of travelling English musicians; I concluded that they
must do very well, if they could afford to make their tours in such
splendid equipages. I asked if he was a musician by profession?

For long I got no answer; finally he drawled out, that he had plenty
of money.

My mistake was obvious to me now, for my question had plainly
offended him. At a loss what to say, I devoured my simple meal in
silence.

After another long inspection of me, the Englishman commenced
afresh.

'Do you know Beethoven?'

I replied that I had never yet been in Vienna, but was on my way
there to fulfil my dearest wish, to see the worshipped master.

'Where do you come from ?' he asked.

'From L . . . .'

'That's not so far! I've come from England, and also with the
intention of seeing Beethoven. We both will make his acquaintance;
he's a very famous composer.'

What a wonderful coincidence! – I thought to myself. Mighty
master, what divers kinds thou drawest to thee! On foot and on wheels
they make their journey. – My Englishman interested me; but I avow
I little envied him his equipage. To me it seemed as though my weary
pilgrimage afoot were holier and more devout, and that its goal must
bless me more than this proud gentleman who drove there in full state.

Then the postilion blew his horn; the Englishman drove off, shouting back to me that he would see Beethoven before I did.

I scarce had trudged a few miles in his wake, when unexpectedly I encountered him again. It was on the high road. A wheel of his carriage had broken down; but in majestic ease he sat inside, with his valet mounted up behind him, notwithstanding that the vehicle was all aslant. I learnt that they were waiting for the return of the postilion, who had run off to a somewhat distant village to fetch a blacksmith. As they had already been waiting a long time, and as the valet spoke nothing but English, I decided to set off for the village myself, to hurry up smith and postilion. In fact I found the latter in a tavern, where spirits were relieving him of any particular care about the Englishman; however, I soon brought him back with the smith to the injured carriage. The damage was mended; the Englishman promised to announce me to Beethoven, and – drove away.

Judge my surprise, when I overtook him again on the high road next day! This time, however, no wheels were broken; drawn up in the middle of the road, he was tranquilly reading a book, and seemed quite pleased to see me coming.

'I've been waiting a good many hours for you,' he said, 'as it occurred to me on this very spot that I did wrong in not inviting you to drive with me to Beethoven. Riding is much better than walking. Come into the carriage.'

I was astonished again. For a moment I really hesitated whether I ought not to accept his invitation; but I soon remembered the vow I had made the previous day when I saw the Englishman rolling off; I had sworn, in any circumstances to pursue my pilgrimage on foot. I told him this openly. It was now the Englishman's turn to be astonished; he could not comprehend me. He repeated his offer, saying that he had already waited many hours expressly for me, notwithstanding his having been very much delayed at his sleeping-quarters through the time consumed in thoroughly repairing the broken wheel. I remained firm, and he drove off, wondering.

Candidly, I had a secret dislike of him; for I was falling prey to a vague foreboding that this Englishman would cause me serious trouble. Moreover his reverence for Beethoven, and his proposal to make his acquaintance, to me seemed more the idle whim of a wealthy coxcomb than the deep inner need of an enthusiastic soul. Therefore I preferred to avoid him, lest his company might desecrate my pious wish.

But, as if my destiny meant to school me for the dangerous association with this gentleman into which I was yet to fall, I met him again on the evening of that same day, halting before an inn, and, as it seemed, still waiting for me. For he sat with his back to the horses, looking down the road, by which I came.

'Sir,' he began, 'I again have waited very many hours for you. Will you drive with me to Beethoven?'

This time my astonishment was mingled with a secret terror. I could only explain his striking obstinacy in the attempt to serve me, on the supposition that the Englishman, having noticed my growing antipathy for him, was bent on thrusting himself upon me for my destruction. With undisguised annoyance, I once more declined his offer. Then he insolently cried:

'Goddam, you little value Beethoven. *I* shall soon see him.' Post haste he flew away. –

And that was really the last time I was to meet this islander on my still lengthy road to Vienna. At last I trod Vienna's streets; the end of my pilgrimage was reached. With what feelings I entered this Mecca of my faith! All the toil and hardships of my weary journey were forgotten; I was at the goal, within the walls that circled Beethoven.

I was too deeply moved, to be able to think of carrying out my aim at once. True, the first thing I did was to inquire for Beethoven's dwelling, but merely in order to lodge myself close by. Almost opposite the house in which the master lived there happened to be a not too stylish hostelry; I engaged a little room on its fifth floor, and there began preparing myself for the greatest event of my life, a visit to Beethoven.

After having rested two days, fasting and praying, but never casting another look on the city, I plucked up heart to leave my inn and march straight across to the house of marvels. I was told Herr Beethoven was not at home. That suited me quite well; for it gave me time to collect myself afresh. But when four times more throughout the day the same reply was given me, and with a certain increasing emphasis, I held that day for an unlucky one, and abandoned my visit in gloom.

As I was strolling back to the inn, my Englishman waved his hand to me from a first-floor window, with a fair amount of affability.

'Have you seen Beethoven?' he shouted.

'Not yet; he wasn't in,' I answered, wondering at our fresh encounter. The Englishman met me on the stairs, and with remarkable friendliness insisted upon my entering his apartment.

'*Mein Herr,*' he said, 'I have seen you go to Beethoven's house five times to-day. I have been here a good many days, and have taken up my quarters in this villainous hotel so as to be near Beethoven. Believe me, it is most difficult to get a word with him; the gentleman is full of crotchets. At first I went six times a day to his house, and each time was turned away. Now I get up very early, and sit at my window till

late in the evening, to see when Beethoven goes out. But the
gentleman seems *never* to go out.'

'So you think Beethoven was at home to-day, as well, and had me
sent away?' I cried aghast.

'Exactly; you and I have each been dismissed. And to me it is very
annoying, for I didn't come here to make Vienna's acquaintance, but
Beethoven's.'

That was very sad news for me. Nevertheless I tried my luck again
on the following day; but once more in vain, – the gates of heaven
were closed against me.

My Englishman, who kept constant watch on my fruitless attempts
from his window, had now gained positive information that
Beethoven's apartments did not face the street. He was very irritating,
but unboundedly persevering. My patience, on the contrary, was
wellnigh exhausted, for I had more reason than he; a week had
gradually slipped by, without my reaching my goal, and the returns
from my galops allowed a by no means lengthy stay in Vienna. Little
by little I began to despair.

I poured my griefs into my landlord's ear. He smiled, and promised
to tell me the cause of my bad fortune if I would undertake not to
betray it to the Englishman. Suspecting my unlucky star, I took the
stipulated vow.

'You see,' said the worthy host, 'quite a number of Englishmen
come here, to lie in wait for Herr von Beethoven. This annoys Herr
von Beethoven very much and he is so enraged by the push of these
gentry that he has made it clean impossible for any stranger to gain
admittance to him. He's a singular gentleman, and one must forgive
him. But it's very good business for my inn, which is generally packed
with English, whom the difficulty of getting a word with Herr
Beethoven compels to be my guests for longer than they otherwise
would. However, as you promise not to scare away my customers, I
hope to find a means of smuggling you to Herr Beethoven.'

This was very edifying; I could not reach my goal because, poor
devil, I was taken for an Englishman. So ho! my fears were verified;
the Englishman was my perdition! At first I thought of quitting the
inn, since it was certain that everyone who lodged there was
considered an Englishman at Beethoven's house, and for that reason I
also was under the ban. However, the landlord's promise, to find me
an opportunity of seeing and speaking with Beethoven, held me back.
Meanwhile the Englishman, whom I now detested from the bottom of
my heart, had been practising all kinds of intrigues and bribery, yet all
without result.

Thus several fruitless days slipped by again, while the revenue from my galops was visibly dwindling, when at last the landlord confided to me that I could not possibly miss Beethoven if I would go to a certain beer-garden, which the composer was in the habit of visiting almost every day at the same hour. At like time my mentor gave me such unmistakable directions as to the master's personal appearance, that I could not fail to recognise him. My spirits revived, and I resolved not to defer my fortune to the morrow. It was impossible for me to meet Beethoven on his going out, as he always left his house by a back-door; so there remained nothing but the beer-garden.

Alas! I sought the master there in vain on that and the two succeeding days. Finally, on the fourth, as I was turning my steps towards the fateful garden at the stated hour, to my despair I noticed that the Englishman was cautiously and carefully following me at a distance. The wretch, posted at his eternal window, had not let it escape him that I went out every day at a certain time in the same direction; struck by this, and guessing that I had found some means of tracking Beethoven, he had decided to reap his profit from my supposed discovery. He told me all this with the calmest impudence, declaring at the same time that he meant to follow wherever I went. In vain were all my efforts to deceive him and make him believe that I was only going to refresh myself in a common beer-garden, far too unfashionable to be frequented by gentlemen of his quality: he remained unshaken, and I could only curse my fate. At last I tried impoliteness, and sought to get rid of him by abuse; but, far from letting it provoke him, he contented himself with a placid smile. His fixed idea was to see Beethoven; nothing else troubled him.

And in truth I was this day, at last, to look on the face of great Beethoven for the first time. Nothing can depict my emotion, and my fury too, as, sitting by side of my gentleman, I saw a man approach whose looks and bearing completely answered the description my host had given me of the master's exterior. The long blue overcoat, the tumbled shock of grey hair; and then the features, the expression of the face, – exactly what a good portrait had long left hovering before my mental eye. There could be no mistake: at the first glance I had recognised him! With short, quick steps, he passed us; awe and veneration held me chained.

Not one of my movements was lost on the Englishman; with avid eyes he watched the newcomer, who withdrew into the farthest corner of the as yet deserted garden, gave his order for wine, and remained for a while in an attitude of meditation. My throbbing heart cried out: 'Tis he. For some moments I clean forgot my neighbour, and watched with eager eye and speechless transport the man whose genius was autocrat of all my thoughts and feeling since ever I had learnt to think and feel. Involuntarily I began muttering to myself, and fell into a sort of monologue, which closed with the but too meaning words: '*Beethoven, it is thou, then, whom I see?*'

Nothing escaped my dreadful neighbour, who, leaning over to me, had listened with bated breath to my aside. From the depths of my ecstasy I was startled by the words:

'*Yes*! this gentleman is Beethoven. Come, let us present ourselves to him at once!'

In utter alarm and irritation, I held the cursed Englishman back by the elbow.

'What are you doing?' I cried, 'Do you want to compromise us – in this place – so entirely without regard for manners?'

'Oh!' he answered, 'it's a capital opportunity; we shall not easily find a better.'

With that he drew a kind of notebook from his pocket and tried to make direct for the man in the blue overcoat. Beside myself, I clutched the idiot's coat-tails, and thundered at him, 'Are you possessed with a devil?'

This scene had attracted the stranger's attention. He appeared to have formed a painful guess that he was the subject of our agitation, and, hastily emptying his glass, he rose to go. No sooner had the Englishman remarked this than he tore himself from my grasp with such violence that he left one of his coat-tails in my hand, and threw himself across Beethoven's path. The master sought to avoid him; but the good-for-nothing stepped in front, made a superfine bow in the latest English fashion, and addressed him as follows:

'I have the honour to present myself to the much renowned composer and very estimable gentleman, Herr Beethoven.'

He had no need to add more, for at his very first words Beethoven, after casting a glance at myself, had sprung on one side and vanished from the garden as quick as lightning. Nevertheless the irrepressible Briton was on the point of running after the fugitive, when I seized his remaining coat-tail in a storm of indignation. Somewhat surprised, he stopped, and bellowed at me:

'Goddam! this gentleman is worthy to be an Englishman! He's a great man, and no mistake, and I shall lose no time in making his acquaintance.'

I was petrified; this ghastly adventure had crushed my last hope of seeing my heart's fondest wish e'er fulfilled.

It was manifest, in fact, that henceforth every attempt to approach Beethoven in an ordinary way had been made completely futile for me. In the utterly threadbare state of my finances I now had only to decide whether I should set out at once for home, with my labour lost, or take one final step to reach my goal. The first alternative sent a shudder to the very bottom of my soul. Who so near the doors of the highest shrine, could see them shut for ever without falling into annihilation?

Ere thus abandoning my soul's salvation, I still would venture on one forlorn hope. But *what* step, what road should I take? For long I could think of nothing coherent. Alas! my brain was paralysed; nothing presented itself to my overwrought imagination, save the memory of what I had to suffer when I held the coat-tail of that terrible Englishman in my hand. Beethoven's side-glance at my unhappy self, in this fearful catastrophe, had not escaped me; I felt what that glance had meant; he had taken me for an Englishman!

What was to be done, to lay the master's suspicion? Everything depended on letting him know that I was a simple German soul, brimful of earthly poverty but over-earthly enthusiasm.

So at last I decided to pour out my heart upon paper. And this I did. I wrote; briefly narrating the history of my life, how I once had come by the wish to know him in person, how I had become a musician, how I worshipped him, how I had spent two years in making a name as galop-composer, how I had begun and ended my pilgrimage, what sufferings the Englishman had brought upon me, and what a terrible plight my present was. As my heart grew sensibly lighter with this recital of my woes, the comfortable feeling led me to a certain tone of familiarity; I wove into my letter quite frank and fairly strong reproaches of the master's unjust treatment of my wretched self. Finally I closed the letter in genuine inspiration; sparks flew before my eyes when I wrote the address: '*An Herrn Ludwig van Beethoven.*' I only stayed to breathe a silent prayer, and delivered the letter with my own hand at Beethoven's house.

Returning to my hotel in the highest spirits – great heavens! what brought the dreaded Englishman again before my eyes? From his window he had spied my latest move, as well; in my face he had read the joy of hope, and that sufficed to place me in his power once more. In effect he stopped me on the steps with the question: 'Good news? When do we see Beethoven?'

'Never, never'! – I cried in despair – '*You* will never see Beethoven again, in all your life. Leave me, wretch, we have nothing in common!'

'We have much in common,' he coolly rejoined, 'where is my coat-tail, sir? Who authorised you to forcibly deprive me of it? Don't you know that you are to blame for Beethoven's behaviour to me? How could he think it *convenable* to have anything to with a gentleman wearing only one coat-tail?'

Furious at seeing the blame thrown back upon myself, I shouted: 'Sir, your coat-tail shall be restored to you; may you keep it as a shameful memento of how you insulted the great Beethoven, and hurled a poor musician to his doom! Farewell; may we never meet again!'

He tried to detain and pacify me, assuring me that he had plenty more coats in the best condition; would I only tell him when Beethoven meant to receive us? – But I rushed upstairs to my fifth-floor attic; there I locked myself in, and waited for Beethoven's answer.

How can I ever describe what took place inside, *around* me, when the next hour actually brought me a scrap of music-paper, on which stood hurriedly written: 'Excuse me, Herr R . . ., if I beg you not to call on me until tomorrow morning, as I am busy preparing a packet of music for the post to-day. To-morrow I shall expect you. – Beethoven.'

My first action was to fall on my knees and thank Heaven for this exceptional mercy; my eyes grew dim with scalding tears. At last, however, my feelings found vent in the wildest joy; I sprang up, and round my tiny room I danced like a lunatic. I'm not quite sure what it was I danced; I only remember that to my utter shame I suddenly became aware that I was whistling one of my galops to it. This mortifying discovery restored me to my senses. I left my garret, the inn, and, drunk with joy, I rushed into the streets of Vienna.

My God, my woes had made me clean forget that I was in Vienna! How delighted I was with the merry ways of the dwellers in this empire-city. I was in a state of exaltation, and saw everything through coloured spectacles. The somewhat shallow sensuousness of the Viennese seemed the freshness of warm life to me; their volatile and none too discriminating love of pleasure I took for frank and natural sensibility to things beautiful. I ran my eye down the five stage-posters for the day. Heavens! On one of them I saw: *Fidelio*, an opera by Beethoven.

To the theatre I must go, however shrunk the profits from my galops. As I entered the pit, the overture began. It was the revised edition of the opera, which, to the honour of the penetrating public of Vienna, had failed under its earlier title, *Leonora*. I had never yet heard the opera in this its second form; judge, then, my delight at making here my first acquaintance with the glorious new! A very young maiden played the rôle of Leonora; but youthful as she was, this singer seemed already wedded to Beethoven's genius. With what a glow, what poetry, what depth of effect, did she portray this extraordinary woman! She was called *Wilhelmine Schröder*. Hers is the high distinction of having set open this work of Beethoven to the German public; for that evening I saw the superficial Viennese themselves aroused to the strongest enthusiasm. For my own part, the heavens were opened to me; I was transported, and adored the genius who had led me – like Florestan – from night and fetters into light and freedom.

I could not sleep that night. What I had just experienced, and what was in store for me next day, were too great and overpowering for me to calmly weave into a dream. I lay awake, building castles in the air and preparing myself for Beethoven's presence. – At last the new day dawned; impatiently I waited till the seemly hour for a morning visit; – it struck, and I set forth. The weightiest event of my life stood before me: I trembled at the thought.

However, I had yet one fearful trial to pass through.

Leaning against the wall of Beethoven's house, as cool as a cucumber, my evil spirit waited for me – the Englishman! – The monster, after suborning all the world, had ended by bribing our landlord; the latter had read the open note from Beethoven before myself, and betrayed its contents to the Briton.

A cold sweat came over me at the sight; all poesy, all heavenly exaltation vanished: once more I was in *his* power.

'Come,' began the caitiff, 'let us introduce ourselves to Beethoven.'

At first I thought of helping myself with a lie, and pretending that I was not on the road to Beethoven at all. But he cut the ground from under my feet by telling me with the greatest candour how he had got to the back of my secret, and declaring that he had no intention of leaving me till we both returned from Beethoven. I tried soft words, to move him from his purpose – in vain! I flew into a rage – in vain! At last I hoped to outwit him by swiftness of foot; like an arrow I darted up the steps, and tore at the bell like a maniac. But ere the door was opened the gentleman was by my side, tugging at the tail of my coat and saying: 'You can't escape me. I've a right to your coat-tail, and shall hold on to it till we are standing before Beethoven.'

Infuriated, I turned about and tried to loose myself; ay, I felt tempted to defend myself against this insolent son of Britain by deeds of violence: – then the door was opened. The old serving-maid appeared, shewed a wry face at our queer position, and made to promptly shut the door again. In my agony I shouted out my name, and protested that I had been invited by Herr Beethoven himself.

The old lady was still hestitating, for the look of the Englishman seemed to fill her with a proper apprehension, when Beethoven himself, as luck would have it, appeared at the door of his study. Seizing the moment, I stepped quickly in, and moved towards the master to tender my apologies. At like time, however, I dragged the Englishman behind me, as he still was holding me tight. He carried out his threat, and never released me till we both were standing before

Beethoven. I made my bow, and stammered out my name; although of course, he did not hear it, the master seemed to guesss that it was I who had written him. He bade me enter his room; without troubling himself at Beethoven's astonished glance, my companion slipped in after me.

Here I was – in the sanctuary; and yet the hideous perplexity into which the awful Briton had plunged me, robbed me of all that sense of well-being so requisite for due enjoyment of my fortune. Nor was Beethoven's outward appearance itself at all calculated to fill one with a sense of ease. He was clad in somewhat untidy house clothes, with a red woollen scarf wrapped around his waist; long, bushy grey hair hung in disorder from his head, and his gloomy, forbidding expression by no means tended to reassure me. We took our seats at a table strewn with pens and paper.

An uncomfortable feeling held us tongue-tied. It was only too evident that Beethoven was displeased at receiving two instead of one.

At last he began, in grating tones: 'You come from L...? I was about to reply, when he stopped me; passing me a sheet of paper and a pencil, he added: 'Please write; I cannot hear.'

I knew of Beethoven's deafness, and had prepared myself for it. Nevertheless it was like a stab through my heart when I heard his hoarse and broken words, 'I cannot hear.' To stand joyless and poor in the world; to know no uplifting but in the might of Tone, and yet to be forced to say, 'I cannot hear!' That moment gave me the key to Beethoven's exterior, the deep furrows on his cheeks, the sombre dejection of his look, the set defiance of his lips – *he heard not!*

Distraught, and scarcely knowing what, I wrote down an apology, with a brief account of the circumstances that had made me appear in the Englishman's company. Meanwhile the latter sat silently and calmly contemplating Beethoven, who, as soon as he had read my lines, turned rather sharply to him and asked what he might want.

'I have the honour – ' commenced the Briton.

'I don't understand you!' cried Beethoven, hastily interrupting him; 'I cannot hear, nor can I speak much. Please write down what you want of me.'

The Englishman placidly reflected for a moment, then drew an elaborate music-case from his pocket, and said to me: 'Very good. You write: "I beg Herr Beethoven to look through my composition; if any passage does not please him, will he have the kindness to set a cross against it."'

I wrote down his request, word for word, in the hope of getting rid of him at last. And so it happened. After Beethoven had read, he laid the Englishman's composition on the table with a peculiar smile, nodded his head, and said, 'I will send it.'

With this my gentleman was mighty pleased; he rose, made an extra-superfine bow, and took his leave. I drew a deep breath: – he was gone.

Now for the first time did I feel myself within the sanctuary. Even Beethoven's features visibly brightened; he looked at me quietly for an instant, then began:

'The Briton has caused you much annoyance? Take comfort from mine; these travelling Englishmen have plagued me wellnigh out of my life. To-day they come to stare at a poor musician, to-morrow at a rare wild beast. I am truly grieved at having confounded you with them. – You wrote me that you liked my compositions. I'm glad of that, for nowadays I count but little on folk being pleased with my things.'

This confidential tone soon removed my last embarrassment; a thrill of joy ran through me at these simple words. I wrote that I certainly was not the only one imbued with such glowing enthusiasm for every creation of his; that I wished nothing more ardently than to be able to secure for my father-town, for instance, the happiness of seeing him in its midst for once; that he then would convince himself what an effect his works produced on the entire public there.

'I can quite believe,' answered Beethoven, 'that my compositions find more favour in Northern Germany. The Viennese annoy me often; they hear too much bad stuff each day, ever to be disposed to take an earnest thing in earnest.'

I ventured to dispute this, instancing the performance of 'Fidelio' I had attended on the previous evening, which the Viennese public had greeted with the most demonstrative enthusiasm.

'H'm, h'm!' muttered the master. 'Fidelio! But I know the little mites are clapping their hands to-day out of pure conceit, for they fancy that in revising this opera I merely followed their own advice. So they want to pay me for my trouble, and cry bravo! 'Tis a good-natured folk, and not too learned; I had rather be with them, than with sober people. – Do you like Fidelio now?'

I described the impression made on me by last night's performance, and remarked that the whole had splendidly gained by the added pieces.

'Irksome work!' rejoined Beethoven. 'I am no opera composer; at least, I know no theatre in the world for which I should care to write another opera! Were I to make an opera after my own heart, everyone would run away from it; for it would have none of your arias, duets, trios, and all the stuff they patch up operas with to-day; and what I should set in their place no singer would sing, and no audience listen to. They all know nothing but gaudy lies, glittering nonsense, and sugared tedium. Whoever wrote a true musical drama, would be taken for a fool; and so indeed he would be, if he didn't keep such a thing to himself, but wanted to set it before these people.'

'And how must one go to work,' I hotly urged, 'to bring such a musical drama about?'

'As Shakespeare did, when he wrote his plays,' was the almost passionate answer. Then he went on: 'He who has to stitch all kinds of pretty things for ladies with passable voices to get *bravi* and hand-claps, had better become a Parisian lady's-tailor, not a dramatic composer. – For my part, I never was made for such fal-lals. Oh, I know quite well that the clever ones say I am good enough at instrumental music, but should never be at home in vocal. They are perfectly right, since vocal music for them means nothing but operatic music; and from being at home in that nonsense, preserve me heaven!'

I here ventured to ask whether he really believed that anyone, after hearing his 'Adelaide,' would dare to deny him the most brilliant calling as a vocal composer too?

'Eh!' he replied after a little pause, – 'Adelaide and the like are but trifles after all, and come seasonably enough to professional virtuosi, as a fresh opportunity for letting off their fireworks. But why should not vocal music, as much as instrumental, form a grand and serious genre, and its execution meet with as much respect from the feather-brained warblers as I demand from an orchestra for one of my symphonies? The human voice is not to be gainsaid. Nay, it is a far more beautiful and nobler organ of tone, than any instrument in the orchestra. Could not one employ it with just the same freedom as these? What entirely new results one would gain from such a procedure! For the very character that naturally distinguishes the voice of man from the mechanical instrument would have to be given especial prominence, and that would lead to the most manifold combinations. The instruments represent the rudimentary organs of Creation and Nature; what they express can never be clearly defined or put into words, for they reproduce the primitive feelings themselves, those feelings which issued from the chaos of the first Creation, when maybe there was not as yet one human being to take them up into his heart. 'Tis quite otherwise with the genius of the human voice; that represents the heart of man and its sharp-cut individual emotion. Its character is consequently restricted, but definite and clear. Now, let us bring these two elements together, and unite them! Let us set the wild, unfettered elemental feelings, represented by the instruments, in contact with the clear and definite emotion of the human heart, as represented by the voice of man. The advent of this second element will calm and smooth the conflict of those primal feelings, will give their waves a definite, united course; whilst the human heart itself, taking up into it those primordial feelings, will be immeasurably reinforced and widened, equipped to feel with perfect clearness its earlier indefinite presage of the Highest, transformed thereby to godlike consciousness.'

Here Beethoven paused for a few moments, as if exhausted. Then he continued with a gentle sigh: 'To be sure, in the attempt to solve this problem one lights on many an obstacle; to let men sing, one must give them words. Yet who could frame in words *that* poesy which needs must form the basis of such a union of all elements? The poem must necessarily limp behind, for words are organs all too weak for such a task. – You soon will make acquaintance with a new composition of mine, which will remind you of what I just have touched on. It is a symphony with choruses. I will ask you to observe how hard I found it, to get over the incompetence of Poetry to render thorough aid. At last I decided upon using our Schiller's beautiful hymn 'To Joy'; in any case it is a noble and inspiring poem, but far from speaking *that* which, certainly in this connection, no verses in the world could say.'

To this day I scarce can grasp my happiness at thus being helped by Beethoven himself to a full understanding of his titanic Last Symphony, which then at most was finished, but known as yet to no man. I conveyed to him my fervent thanks for this rare condescension. At the same time I expressed the delightful surprise it had been to me, to hear that we might look forward to the appearance of a new great work of his composition. Tears had welled into my eyes, – I could have gone down on my knees to him.

Beethoven seemed to remark my agitation. Half mournfully, half roguishly, he looked into my face and said: 'You might take my part, when my new work is discussed. Remember me: for the clever ones will think I am out of my senses; at least, that is what they will cry. But perhaps you see, Herr R., that I am not quite a madman yet, though unhappy enough to make me one. – People want me to write according to *their* ideas of what is good and beautiful; they never reflect that I, a poor deaf man, must have my very own ideas, – that it would be impossible for me to write otherwise than I feel. And that I cannot think and feel their beautiful affairs,' he added in irony, 'is just what makes out my misfortune!'

With that he rose, and paced the room with short, quick steps. Stirred to my inmost heart as I was, I stood up too; – I could feel myself trembling. It would have been impossible for me to pursue the conversation either by pantomimic signs or writing. I was conscious also that the point had been reached when my visit might become a burden to the master. To *write* a farewell word of heartfelt thanks, seemed too matter-of-fact; so I contented myself with seizing my hat, approaching Beethoven, and letting him read in my eyes what was passing within me.

He seemed to understand. 'You are going?' he asked. 'Shall you remain in Vienna awhile?'

I wrote that my journey had no other object than to gain his personal acquaintance; since he had honoured me with so unusual a reception, I was overjoyed to view my goal as reached, and should start for home again next day.

Smiling, he replied: 'You wrote me, in what manner you had procured the money for this journey. – You ought to stop in Vienna and write galops, – that sort of ware is much valued here.'

I declared that I had done with all that, as I now knew nothing worth a similar sacrifice.

'Well, well,' he said, 'one never knows! Old fool that I am, I should have done better, myself, to write galops; the way I have gone, I shall always famish. A pleasant journey,' – he added – 'think of me, and let that console you in all your troubles.'

My eyes full of tears, I was about to withdraw, when he called to me: 'Stay, we must polish off the musical Englishman! Let's see where to put the crosses!'

He snatched up the Briton's music case, and smilingly skimmed its contents; then he carefully put it in order again, wrapped it in a sheet of paper, took a thick scoring pen, and drew a huge cross from one end of the cover to the other. Whereupon he handed it to me with the words: 'Kindly give the happy man his masterwork! He's an ass, and yet I envy him his long ears! – Farewell, dear friend, and hold me dear!'

And so he dismissed me. With staggering steps I left his chamber and the house.

At the hotel I found the Englishman's servant packing away his master's trunks in the travelling-carriage. So his goal, also, was reached; I could but admit that *he*, too, had proved his endurance. I ran up to my room, and likewise made ready to commence my homeward march on the morrow. A fit of laughter seized me when I looked at the cross on the cover of the Englishman's composition. That cross, however, was a souvenir of Beethoven, and I grudged it to the evil genius of my pilgrimage. My decision was quickly taken. I removed the cover, hunted out my galops, and clapped them in this damning shroud. To the Englishman I sent his composition wrapperless, accompanying it with a little note in which I told him that Beethoven envied him and had declared he didn't know where to set a cross.

As I was leaving the inn, I saw my wretched comrade mount into his carriage.

'Goodbye,' he cried. 'You have done me a great service. I am glad to have made Beethoven's acquaintance. – Will you come with me to Italy?'

'What would you there?' – I asked in reply.

'I wish to know Mr Rossini, as he is a very famous composer.'

'Good luck!' – called I: 'I know Beethoven, and that's enough for my lifetime!'

We parted. I cast one longing glance at Beethoven's house, and turned to the north, uplifted in heart and ennobled.

Louis Spohr

On Beethoven

Immediately on my arrival in Vienna I paid a visit to Beethoven, but not finding him at home I left my card. I hoped to meet him at some musical party but was informed that, when his deafness increased and he could not well hear music, he had become shy of society and had given up attending parties. I tried another visit but was again unsuccessful. Finally, I ran him to earth at the eating-house where I was in the habit of going with my wife. I had already given concerts which had been favourably commented upon by the Vienna Press and as I introduced myself, Beethoven, who must have heard of me, received me in an unusually gracious manner. We sat down at the same table and Beethoven became very talkative, surprising the other guests, for he was usually very taciturn. It was difficult to make him hear me and I was obliged to talk loudly enough to be heard a long distance off. We met again at the restaurant and he ended by visiting me at home. We thus became well acquainted. He was a little blunt, not to say uncouth, in his manner, but there was a truthful eye under his bushy eyebrows. After my return from Gotha I met him at the Theatre An der Wien where Count Palffy had given him a free seat behind the orchestra. After the opera he would accompany me to my house and spend the rest of the evening with us. He would then be very friendly with my wife and the children. He very seldom spoke of music. When he did, his opinions were very decided and he could not bear to be contradicted. He took no interest whatever in the work of others and I therefore had not the courage to show him my compositions. His favourite topic was criticism of the way Prince Lobkowitz and Count Palffy were running the theatres. He frequently abused the Count while we were still inside the theatre and in so loud a voice that the Count himself in his office could hear him. This embarrassed me greatly.

Beethoven's rough and even repulsive manner at the time arose partly from his deafness and partly from his poverty. He was a bad housekeeper and, moreover, was plundered by all those about him. In the early part of our acquaintance, not having seen him for several days, I asked him: 'I hope you were not sick?' He replied: 'I was not; but one of my shoes was; and as I have only one pair I was under "house arrest".' Sometime afterwards he was relieved by his friends in the following circumstances.

Fidelio, performed in unfavourable circumstances during the French occupation, had met with little success in 1805. Now the director of the Karthnerthor theatre produced it again for his benefit. Beethoven had been persuaded to write a new overture (in E) as well as a song for the jailer and the grand aria for Fidelio with horns obbligati. In this new form the opera had been a great success and kept its place for a long succession of crowded performances. His friends availed themselves of the favourable moment to give a concert for his benefit in the great Redouten-Saal where the most recent works of his were given. All who could fiddle, blow or sing were invited to assist and all the most celebrated artists in Vienna turned up, including myself and my orchestra. I then for the first time saw Beethoven conduct. His manner surprised me, although I had already heard a good deal about his behaviour on the rostrum. He indicated marks of expression to the orchestra with extraordinary motions of his body. The arms that were crossed on his breast were suddenly and violently thrust out when a 'sforzando' occurred. When he wanted soft tones he would crouch down; when a 'crescendo' was needed he raised himself by degrees, springing bolt upright when the 'forte' was reached. If he wanted still louder sounds he would shout to the orchestra without being actually aware of it.

On my expressing astonishment at this extraordinary method of conducting, I was told the tragi-comical events that happened at Beethoven's last concert at the Theatre An der Wien.

He was playing his new piano concerto, but at the very first 'Tutti', forgetting that he was the soloist, he began to conduct. When he came to the first sforzando he threw out his arms with such force that he knocked down the lights on the piano. The audience laughed and Beethoven, annoyed, stopped the orchestra and the concerto started again from the beginning. This time the leader took the precaution to order two choirboys to hold the lights for the pianist. When the sforzando was reached a second time, Beethoven acted as before, but instead of hitting the lights he hit one of the boys who, receiving a smart blow, dropped the light in terror. The other lad, guessing what was coming, had saved himself by suddenly bending and dodging the blow. If the public had laughed before, they now became hysterical and Beethoven, enraged, struck the piano with such force that at the very first chord six strings broke.

The concert got up by his friends was a great success. The new compositions were much applauded and the Seventh Symphony in particular made a deep impression, the second movement being encored. In spite of Beethoven's uncertain and, at times, laughable directions the execution was masterly.

It was easy to see that the poor deaf maestro could no longer hear his music. It was particularly noticeable in the second part of the first movement where occur two pauses in succession. The second is marked pianissimo and obviously Beethoven had overlooked it as he beat time before the orchestra had finished the pause. As usual with him he marked crescendo and diminuendo by crouching down and rising, but in this instance when he sprang up for the forte nothing happened. He looked round frightened and only recovered when he realized that the forte was on the way. Fortunately this happened at the rehearsal. The hall being crowded for the concert, Beethoven's friends arranged for a repetition of the event and this realized an equally conspicuous sum so that Beethoven was relieved of financial worries for some time. But before his death he found himself once more in poverty and owing to the same cause.

As at the time I made Beethoven's acquaintance he had already given up playing in public I only had an opportunity to hear him when I accidentally dropped in during the rehearsal of a new trio (in D major). It was by no means an enjoyable experience. The piano was woefully out of tune – a fact which troubled him little since he could hear nothing – and of his excellence as a virtuoso there was hardly any evidence because of his deafness. In the 'fortes' the poor deaf man hammered upon the keys in such a way that whole groups of notes became inaudible; the only way of knowing what was happening was to follow the performance on the score. I was deeply moved by so hard a fate. It is a sad thing for anyone to be afflicted with deafness; a musician cannot endure it without being driven to despair. The cause of Beethoven's continual melancholy was no longer a mystery to me.

W. H. Auden

The Composer

All the others translate: the painter sketches
A visible world to love or reject;
Rummaging into his living, the poet fetches
The images out that hurt and connect.

From Life to Art by painstaking adaption,
Relying on us to cover the rift;
Only your notes are pure contraption,
Only your song is an absolute gift.

Pour out your presence, O delight, cascading
The falls of the knee and the weirs of the spine,
Our climate of silence and doubt invading;

You alone, alone, O imaginary song,
Are unable to say an existence is wrong,
And pour out your forgiveness like a wine.

Delmore Schwartz

Vivaldi

I

In the dark church of music
Which never is of land or sea alone
But blooms within the air inside the mind,
Patterns in motion and in action – successions
Of processionals, moving with the majesty of certainty
To part the unparted curtains, to bring the chandeliers
Into the sarabande of courtiers who have bowed and curtsied,
Turned somersaults in circuses, climbed masts and towers,
Or dived as from a glistening tower toward a glittering lake,
Springing, daring and assured, fearless and precise –
Find, in the darkness of the dark church
That music is: This is what music is:
It has no meaning and is possessed by all meaning,
For music says,

> Remorse, here is the scar of healing.
> Here is a window, curiosity!
> And here, O sensuality, a sofa!
> Behold, for ambition's purposeless energy,
> Mountains rising beyond mountains
> More tense and steep than any known before.

Devout
The processional (having a solemn majesty,
Though childlike acrobats like flowers decorate
With flourishes and *entrechats* the passage to success.

As queens serene, crowned by poise, slowly
Are drawn in cars by dragons domesticated in the last of
    wars)
Is uttered again, freshly and fully, newly and uniquely,
Uniquely and newly, fully and freshly uttered again.

II

O clear soprano like the morning peal of bluebells!
O the water colors of the early morning,
Con amore and *vivace*, dancing, prancing, galloping,
        rollicking!

This is the surrender to the splendor of being's becoming
     and being!
Here are all the flowers and the images of faces as flowers, of
     fear and hope, longing and despair;
Here is the hour of the new blue flower
Dissolved, consumed in this being that is the being of beings.
So we are to be contained, so we are to be consumed –
The iron petal of the flute possesses morning's intuition;
The cellist is as Gautama Buddha, curved like an almond;
The first violinist is St. Francis of Assisi,
Blessing the trees, the cats, the birds, calling to them, and
     calling them his brothers and his sisters;
The full orchestra responds to the virtuoso's cadenza:
'Love is the dark secret of everything,
Love is the open secret of everything,
An open secret as useless as the blue!'

Music is not water, but it moves like water;
It is not fire, but it soars as warm as the sun.
It is not rock, it is not fountain,
But rock and fountain, clock and mountain
Abide within it, bound together
In radiance, pulsing, vibrating, and reverberating,
Dominating the domination of the weather.

III

The music declares
'Is this what you want? Is this the good news for which you
     have been here convened –
To be, to become, and to participate in the sweet congress of
     serene attention,
Silent, attentive, motionless, waiting,
Save for the heart clutching itself and the hushed breathing?'

The answered question is: Our being. Our presence. Our
    surrender.
Consciousness has consented, is consumed, has surrendered,
    to hear only the players playing.
Consciousness has become only and purely listening.

    The vivid world has been barred,
    The press of desire shut out.
This is the dark city of the innermost wish,
    The motion beyond emotion,
    The power beyond and free of power.
This is the dark city of the hidden innermost wish,
This is the immortality of mortality, this
Is supreme consciousness, the grasped reality of reality,
moving
        forward,
    Now and forever.

—

Gottfried Benn

Chopin

Not very forthcoming in conversation,
opinions were not his forte,
opinions don't get to the centre;
when Delacroix expounded a theory
he became restive, he for his part was unable
to explicate his Nocturnes.

Weak as a lover;
shadows at Nohant,
where George Sand's children
would not accept
his pedagogic advice.

Consumptive, of the kind
with haemorrhages and cicatrization,
the kind that drags on for years;
quiet death
as opposed to one
with paroxysms of pain
or one by the firing-squad:
They moved his grand piano (Erard) up to the door
and Delphine Potocka
sang for him at his dying hour
a violet song.

To England he went with three pianos:
Pleyel, Erard, Broadwood,
gave for twenty minutes
fifteen-minute recitals
at Rothschild's, the Wellingtons, at Stratford House,
and to countless garters:
darkened by weariness and approaching death,
he went home
to the Square d'Orléans.

Then he burnt his sketches
and manuscripts;
no residues please, no fragments or notes,
they grant such revealing insights –
and said at the end:
'My endeavours are as complete
as it was in my power to make them.'

Every finger was to play
with the force appropriate to its structure;
the fourth is the weakest
(mere siamese twin to the middle finger).
When he began they rested
on E, F sharp, G sharp, B, C.

The man who has ever heard
certain Preludes by him,
whether in country houses or
in a mountain landscape
or on a terrace, through open doors,
a sanatorium's for instance,
will hardly forget it.

Never composed an opera,
no symphony,
only these tragic progressions
out of artistic conviction
and with a slender hand.

Translated by Michael Hamburger

Hector Berlioz

The Composer-Conductor

From *Mémoires*

Letter to Liszt – from Mannheim, Weimar

On my return from Hechingen, I stayed several more days at Stuttgart, a prey to new uncertainties. To all the questions asked me about my plans and the future direction of my travels which had scarcely begun, I could have truthfully replied like the character in Molière:

> No, I am not returning, for I have not been;
> Nor am I going, for I am detained,
> But I am not staying, for all the same
> I intend to go away . . .

Go away . . . where? I hardly knew. I had written to Weimar, it is true, but a reply had not arrived, and I certainly had to wait for one before making any decision.

You do not know about such uncertainties, my dear Liszt; it does not matter much to you whether there is a select musical group in the town you intend to visit; if the theatre is open; if the manager will place it at your disposal, etc. What do you care about having all this information? You can, to adapt the words of Louis XIV, say confidently: 'The orchestra, c'est moi! the choir, c'est moi! the conductor, c'est moi! My piano sings, dreams, flashes, resounds; it challenges the flight of the most skilful bow; like the orchestra it has its brassy harmonies, and, like the orchestra also but without any of its contrivances it can release on to the evening air a cloud of fairylike sounds and haunting melodies; I need neither theatre, nor special enclosure, nor vast tiers; I do not need to wear myself out with long rehearsals; I do not ask for a hundred, fifty, or even twenty musicians; I do not ask for anything at all; I do not even need music. A large room, a grand piano and I can have an audience at my feet. I have only to show myself and I am greeted with applause. My memory stirs, dazzling fantasies come to life at the touch of my fingers and are enthusiastically acclaimed; I play Schubert's *Ave Maria* or Beethoven's *Adelaide* and all hearts are softened towards me, everyone holds their breath . . . there is a moving silence, a deep and stilled hush of admiration. Then come the sparkling explosions, the fireworks, and the cheers of the audience, the flowers and the crowns of glory raining around this high priest of harmony quivering on his tripod, and the young girls who, in their sacred frenzy, tearfully embrace the hem of his garment; and the sincere homage given by earnest admirers and the feverish applause wrung from the envious, the superior minds who stoop to admire, the narrow-minded surprised at being expanded . . .' And next day when the young genius has dispensed as much as he wishes to dispense of his inexhaustible gift, he goes away, he disappears, leaving behind him a lambent glow of glory and success. What a dream! It's one of those golden dreams one has when one thinks of Liszt or Paganini.

But the composer who tries, as I have done, to travel to perform his own works, what stresses and thankless labour, endlessly repeated, await him. Does anyone know what torture rehearsals can be for him? First he has to face the frosty looks of all the musicians, not at all pleased to have to put themselves to some inconvenience and give unaccustomed study to his work. 'What does this Frenchman want? Why doesn't he stay at home?' Nevertheless each one takes his place at his desk: but with his first glance at the assembled orchestra, the composer perceives quickly enough that there are some worrying gaps. He asks the musical director why this is: 'The first clarinet is sick, the oboist's wife is in labour, the first violin's child has croup, the trombones are on parade – they forgot to ask exemption from military duties for today; the tympanist has strained his wrist, the harpist will never come to rehearsals because he needs the time to study his part, etc., etc.' All the same things begin, the notes are read, just about, and the tempo goes twice as slow as the composer intended; nothing is more awful for him than this languishing rhythm! Little by little his instincts take over, his blood warms, he gets carried away, the beat quickens and in spite of himself, approaches the right tempo; then, what a mess results, a very cacophony assaults his ears and his heart; he must stop and take the tempo again slowly and practise bit by bit the long phrases which, so many times before with other orchestras he has directed without pause or hindrance. This is still not sufficient; in spite of the slowness of the tempo, certain strange discords can be heard coming from certain sections of the wind instruments; the cause has to be traced. 'Let me hear the trumpets by themselves . . . . What are you doing there? I must have a third and you're giving me a second. The second trumpet in C has a D, give me your D. Very good. The first has a C which sounds F, give me your C! Good heavens! You gave me an E flat.'

'No, sir. I'm playing what is written!'

'But you're not, you mistook the tone!'

'All the same, I'm sure I played a C.'

'What key is your trumpet in ?'

'E flat.'

'Oh, there you are, that's what's causing the mistake, you ought to have a trumpet in F.'

'Oh I didn't read the instructions properly; that's true, I'm sorry.'

'Let's get on then! What a devil of a din you're making, you there, the tympanist!'

'Sir, I have a fortissimo.'

'Not at all, it's a mezze forte, it's not two ffs, but an m and an f. Besides you're using wooden drumsticks and you must use sticks with sponge heads; it's the difference between black and white.'

'We don't know them,' says the musical director. 'What do you mean by sticks with sponge heads? We only have a single type of drumstick.'

'I am not surprised; I have brought some from Paris. Take a pair which I put on that table. Now, are we ready? . . . My God, it's twenty times too loud! And you haven't got the mutes!'

'We haven't got them, the boy forgot to put them out on the desks; we'll have them tomorrow, etc. etc. . . . '

After three or four hours of these antiharmonical wranglings, not one bit has been made intelligible. Everything is disjointed, muddled, false, cold, flat, noisy, discordant, horrible! And then sixty or eighty musicians leave, going home tired and discontented, all with the same impression; all of them saying that they don't know what this music means, that it's hellish, chaotic, that they've never endured anything like it. The next day there's hardly any progress; it is not until the third day that things begin to take shape. Only then does the poor composer begin to breathe; the carefully arranged harmonies become clear, the rhythms skip, the melodies weep and smile; the whole united ensemble advances boldly; after so many stumblings and stutterings the orchestra grows up, it walks, it speaks, it becomes a man! Understanding gives courage to the astonished musicians; the composer asks for a further proof; his interpreters who, when all is said and done, are the best fellows in the world, respond to him with eagerness. This time, let there be light! 'Think of the nuances! You are no longer afraid? No! then give us the right tempo! Let's go!' And there is light, art becomes manifest, the thought is illuminated, the work is understood! And the orchestra rises to its feet, applauding and saluting the composer; the musical director congratulates him; curious listeners who have hidden themselves in dark corners of the hall approach, climb up on to the platform and exchange exclamations of pleasure and astonishment with the musicians while gazing in wonder at the foreigner whom they had at first taken for a madman or a barbarian. It's now that he might feel tempted to relax. But the poor fellow should beware of that! Now, on the contrary, it's time for him to redouble his efforts and his concentration. He must go back before the concert to supervise the arrangement of the desks, to inspect the orchestra's parts and make sure that they are not mixed up. He must walk up and down the rows, a red pencil in his hand, and mark on the music of the wind instruments the key indications used in Germany in place of those used in France (putting everything in C, in D, in Des, in Fis, instead of in ut, re, re bemol, fa diese). He has to transpose for the oboe a solo of the cor anglais because this instrument is not available in the orchestra he is going to conduct and the player is reluctant to transpose it himself. He has to rehearse the choirs and the singers separately if they are still unsure of themselves. But the audience is arriving, the hour strikes; exhausted, overwhelmed with fatigue in both body and mind, the composer comes out to the conductor's desk, scarcely able to hold himself up, uncertain, drained, dejected, until the transforming moment when the applause of the audience and the excitement of the musicians, the love which he has for his own work turn him into a dynamo of energy from which pour out invisible, but real enough, galvanising rays. And then the recompense begins. Oh, it's then, I am sure, that the composer-conductor lives a life quite unknown to the virtuoso. Now he can abandon himself to the incomparable ecstasy of 'playing' the orchestra! How he holds, how he embraces, how he sways this immense and fiery instrument. Once more he is all attention. His eye is everywhere; he indicates with a glance the entry of voices and instruments, from above, below, to the right, to the left. He dispatches with his right arm terrible chords which seem to burst in the distance like harmonious projectiles; then he arrests, with the notes of the organ, all the movement which he has initiated; everyone's attention is riveted, every arm suspended, every sound stilled, he listens a moment to the silence . . . then unleashes once more the frenzied turbulence which he has restrained.

> The rearing winds and roaring tempests
> He subdues to his dominion, and curbs and confines them.

And in the long adagios, how happy he is to rock gently on his beautiful sea of harmony! listening to a hundred mingled voices singing his songs of love, or confiding the sorrows of today and past regrets to the solitude of the night. Then often, but only then, the composer-conductor is completely oblivious of the audience; he listens to himself, he judges himself; and if deeply stirred, like the artists who surround him, he pays no further attention to the impression of the audience now too far removed from him. If his heart has trembled in its contact with the poetic melody, if he has felt a consuming sensation in his inmost soul, he has his reward, the heaven of art is open to him, what does earth matter!

Then at the end of the evening when great success has been achieved his joy is multiplied, shared as it is by all the gratified satisfaction of his army. So you, great virtuosos, you are princes and kings by the grace of God, you are born on the steps of the throne; composers must fight, win and conquer in order to rule. But the very weariness and dangers of the struggle add to the intoxicating glory of their victories and they will always perhaps be happier than you – as long as they have soldiers.

Translated by Joan Abse

Roald Dahl

Edward the Conqueror

Louisa, holding a dishcloth in her hand, stepped out the kitchen door at the back of the house into the cool October sunshine.

'Edward!' she called. '*Ed-ward*! Lunch is ready!'

She paused a moment, listening; then she strolled out on to the lawn and continued across it – a little shadow attending her – skirting the rose bed and touching the sundial lightly with one finger as she went by. She moved rather gracefully for a woman who was small and plump, with a lilt in her walk and a gentle swinging of the shoulders and the arms. She passed under the mulberry tree on to the brick path, then went all the way along the path until she came to the place where she could look down into the dip at the end of this large garden.

'*Edward!* Lunch!'

She could see him now, about eighty yards away, down in the dip on the edge of the wood – the tallish narrow figure in khaki slacks and dark-green sweater, working beside a big bonfire with a fork in his hands, pitching brambles on to the top of the fire. It was blazing fiercely, with orange flames and clouds of milky smoke, and the smoke was drifting back over the garden with a wonderful scent of autumn and burning leaves.

Louisa went down the slope towards her husband. Had she wanted, she could easily have called again and made herself heard, but there was something about a first-class bonfire that impelled her towards it, right up close so she could feel the heat and listen to it burn.

'Lunch,' she said, approaching.

'Oh, hello. All right – yes. I'm coming.'

'*What* a good fire.'

'I've decided to clear this place right out,' her husband said. 'I'm sick and tired of all these brambles.' His long face was wet with perspiration.There were small beads of it clinging all over his moustache like dew, and two little rivers were running down his throat on to the turtleneck of the sweater.

'You better be careful you don't overdo it, Edward.'

'Louisa, I do wish you'd stop treating me as though I were eighty. A bit of exercise never did anyone any harm.'

'Yes, dear. I know. Oh, Edward! Look! Look!'

The man turned and looked at Louisa, who was pointing now to the far side of the bonfire.

'Look, Edward! The cat!'

Sitting on the ground, so close to the fire that the flames sometimes seemed actually to be touching it, was a large cat of a most unusual colour. It stayed quite still, with its head on one side and its nose in the air, watching the man and woman with a cool yellow eye.

'It'll get burnt!' Louisa cried, and she dropped the dishcloth and darted swiftly in and grabbed it with both hands, whisking it away and putting it on the grass well clear of the flames.

'You crazy cat,' she said, dusting off her hands. 'What's the matter with you?'

'Cats know what they're doing,' the husband said. 'You'll never find a cat doing something it doesn't want. Not cats.'

'Whose is it? You ever seen it before?'

'No, I never have. Damn peculiar colour.'

The cat had seated itself on the grass and was regarding them with a sidewise look. There was a veiled inward expression about the eyes, something curiously omniscient and pensive, and around the nose a most delicate air of contempt, as though the sight of these two middle aged persons – the one small, plump, and rosy, the other lean and extremely sweaty – were a matter of some surprise but very little importance. For a cat, it certainly had an unusual colour – a pure silvery grey with no blue in it at all – and the hair was very long and silky.

Louisa bent down and stroked its head. 'You must go home,' she said. 'Be a good cat now and go on home to where you belong.'

The man and wife started to stroll back up the hill towards the house. The cat got up and followed, at a distance at first, but edging closer and closer as they went along. Soon it was alongside them, then it was ahead, leading the way across the lawn to the house, and walking as though it owned the whole place, holding its tail straight up in the air, like a mast.

'Go home,' the man said. 'Go on home. We don't want you.'

But when they reached the house, it came in with them, and Louisa gave it some milk in the kitchen. During lunch, it hopped up on to the spare chair between them and sat through the meal with its head just above the level of the table, watching the proceedings with those dark-yellow eyes which kept moving slowly from the woman to the man and back again.

'I don't like this cat,' Edward said.

'Oh, I think it's a beautiful cat. I do hope it stays a little while.'

'Now, listen to me, Louisa. The creature can't possibly stay here. It belongs to someone else. It's lost. And if it's still trying to hang around this afternoon, you'd better take it to the police. They'll see it gets home.'

After lunch, Edward returned to his gardening. Louisa, as usual, went to the piano. She was a competent pianist and a genuine music-lover, and almost every afternoon she spent an hour or so playing for herself. The cat was now lying on the sofa, and she paused to stroke it as she went by. It opened its eyes, looked at her a moment, then closed them again and went back to sleep.

'You're an awfully nice cat,' she said.'And such a beautiful colour. I wish I could keep you.' Then her fingers, moving over the fur on the cat's head, came into contact with a small lump, a little growth just above the right eye.

'Poor cat,' she said.'You've got bumps on your beautiful face.You must be getting old.'

She went over and sat down on the long piano bench, but she didn't immediately start to play. One of her special little pleasures was to make every day a kind of concert day, with a carefully arranged programme which she worked out in detail before she began. She never liked to break her enjoyment by having to stop while she wondered what to play next. All she wanted was a brief pause after each piece while the audience clapped enthusiastically and called for more. It was so much nicer to imagine an audience, and now and again while she was playing – on the lucky days, that is – the room would begin to swim and fade and darken, and she would see nothing but row upon row of seats and a sea of white faces upturned towards her, listening with a rapt and adoring concentration.

Sometimes she played from memory, sometimes from music. Today she would play from memory; that was the way she felt. And what should the programme be? She sat before the piano with her small hands clasped on her lap, a plump rosy little person with a round and still quite pretty face, her hair done up in a neat bun at the back of her head. By looking slightly to the right, she could see the cat curled up asleep on the sofa, and its silvery-grey coat was beautiful against the purple of the cushion. How about some Bach to begin with? Or, better still, Vivaldi. The Bach adaptation for organ of the D minor Concerto Grosso. Yes – that first. Then perhaps a litle Schumann. *Carnaval?* That would be fun. And after that – well, a touch of Liszt for a change. One of the *Petrarch Sonnets*. The second one – that was the loveliest – the E major. Then another Schumann, another of his gay ones – *Kinderscenen*. And lastly, for the encore, a Brahms waltz, or maybe two of them if she felt like it.

Vivaldi, Schumann, Liszt, Schumann, Brahms. A very nice pro-gramme, one that she could play easily without the music. She moved herself a little closer to the piano and paused a moment while someone in the audience – already she could feel that this was one of the lucky days – while someone in the audience had his last cough; then, with the slow grace that accompanied nearly all her movements, she lifted her hands to the keyboard and began to play.

She wasn't, at that particular moment, watching the cat at all – as a matter of fact she had forgotten its presence – but as the first deep notes of the Vivaldi sounded softly in the room, she became aware, out of the corner of one eye, of a sudden flurry, a flash of movement, on the sofa to her right. She stopped playing at once. 'What is it?' she said, turning to the cat. 'What's the matter?'

The animal, who a few seconds before had been sleeping peacefully, was now sitting bolt upright on the sofa, very tense, the whole body aquiver, ears up and eyes wide open, staring at the piano.

'Did I frighten you?' she asked gently. 'Perhaps you've never heard music before.'

No, she told herself. I don't think that's what it is. On second thoughts, it seemed to her that the cat's attitude was not one of fear. There was no shrinking or backing away. If anything, there was a leaning forward, a kind of eagerness about the creature, and the face – well, there was rather an odd expression on the face, something of a mixture between surprise and shock. Of course, the face of a cat is a small and fairly expressionless thing, but if you watch carefully the eyes and ears working together, and particularly that little area of mobile skin below the ears and slightly to one side, you can occasionally see the reflection of very powerful emotions. Louisa was watching the face closely now, and because she was curious to see what would happen a second time, she reached out her hands to the keyboard and began again to play the Vivaldi.

This time the cat was ready for it, and all that happened to begin with was a small extra tensing of the body. But as the music swelled and quickened into that first exciting rhythm of the introduction to the fugue, a strange look that amounted almost to ecstasy began to settle upon the creature's face. The ears, which up to then had been pricked up straight, were gradually drawn back, the eyelids drooped, the head went over to one side, and at that moment Louisa could have sworn that the animal was actually *appreciating* the work.

What she saw (or thought she saw) was something she had noticed many times on the faces of people listening very closely to a piece of music. When the sound takes complete hold of them and drowns them in itself, a peculiar, intensely ecstatic look comes over them that you can recognize as easily as a smile. So far as Louisa could see, the cat was now wearing almost exactly this kind of look.

Louisa finished the fugue, then played the siciliana, and all the way through she kept watching the cat on the sofa. The final proof for her that the animal was listening came at the end, when the music stopped. It blinked, stirred itself a little, stretched a leg, settled into a more comfortable position, took a quick glance round the room, then looked expectantly in her direction. It was precisely the way a concert-goer reacts when the music momentarily releases him in the pause between two movements of a symphony. The behaviour was so thoroughly human it gave her a queer agitated feeling in the chest.

'You like that?' she asked. 'You like Vivaldi?'

The moment she'd spoken, she felt ridiculous, but not – and this to her was a trifle sinister – not quite so ridiculous as she knew she should have felt.

Well, there was nothing for it now except to go straight ahead with the next number on the programme, which was *Carnaval*. As soon as she began to play, the cat again stiffened and sat up straighter; then, as it became slowly and blissfully saturated with the sound, it relapsed into that queer melting mood of ecstasy that seemed to have something to do with drowning and with dreaming. It was really an extravagant sight – quite a comical one, too – to see this silvery cat sitting on the sofa and being carried away like this. And what made it more screwy than ever, Louisa thought, was the fact that this music, which the animal seemed to be enjoying so much, was manifestly too *difficult*, too *classical*, to be appreciated by the majority of humans in the world.

Maybe, she thought, the creature's not really enjoying it at all. Maybe it's a sort of hypnotic reaction, like with snakes. After all, if you can charm a snake with music, then why not a cat? Except that millions of cats hear the stuff every day of their lives, on radio and gramophone and piano, and, as far as she knew, there'd never yet been a case of one behaving like this. This one was acting as though it were following every single note. It was certainly a fantastic thing.

But was it not also a wonderful thing? Indeed it was. In fact, unless she was much mistaken, it was a kind of miracle, one of those animal miracles that happen about once every hundred years.

'I could see you *loved* that one,' she said when the piece was over. 'Although I'm sorry I didn't play it any too well today. Which did you like best – the Vivaldi or the Schumann?'

The cat made no reply, so Louisa, fearing she might lose the attention of her listener, went straight into the next part of the programme – Liszt's second *Petrarch Sonnet*.

And now an extraordinary thing happened. She hadn't played more than three or four bars when the animal's whiskers began perceptibly to twitch.

Slowly it drew itself up to an extra height, laid its head on one side, then on the other, and stared into space with a kind of frowning concentrated look that seemed to say, 'What's this? Don't tell me. I know it so well, but just for the moment I don't seem to be able to place it.' Louisa was fascinated, and with her little mouth half open and half smiling, she continued to play, waiting to see what on earth was going to happen next.

The cat stood up, walked to one end of the sofa, sat down again, listened some more; then all at once it bounded to the floor and leaped up on to the piano bench beside her. There it sat, listening intently to the lovely sonnet, not dreamily this time, but very erect, the large yellow eyes fixed upon Louisa's fingers.

'Well!' she said as she struck the last chord. 'So you came up to sit beside me, did you? You like this better than the sofa? All right, I'll let you stay, but you must keep still and not jump about.' She put out a hand and stoked the cat softly along the back, from head to tail. 'That was Liszt,' she went on. 'Mind you, he can sometimes be quite horribly vulgar, but in things like this he's really charming.'

She was beginning to enjoy this odd animal pantomime, so she went straight on into the next item on the programme, Schumann's *Kinderscenen*.

She hadn't been playing for more than a minute or two when she realized that the cat had again moved, and was now back in its old place on the sofa. She'd been watching her hands at the time, and presumably that was why she hadn't even noticed its going; all the same, it must have been an extremely swift and silent move. The cat was still staring at her, still apparently attending closely to the music, and yet it seemed to Louisa that there was not now the same rapturous enthusiasm there'd been during the previous piece, the Liszt. In addition, the act of leaving the stool and returning to the sofa appeared in itself to be a mild but positive gesture of disappointment.

'What's the matter?' she asked when it was over. 'What's wrong with Schumann? What's so marvellous about Liszt?' The cat looked straight back at her with those yellow eyes that had small jet-black bars lying vertically in their centres.

This, she told herself, is really beginning to get interesting – a trifle spooky, too, when she came to think of it. But one look at the cat sitting there on the sofa, so bright and attentive, so obviously waiting for more music, quickly reassured her.

'All right,' she said. 'I'll tell you what I'm going to do. I'm going to alter my programme specially for you. You seem to like Liszt so much, I'll give you another.'

She hesitated, searching her memory for a good Liszt; then softly she began to play one of the twelve little pieces from *Der Weihnachtsbaum*. She was now watching the cat very closely, and the first thing she noticed was that the whiskers again began to twitch. It jumped down to the carpet, stood still a moment, inclining its head, quivering with excitement, and then, with a slow, silky stride, it walked round the piano, hopped up on the bench, and sat down beside her.

They were in the middle of all this when Edward came in from the garden.

'Edward!' Louisa cried, jumping up. 'Oh, Edward, darling! Listen to this! Listen what's happened!'

'What is it now?' he said. 'I'd like some tea.' He had one of those narrow, sharp-nosed, faintly magenta faces, and the sweat was making it shine as though it were a long wet grape.

'It's the cat!' Louisa cried, pointing to it sitting quietly on the piano bench. 'Just *wait* till you hear what's happened!'

'I thought I told you to take it to the police.'

'But, Edward, *listen* to me. This is *terribly* exciting. This is a *musical* cat.'

'Oh, yes?'

'This cat can appreciate music, and it can understand it too.'

'Now stop this nonsense, Louisa, and let's for God's sake have some tea. I'm hot and tired from cutting brambles and building bonfires.' He sat down in an armchair, took a cigarette from a box beside him, and lit it with an immense patent lighter that stood near the box.

'What you don't understand,' Louisa said, 'is that something extremely exciting has been happening here in our own house while you were out, something that may even be ... well ... almost momentous.'

'I'm quite sure of that.'

'Edward, *please*!'

Louisa was standing by the piano, her little pink face pinker than ever, a scarlet rose high up on each cheek. 'If you want to know,' she said, 'I'll tell you what I think.'

'I'm listening, dear.'

'I think it might be possible that we are at this moment sitting in the presence of – ' She stopped, as though suddenly sensing the absurdity of the thought.

'Yes?'

'You may think it silly, Edward, but it's honestly what I think.'

'In the presence of who, for heaven's sake?'

'Of Franz Liszt himself!'

Her husband took a long slow pull at his cigarette and blew the smoke up at the ceiling. He had the tight-skinned, concave cheeks of a man who has worn a full set of dentures for many years, and every time he sucked at a cigarette, the cheeks went in even more, and the bones of his face stood out like a skeleton's. 'I don't get you,' he said.

'Edward, listen to me. From what I've seen this afternoon with my own eyes, it really looks as though this might actually be some sort of a reincarnation.'

'You mean this lousy cat?'

'Don't talk like that, dear, please.'

'You're not ill, are you, Louisa?'

'I'm perfectly all right, thank you very much. I'm a bit confused – I don't mind admitting it, but who wouldn't be after what's just happened? Edward, I swear to you – '

'What *did* happen, if I may ask?'

Louisa told him, and all the while she was speaking, her husband lay sprawled in the chair with his legs stretched out in front of him, sucking at his cigarette and blowing the smoke up at the ceiling. There was a thin cynical smile on his mouth.

'I don't see anything very unusual about that,' he said when it was over. 'All it is – it's a trick cat. It's been taught tricks, that's all.'

'Don't be silly, Edward. Every time I play Liszt, he gets all excited and comes running over to sit on the stool beside me. But only for Liszt, and nobody can teach a cat the difference between Liszt and Schumann. You don't even know it yourself. But this one can do it every single time. Quite obscure Liszt, too.'

'Twice,' the husband said. 'He's only done it twice.'

'Twice is enough.'

'Let's see him do it again. Come on.'

'No,' 'Louisa said. 'Definitely not. Because if this *is* Liszt, as I believe it is, or anyway the soul of Liszt or whatever it is that comes back, then it's certainly not right or even very kind to put him through a lot of silly undignified tests.'

'My dear woman! This is a *cat* – a rather stupid grey cat that nearly got its coat singed by the bonfire, this morning in the garden. And anyway, what do you know about reincarnation?'

'If his soul is there, that's enough for me,' Louisa said firmly. 'That's all that counts.'

'Come on, then. Let's see him perform. Let's see him tell the difference between his own stuff and someone else's.'

'No, Edward. I've told you before. I refuse to put him through any more silly circus tests. He's had quite enough of that for one day. But I'll tell you what I *will* do. I'll play him a little more of his own music.'

'A fat lot that'll prove.'

'You watch. And one thing is certain – as soon as he recognizes it, he'll refuse to budge off that bench where he's sitting now.'

Louisa went to the music shelf, took down a book of Liszt, thumbed through it quickly, and chose another of his finger compositions – the B minor Sonata. She had meant to play only the first part of the work, but once she got started and saw how the cat was sitting there literally quivering with pleasure and watching her hands with that rapturous concentrated look, she didn't have the heart to stop. She played it all the way through. When it was finished, she glanced up at her husband and smiled. 'There you are,' she said. 'You can't tell me he wasn't absolutely *loving* it.'

'He just likes the noise, that's all.'

'He was *loving* it. Weren't you, darling?' she said, lifting the cat in her arms. 'Oh, my goodness, if only he could talk. Just think of it, dear – he met Beethoven in his youth! He knew Schubert and Mendelssohn and Schumann and Berlioz and Grieg and Delacroix and Ingres and Heine and Balzac. And let me see . . . My heavens, he was Wagner's father-in-law! I'm holding Wagner's father-in-law in my arms!'

'Louisa!' her husband said sharply, sitting up straight. 'Pull yourself together.' There was a new edge to his voice now, and he spoke louder.

Louisa glanced up quickly. 'Edward, I do believe you're jealous!'

'Oh, sure, sure I'm jealous – of a lousy grey cat!'

'Then don't be so grumpy and cynical about it all. If you're going to behave like this, the best thing you can do is to go back to your gardening and leave the two of us together in peace. That will be best for all of us, won't it, darling?' she said, addressing the cat, stroking its head. 'And later on this evening, we shall have some more music together, you and I, some more of your own work. Oh, yes,' she said, kissing the creature several times on the neck, 'and we might have a little Chopin, too. You needn't tell me – I happen to know you adore Chopin. You used to be great friends with him, didn't you, darling? As a matter of fact – if I remember rightly – it was in Chopin's apartment that you met the great love of your life, Madame Something-or-Other. Had three illegitimate children by her, too, didn't you? Yes, you did, you naughty thing, and don't go trying to deny it. So you shall have some Chopin,' she said, kissing the cat again, 'and that'll probably bring back all sorts of lovely memories to you, won't it?'

'Louisa, stop this at once!'

'Oh, don't be so stuffy, Edward.'

'You're behaving like a perfect idiot, woman. And anyway, you forget we're going out this evening, to Bill and Betty's for canasta.'

'Oh, but I couldn't *possibly* go out now. There's no question of that.'

Edward got up slowly from his chair, then bent down and stubbed his cigarette hard into the ashtray. 'Tell me something,' he said quietly. 'You don't really believe this – this twaddle you're talking, do you?'

'But of *course* I do. I don't think there's any question about it now. And what's more, I consider that it puts a tremendous responsiblity upon us, Edward – upon both of us. You as well.'

'You know what I think,' he said. 'I think you ought to see a doctor. And damn quick too.'

With that, he turned and stalked out of the room, through the French windows back into the garden.

Louisa watched him striding across the lawn towards his bonfire and his brambles, and she waited until he was out of sight before she turned and ran to the front door, still carrying the cat.

Soon she was in the car, driving to town.

She parked in front of the library, locked the cat in the car, hurried up the steps into the building, and headed straight for the reference room. There she began searching the cards for books on two subjects – REINCARNATION and LISZT.

Under REINCARNATION she found something called *Recurring Earthlives – How and Why*, by a man called F.Milton Willis, published in 1921. Under LISZT she found two biographical volumes. She took out all three books, returned to the car, and drove home.

Back in the house, she placed the cat on the sofa, sat herself down beside it with her three books, and prepared to do some serious reading. She would begin, she decided, with Mr F.Milton Willis's work. The volume was thin and a trifle soiled, but it had a good heavy feel to it, and the author's name had an authoritative ring.

The doctrine of reincarnation, she read, states that spiritual souls pass from higher to higher forms of animals. 'A man can, for instance, no more be reborn as an animal than an adult can re-become a child.'

She read this again. But how did he know? How could he be so sure? He couldn't. No one could possibly be certain about a thing like that. At the same time, the statement took a great deal of the wind out of her sails.

'Around the centre of consciousness of each of us, there are, besides the dense outer body, four other bodies, invisible to the eye of flesh, but perfectly visible to people whose faculties of perception of superphysical things have undergone the requisite development . . . '

She didn't understand that one at all, but she read on, and soon she came to an interesting passage that told how long a soul usually stayed away from the earth before returning in someone else's body. The time varied according to type, and Mr Willis gave the following breakdown:

Drunkards and the unemployable	40/50	YEARS
Unskilled labourers	60/100	,,
Skilled workers	100/200	,,
The bourgeoisie	200/300	,,
The upper-middle classes	500	,,
The highest class of gentleman farmers	600/1,000	,,
Those in the Path of Initiation	1,500/2,000	,,

Quickly she referred to one of the other books, to find out how long Liszt had been dead. It said he died in Bayreuth in 1886. That was sixty-seven years ago. Therefore, according to Mr Willis, he'd have to have been an unskilled labourer to come back so soon. That didn't seem to fit at all. On the other hand, she didn't think much of the author's methods of grading. According to him, 'the highest class of gentleman farmer' was just about the most superior being on the earth. Red jackets and stirrup cups and the bloody, sadistic murder of the fox. No, she thought, that isn't right. It was a pleasure to find herself beginning to doubt Mr Willis.

Later in the book, she came upon a list of some of the more famous reincarnations. Epictetus, she was told, returned to earth as Ralph Waldo Emerson. Cicero came back as Gladstone. Alfred the Great as Queen Victoria, William the Conqueror as Lord Kitchener. Ashoka Vardhana, King of India in 272 B.C., came back as Colonel Henry Steel Olcott, an esteemed American lawyer. Pythagoras returned as Master Koot Hoomi, the gentleman who founded the Theosophical Society with Mme Blavatsky and Colonel H. S. Olcott (the esteemed American lawyer, alias Ashoka Vardhana, King of India). It didn't say who Mme Blavatsky had been. But 'Theodore Roosevelt,' it said,

has for numbers of incarnations played great parts as a leader of men . . . From him descended the royal line of ancient Chaldea, he having been, about 30,000 B.C., appointed governor of Chaldea by the Ego we know as Caesar who was then ruler of Persia. . . Roosevelt and Caesar have been together time after time as military and administrative leaders; at one time, many thousands of years ago, they were husband and wife. . .

That was enough for Louisa. Mr F. Milton Willis was clearly nothing but a guesser. She was not impressed by his dogmstic assertions. The fellow was probably on the right track, but his pronouncements were extravagant, especially the first one of all, about animals. Soon she hoped to be able to confound the whole Theosophical Society with her proof that man could indeed reappear as a lower animal. Also that he he did not have to be an unskilled labourer to come back within a hundred years.

She now turned to one of the Liszt biographies, and she was glancing through it casually when her husband came in again from the garden.

'What are you doing now?' he asked.

'Oh – just checking up a little here and there. Listen, my dear, did you know that Theodore Roosevelt once was Caesar's wife?'

'Louisa,' he said, 'look – why don't we stop this nonsense? I don't like to see you making a fool of yourself like this. Just give me that goddam cat and I'll take it to the police station myself.'

Louisa didn't seem to hear him. She was staring open-mouthed at a picture of Liszt in the book that lay on her lap. 'My God!' she cried. 'Edward, look!'

'What?'

'Look! The warts on his face! I forgot all about them! He had these great warts on his face and it was a famous thing. Even his students used to cultivate little tufts of hair on their own faces in the same spots, just to be like him.'

'What's that got to do with it?'

'Nothing. I mean not the students. But the warts have.'

'Oh, Christ,' the man said. 'Oh, Christ God Almighty.'

'The cat has them, too! Look, I'll show you.'

She took the animal on to her lap and began examining its face. 'There! There's one! And there's another! Wait a minute! I do believe they're in the same places! Where's that picture?'

It was a famous portrait of the musician in his old age, showing the fine powerful face framed in a mass of long grey hair that covered his ears and came halfway down his neck. On the face itself, each large wart had been faithfully reproduced, and there were five of them in all.

'Now, in the picture there's *one* above the right eyebrow.' She looked above the right eyebrow of the cat. 'Yes! It's there! In exactly the same place! And another on the left, at the top of the nose. That one's there, too! And one just below it on the cheek. And two fairly close together under the chin on the right side. Edward! Edward! Come and look! They're exactly the same.'

'It doesn't prove a thing.'

She looked up at her husband who was standing in the centre of the room in his green sweater and khaki slacks, still perspiring freely. 'You're scared, aren't you. Edward? Scared of losing your precious dignity and having people think you might be making a fool of yourself just for once.'

'I refuse to get hysterical about it, that's all.'

Louisa turned back to the book and began reading some more. 'This is interesting,' she said. 'It says here that Liszt loved all of Chopin's works except one – the Scherzo in B flat minor. Apparently he hated that. He called it the "Governess Scherzo", and said that it ought to be reserved solely for people in that profession.'

'So what?'

'Edward, listen. As you insist on being so horrid about all this, I'll tell you what I'm going to do. I'm going to play this scherzo right now and you can stay here and see what happens.'

'And then maybe you will deign to get us some supper.'

Louisa got up and took from the shelf a large green volume containing all of Chopin's works. 'Here it is. Oh yes, I remember it. It *is* rather awful. Now, listen – or, rather, watch. Watch to see what he does.'

She placed the music on the piano and sat down. Her husband remained standing. He had his hands in his pockets and a cigarette in his mouth, and in spite of himself he was watching the cat, which was now dozing on the sofa. When Louisa began to play, the first effect was as dramatic as ever. The animal jumped up as though it had been stung, and it stood motionless for at least a minute, the ears pricked up, the whole body quivering. Then it became restless and began to walk back and forth along the length of the sofa. Finally, it hopped down on to the floor, and with its nose and tail held high in the air, it marched slowly, majestically, from the room.

'There!' Louisa cried, jumping up and running after it. 'That does it! That really proves it!' She came back carrying the cat which she put down again on the sofa. Her whole face was shining with excitement now, her fists were clenched white, and the little bun on top of her head was loosening and going over to one side. 'What about it, Edward? What d'you think?' She was laughing nervously as she spoke.

'I must say it was quite amusing.'

'*Amusing!* My dear Edward, it's the most wonderful thing that's ever happened! Oh, goodness me!' she cried, picking up the cat again and hugging it to her bosom. 'Isn't it marvellous to think we've got Franz Liszt staying in the house?'

'Now, Louisa. Don't let's get hysterical.'

'I can't help it, I simply can't. And to *imagine* that he's actually going to live with us for always!'

'I beg your pardon?'

'Oh, Edward! I can hardly talk from excitement. And d'you know what I'm going to do next? Every musician in the whole world is going to want to meet him, that's a fact, and ask him about the people he knew – about Beethoven and Chopin and Schubert – '

'He can't talk,' her husband said.

'Well – all right. But they're going to want to meet him anyway, just to see him and touch him and to play their music to him, modern music he's never heard before.'

'He wasn't that great. Now, if it had been Bach or Beethoven ...'

'Don't interrupt, Edward, please. So what I'm going to do is notify all the important living composers everywhere. It's my duty. I'll tell them Liszt is here, and invite them to visit him. And you know what? They'll come flying in from every corner of the earth!'

'To see a grey cat?'

'Darling, it's the same thing. It's *him*. No one cares what he *looks* like. Oh, Edward, it'll be the most exciting thing there ever was!'

'They'll think you're mad.'

'You wait and see.' She was holding the cat in her arms and petting it tenderly but looking across at her husband, who now walked over to the French windows and stood there staring out into the garden. The evening was beginning, and the lawn was turning slowly from green to black, and in the distance he could see the smoke from his bonfire rising straight up in a white column.

'No,' he said, without turning round, 'I'm not having it. Not in this house. It'll make us both look perfect fools.'

'Edward, what do you mean?'

'Just what I say. I absolutely refuse to have you stirring up a lot of publicity about a foolish thing like this. You happen to have found a trick cat. O.K. – that's fine. Keep it, if it pleases you. I don't mind. But I don't wish you to go any further than that. Do you understand me, Louisa?'

'Further than what?'

'I don't want to hear any more of this crazy talk. You're acting like a lunatic.'

Louisa put the cat slowly down on the sofa. Then slowly she raised herself to her full small height and took one pace forward. '*Damn* you, Edward!' she shouted, stamping her foot. 'For the first time in our lives something really exciting comes along and you're scared to death of having anything to do with it because someone may laugh at you! That's right, isn't it? You can't deny it, can you?'

'Louisa,' her husband said. 'That's quite enough of that. Pull yourself together now and stop this at once.' He walked over and took a cigarette from the box on the table, then lit it with the enormous patent lighter. His wife stood watching him, and now the tears were beginning to trickle out of the inside corners of her eyes, making two little shiny rivers where they ran through the powder on her cheeks.

'We've been having too many of these scenes just lately, Louisa,' he was saying. 'No no, don't interrupt. Listen to me. I make full allowance for the fact that this may be an awkward time of life for you, and that – '

'Oh, my God! You idiot! You pompous idiot! Can't you see that this is different, this is – this is something miraculous? Can't you see *that*?'

At that point, he came across the room and took her firmly by the shoulders. He had the freshly lit cigarette between his lips, and she could see faint contours on his skin where the heavy perspiration had dried in patches. 'Listen,' he said. 'I'm hungry. I've given up my golf and I've been working all day in the garden, and I'm tired and hungry and I want some supper. So do you. Off you go now to the kitchen and get us both something good to eat.'

Louisa stepped back and put both hands to her mouth. 'My heavens!' she cried. 'I forgot all about it. He must be absolutely famished. Except for some milk, I haven't given him a thing to eat since he arrived.'

'Who?'

'Why, *him*, of course. I must go at once and cook something really special. I wish I knew what his favourite dishes used to be. What do you think he would like best, Edward?'

'*Goddam* it, Louisa!'

'Now, Edward, please. I'm going to handle this *my* way just for once. You stay here,' she said, bending down and touching the cat gently with her fingers. 'I won't be long.'

Louisa went into the kitchen and stood for a moment, wondering what special dish she might prepare. How about a soufflé? A nice cheese soufflé? Yes, that would be rather special. Of course, Edward didn't much care for them, but that couldn't be helped.

She was only a fair cook, and she couldn't be sure of always having a soufflé come out well, but she took extra trouble this time and waited a long while to make certain the oven had heated fully to the correct temperature. While the soufflé was baking and she was searching around for something to go with it, it occurred to her that Liszt had probably never in his life tasted either avocado pears or grapefruit, so she decided to give him both of them at once in a salad. It would be fun to watch his reaction. It really would.

When it was all ready, she put it on a tray and carried it into the living room. At the exact moment she entered, she saw her husband coming in through the French windows from the garden.

'Here's his supper,' she said, putting it on the table and turning towards the sofa. 'Where is he?'

Her husband closed the garden door behind him and walked across the room to get himself a cigarette.

'Edward, where is he?'

'Who?'

'You know who.'

'Ah, yes. Yes, that's right. Well – I'll tell you.' He was bending forward to light the cigarette, and his hands were cupped around the enormous patent lighter. He glanced up and saw Louisa looking at him – at his shoes and the bottoms of his khaki slacks which were damp from walking in the long grass.

'I just went to see how the bonfire was going,' he said.

Her eyes travelled slowly upward and rested on his hands.

'It's still burning fine,' he went on. 'I think it'll keep going all night.'

But the way she was staring made him uncomfortable.

'What is it?' he said, lowering the lighter. Then he looked down and noticed for the first time the long thin scratch that ran diagonally clear across the back of one hand, from the knuckle to the wrist.

'*Edward!*'

'Yes,' he said, 'I know. Those brambles are terrible. They tear you to pieces. Now, just a minute, Louisa. What's the matter?'

'*Edward!*'

'Oh, for God's sake, woman, sit down and keep calm. There's nothing to get worked up about. Louisa! Louisa, *sit down*!'

Charles Lamb

Free Thoughts on Several Eminent Composers

Some cry up Haydn, some Mozart,
Just as the whim bites. For my part,
I do not care a farthing candle
For either of them nor for Handel.
Cannot a man live free and easy,
Without admiring Pergolesi?
Or thro' the world with comfort go,
That never heard of Doctor Blow?
So help me God, I hardly have;
And yet I eat, and drink, and shave,
Like other people if you watch it,
And know no more of Stave or Crotchet,
Than did the primitive Peruvians,
Or those old ante-queer-Diluvians
That lived in the unwash'd world with Tubal,
Before that dirty blacksmith Jubal,
By stroke on anvil, or by summ'at,
Found out, to his great surprise, the gamut.
I care no more for Cimarosa,
Than he did for Salvator Rosa,
Being no painter; and bad luck
Be mine, if I can bear that Gluck.
Old Tycho Brahe, and modern Herschel,
Had something in 'em:but who's Purcel?
The devil, with his foot so cloven,
For aught I care, may take Beethoven;
And, if the bargain does not suit,
I'll throw him Weber in to boot.
There's not the splitting of a splinter
To chuse 'twixt *him last named*, and Winter.
Of Doctor Pepusch old Queen Dido
Knew just as much, God knows, as I do,
I would not go four miles to visit
Sebastian Bach – or Batch – which is it?
No more I would for Bononcini.
As for Novello, and Rossini,
I shall not say a word to grieve 'em,
Because they're living. So I leave 'em!

George Bernard Shaw

Mr. Jack, Composer

From *Love Among the Artists*

The year after began with a General Election, followed by a change in the Ministry, a revival of trade, a general fancy that things were going to mend, and a sudden access of spirit in political agitation, commercial enterprise, public amusements, and private expenditure. The wave even reached a venerable artistic institution called the Antient Orpheus Society, established nearly a century ago for the performance of orchestral music, and since regarded as the pioneer of musical art in England. It had begun by producing Beethoven's symphonies: it had ended by producing a typical collection of old fogies, who pioneered backwards so fast and so far that they had not finished shaking their heads over the innovations in the overture to *William Tell* when the rest of the world were growing tired of the overture to *Tannhäuser*. The younger critics had introduced a fashion of treating the Antient Orpheus as obsolescent; and even their elders began to forebode the extinction of the Society unless it were speedily rejuvenated by the supersession of the majority of the committee. But the warnings of the press, as usual, did not come until long after the public had begun to abstain from the Antient Orpheus concerts; and as the Society in its turn resisted the suggestions of the press until death or dotage reduced the conservative majority of the committee to a minority, the credit of the Antient Orpheus was almost past recovery when reform was at last decided on. When the new members of the rejuvenated committee – three of whom were under fifty – realized this, they became as eager to fill the concert programmes with new works as their predecessors had been determined to exclude them. But when the business of selecting the new works came to be considered, all was discord. Some urged the advisability of performing the works of English composers, a wilful neglect of which had been that one of the practices of the old committee of which the press had most persistently complained. To this it was objected that in spite of the patriotic complaints of critics, the public had showed their opinion of English composers by specially avoiding the few concerts to which they had been allowed to contribute. At last it was arranged that an English work should be given at the first concert of the season, and that care should be taken to neutralize its repellent effect on the public by engaging a young Polish lady, who had recently made an extraordinary success abroad as a pianist, to make her first appearance in England on the occasion. Matters being settled so far, question now arose as to what the new English work should be. Most of the committee had manuscript scores of their own, composed thirty years before in the interval between leaving the academy and getting enough teaching to use up all their energy; but as works of this class had already been heard once or twice by the public with undisguised tedium; and as each composer hesitated to propose his own opus, the question was not immediately answered. Then a recently elected member of the committee, not a professional musician, mentioned a fantasia for pianoforte and orchestra of which he had some private knowledge. It was composed, he said, by a young man, a Mr. Owen Jack. The chairman coughed and remarked coldly that he did not recollect the name. A member asked bluntly who Mr. Jack was, and whether anybody had ever heard of him. Another member protested against the suggestion of a fantasia and declared that if this illustrious obscure did not know enough about musical form to write a concerto, the Antient Orpheus Society, which had subsisted for nearly a century without his assistance, could probably do so a little longer. When the laughter and applause which this speech evoked had subsided, a good-natured member remarked that he had met a man of the name of Jack at somebody's place in Windsor, and had heard him improvise variations on a song of the hostess's in a rather striking manner. He therefore seconded the proposal that Jack's fantasia should be immediately examined with a view to its performance by the Polish lady at the next concert. Another member, not good natured but professionally jealous of the last speaker but one, supported the proposal on the ground that the notion that the Society could get on high-and-mightily without ever doing anything new was just what had brought it to death's door. This naturally elicited a defiant statement that the Society had never been more highly esteemed than at that hour; and a debate ensued, in the course of which Jack's ability was hotly attacked and defended in turn by persons who had never heard of him before that day. Eventually the member who had introduced the subject obtained permission to invite Mr. Jack to submit his fantasia to the committee.

At the next meeting an indignant member begged leave to call the attention of his colleagues to a document which had accompanied the score forwarded in response to the invitation by which the Antient Orpheus Society had honoured Mr. Owen Jack. It was a letter to the secretary, in the following terms:

Sir:Herewith you will find the instrumental partition of a fantasia composed by me for pianoforte and orchestra. I am willing to give the use of it to the Antient Orpheus Society gratuitously for one concert, on condition that the rehearsal be superintended by me, and that, if I require it, a second rehearsal be held.

The member said he would not dwell on the propriety of this communication to the foremost musical society in Europe from a minor teacher, as he had ascertained Mr. Jack to be. It had been sufficiently rebuked by the secretary's reply, despatched after the partition had been duly examined, to the effect that the work, though not destitute of merit, was too eccentric in form, and crude in harmonic structure, to be suitable for public performance at the concerts of the Society. This had elicited a second letter from Mr. Jack, of which the member would say nothing, as he preferred to leave it to speak for itself and for the character of the writer.

> Church Street, Kensington, W.
>
> Sir: Your criticism was uninvited, and is valueless except as an illustration of the invincible ignorance of the pedants whose mouthpiece you are. I am, sir,
>
> Yours truly,
> Owen Jack

The most astute diplomatist could not have written a more effective letter in Jack's favour than this proved. The party of reform took it as an exquisite slap at their opponents and at once determined to make the secretary smart for rejecting the work without the authority of the whole committee. Jack's advocate produced a note from the Polish lady acknowledging the receipt of a pianoforte fantasia and declaring that she should be enchanted to play for the first time to an English audience a work so poetic by one of their own nation. He explained that having borrowed a copy of the pianoforte part from a young lady relative of his who was studying it, he had sent it to the Polish artist, who had just arrived in England. Her opinion of it, he contended, was sufficient to show that the letter of the secretary was the result of an error of judgment which deserved no better answer than it had elicited. The secretary retorted that he had no right to avail himself of his private acquaintance with the pianist to influence the course of the Society and stigmatized Jack's letter as the coarse abuse natural to the vulgar mind of a self-assertive charlatan. On the other hand, it was maintained that Jack had only shown the sensitiveness of an artist, and that to invite a composer to send in a work and then treat it as if it were an examination paper filled by a presumptuous novice was an impertinence likely to bring ridicule as well as odium upon the Antient Orpheus. The senior member, who occupied the chair, now declared very solemnly that he had seen the fantasia, and that it was one of those lawless compositions unhappily too common of late years, which were hurrying the beautiful art of Haydn and Mozart into the abyss of modern sensationalism. Hereupon someone remarked that the gentleman had frequently spoken of the works of Wagner in the same terms, although they all knew that Richard Wagner was the greatest composer of that or any other age. This assertion was vehemently repudiated by some and loudly cheered by others. In the hubbub which followed, Jack's cause became identified with that of Wagner: and a motion to set aside the unauthorized rejection of the fantasia was carried by a majority of the admirers of the Prussian composer, not one of whom knew or cared a straw about the English one.

'I am glad we have won the day,' said Mr. Phipson, the proposer of this motion, to a friend as the meeting broke up; 'but we have certainly experienced the truth of Mary's remark that this Jack creates nothing but discord in real life, whatever he may do in music.'

Jack at first refused to have anything further to do with the Antient Orpheus; but as it was evident that his refusal would harm nobody except himself, he yielded to the entreaties of Mary Sutherland and consented to make use of the opportunity she had, through Mr. Phipson, procured for him. So the negotiation proceeded; and at last, one comfortless wet spring morning, Jack got out of an omnibus in Piccadilly and walked through the mud to St. James's Hall, where, in the gloomy rooms beneath the orchestra, he found a crowd of about eighty men, chatting, hugging themselves, and stamping because of the cold; stooping over black bags and boxes containing musical instruments; or reluctantly unwinding woollen mufflers and unbuttoning greatcoats. He passed them into a lower room, where he found three gentlemen standing in courtly attitudes before a young lady wrapped in furs, with a small head, light brown hair, and a pale face, rather toilworn. She received them with that natural air of a princess in her own right which is so ineffectually striven for by the ordinary princess in other people's rights. As she spoke to the gentlemen in French, occasionally helping them to understand her by a few words of broken English, she smiled occasionally, apparently more from kindness than natural gaiety, for her features always relapsed into an expression of patient but not unhappy endurance. Near her sat an old foreign lady, brown skinned, tall, and very grim.

Jack advanced a few steps into the room; glanced at the gentlemen; and took a long look at the younger lady, who, like the rest, had had her attention arrested by his impressive ugliness. He scrutinized her so openly that she turned away displeased, and a little embarrassed. Two of the gentlemen stared at him stiffly. The third came forward and said with polite severity, 'What is your business here, sir?'

Jack looked at him for a moment, wrinkling his face hideously. 'I am Jack,' he said, in the brassiest tone of his powerful voice. 'Who are you?'

'Oh!' said the gentleman, relaxing a little. 'I beg your pardon. I had not the pleasure of knowing you by sight, Mr. Jack. My name is Manlius, at your service.' Mr. Manlius was the conductor of the Antient Orpheus orchestra. He was a learned musician, generally respected because he had given instruction to members of the Royal family, and, when conducting, never allowed his orchestra to forget the restraint due to the presence of ladies and gentlemen in the sofa stalls.

Jack bowed. Mr. Manlius considered whether he should introduce the composer to the young lady. Whilst he hesitated, a trampling overhead was succeeded by the sounding of a note first on the pianoforte and then on the oboe, instantly followed by the din of an indescribable discord of fifths from innumerable strings varied by irrelevant chromatic scales from the woodwind, and a doleful tuning of slides from the brass. Jack's eyes gleamed. Troubling himself no further about Mr. Manlius, he went out through a door leading to the stalls, where he found a knot of old gentlemen disputing. One of them immediately whispered something to the others: and they continued their discussions in a lower tone. Jack looked at the orchestra for a few minutes and then returned to the room he had left, where the elder lady was insisting in French that the pianoforte fantasia should be rehearsed before anything else, as she was not going to wait in the cold all day. Mr. Manlius assured her that he had anticipated her suggestion and should act upon it as a matter of course.

'It is oll the same thinks,' said the young lady in English. Then in French, 'Even if you begin with the fantasia, Monsieur, I shall assuredly wait to hear for the first time your famous band perform in this ancient hall.'

Manlius bowed. When he straightened himself again, he found Jack standing at his elbow. 'Allow me to present to you Monsieur Jack,' he said.

'It is for Monsieur Jacques to allow,' she replied. 'The poor artist is honoured by the presence of the illustrious English composer.'

Jack nodded gravely as acknowledging that the young woman expressed herself becomingly. Manlius grinned covertly and proposed that they should go upon the orchestra, as the band was apt to get out of humour when too much time was wasted. She rose at once and ascended the steps on the arm of the conductor. She was received with an encouraging clapping of hands and tapping of fiddle backs.

Jack followed with the elder lady, who sat down on the top stair and began to knit.

'If you wish to conduct the rehearsal,' said Manlius politely to Jack, 'you are, of course, quite welcome to do so.'

'Thank you,' said Jack. 'I will.' Manlius, who had hardly expected him to accept the offer, retired to the pianoforte and prepared to turn over the leaves for the player.

'I think I can play it from memory,' she said to him, 'unless Monsieur Jacques puts it all out of my head. Judging by his face, it is certain that he is not very patient – Ah! Did I not say so?'

Jack had rapped the desk sharply with his stick and was looking balefully at the men, who did not seem in any hurry to attend to him. He put down the stick; stepped from the desk; and stooped to the conductor's ear.

'I mentioned,' he said, 'that some of the parts ought to be given to the men to study before rehearsal. Has that been done?'

Manlius smiled. 'My dear sir,' he said, 'I need hardly tell you that players of such standing as the members of the Antient Orpheus orchestra do not care to have suggestions of that kind offered to them. You have no cause to be uneasy. They can play anything – absolutely anything – at sight.'

Jack looked black and returned to his desk without a word. He gave one more rap with his stick and began. The players were attentive, but many of them tried not to look so. For a few bars Jack conducted under some restraint, apparently striving to repress a tendency to extravagant gesticulation. Then, as certain combinations and progressions sounded strange and farfetched, slight bursts of laughter were heard. Suddenly the first clarinetist, with an exclamation of impatience, put down his instrument.

'Well?' shouted Jack. The music ceased.

'I can't play that,' said the clarinetist shortly.

'Can *you* play it?' said Jack, with suppressed rage, to the second clarinetist.

'No,' said he. 'Nobody could play it.'

'That passage *has* been played; and it must be played. It has been played by a common soldier.'

'If a common soldier even attempted it, much less played it,' said the first clarinetist, with some contemptuous indignation at what he considered an evident falsehood,'he must have been drunk.' There was a general titter at this.

Jack visibly wrestled with himself for a moment. Then, with a gleam of humour like a flash of sunshine through a black thunder-cloud, he said, 'You are right. He *was* drunk.' The whole band roared with laughter.

'Well, *I* am not drunk,' said the clarinetist, folding his arms.

'But will you not just try wh – ' Here Jack, choked by the effort to be persuasive and polite, burst out raging, 'It can be done. It shall be done. It must be done. You are the best clarinet player in England. I know what you can do.' And Jack shook his fists wildly at the man as if he were accusing him of some infamous crime. But the compliment was loudly applauded, and the man reddened, not altogether displeased. A cornist who sat near him said soothingly in an Irish accent, 'Aye, do, Joe. Try it.'

'You will: you can,' shouted Jack reassuringly, recovering his self-command. 'Back to the double bar. Now!' The music recommenced; and the clarinetist, overborne, took up his instrument and, when the passage was reached, played it easily, greatly to his own astonishment. The brilliancy of the effect, too, raised him for a time into a prominence which rivalled that of the pianist. The orchestra positively interrupted the movement to applaud it; and Jack joined in with high good humour.

'If you are uneasy about it,' said he, with an undisguised chuckle, 'I can hand it over to the violins.'

'Oh, no, thank you,' said the clarinetist. 'Now I've got it, I'll keep it.'

Jack rubbed his nose until it glowed like a coal; and the movement proceeded without another stoppage, the men now seeing that Jack was in his right place.

But when a theme marked *andante cantabile*, which formed the middle section of the fantasia, was commenced by the pianist, Jack turned to her; said 'Quicker, quicker. *Plus vite*'; and began to mark his beat by striking the desk. She looked at him anxiously; played a few bars in the time indicated by him: and then threw up her hands and stopped.

'I cannot,' she exclaimed. 'I must play it more slowly or not at all.'

'Certainly, it shall be slower if you desire it,' said the elder lady from the steps. Jack looked at her as he sometimes looked at Mrs. Simpson. 'Certainly it shall not be slower, if all the angels desired it,' he said, in well-pronounced but barbarously ungrammatical French. 'Go on; and take the time from my beat.'

The Polish lady shook her head; folded her hands in her lap; and looked patiently at the music before her. There was a moment of silence, during which Jack, thus mutely defied, glared at her with distorted features. Manlius rose irresolutely. Jack stepped down from the desk; handed him the stick; and said in a smothered voice, 'Be good enough to conduct this lady's portion of the fantasia. When *my* music recommences, I will return.'

Manlius took the stick and mounted the desk, the orchestra receiving him with applause. In the midst of it Jack went out, giving the pianist a terrible look as he passed her, transferring it to her companion, who raised her eyebrows and shoulders contemptuously.

Manlius was not the man to impose his own ideas of a composition on a refractory artist; and though he was privately disposed to agree with Jack that the Polish lady was misjudging the speed of the movement, he obediently followed her playing with his beat. But he soon lost his first impression and began to be affected by a dread lest anyone should make a noise in the room. He moved his stick as quietly as possible, and raised his left hand as if to still the band, who were, however, either watching the pianist intently or playing without a trace of the expert offhandedness which they had affected at first. The pleasure of listening made Manlius forget to follow the score. When he roused himself and found his place, he perceived that the first horn player was altering a passage completely, though very happily. Looking questioningly in that direction, he saw Jack sitting beside the man with a pencil in his hand. Manlius observed for the first time that he had an expressive face and remarkable eyes and was not, as he had previously seemed, unmitigatedly ugly. Meanwhile the knot of old gentlemen in the stalls, who had previously chattered subduedly, became quite silent, and a few of them closed their eyes rapturously. The lady on the steps alone did not seem to care about the music. At last the flow of melody waned and broke into snatches. The pianoforte seemed to appeal to the instruments to continue the song. A melancholy strain from the violas responded hopelessly; but the effect of this was marred by a stir in the orchestra. The trombone and trumpet players, hitherto silent, were taking up their instruments and pushing up their moustaches. The drummer, after some hasty screwing round his third drum, poised his sticks; and a super-numerary near him rose, cymbals in hand; fixed his eye on Manlius, and apparently stood ready to clap the head of the trumpet player in front of him as a lady claps a moth flying from a woollen curtain. Manlius looked at the score as if he did not quite understand the sequel. Suddenly, as the violas ceased, Jack shouted in a startling voice, 'Let it be an avalanche. From the top to bottom of the Himalayas'; and rushed to the conductor's desk. Manlius made way for him precipitately; and a tremendous explosion of sound followed. 'Louder,' roared Jack. 'Louder. Less noise and more tone. Out with it like fifty million devils.' And he led the movement at a merciless speed. The pianist looked bewildered, like the band, most of whom lost their places after the first fifty bars; but when the turn of each player came, he found the conductor glaring at him and was swept into his part without clearly knowing how. It was an insensate orgy of sound. Gay melodies, daintily given out by the pianoforte, or by the string instruments, were derisively brayed out immediately afterwards by cornets, harmonized in thirds with the most ingenious vulgarity. Cadenzas, agilely executed by the Polish lady, were uncouthly imitated by the double basses. Themes constructed like ballads with choruses were introduced instead of orthodox 'subjects'. The old gentlemen in the stalls groaned and protested. The Polish lady, incommoded by the capricious and often excessive speed required of her, held on gallantly, Jack all the time grinding his teeth, dancing, gesticulating, and by turns shshsh-shing at the orchestra or shouting to them for more tone and less noise. Even the lady on the steps had begun to nod to the impetuous rhythm, when the movement ended as suddenly as it had begun; and all the players rose to their feet, laughing and applauding heartily. Manlius, from whose mind the fantasia had banished all prejudice as to Jack's rank as a musician, shook his hand warmly. The Polish lady, her face transfigured by musical excitement, offered her hand too. Jack took it and held it, saying abruptly, 'Listen to me. You were quite right; and I am a fool. I did not know what there was in my own music and would have spoiled it if you had not prevented me. You are a great player, because you get the most beautiful tone possible from every note you touch, and you make every phrase say all that it was meant to say, and more. You are an angel. I would rather hear you play scales than hear myself play sonatas. And' – here he lowered his voice and drew her aside – 'I rely on you to make my work succeed at the concert. Manlius will conduct the band; but you must conduct Manlius. It is not enough to be a gentleman and a contrapuntist in order to conduct. You comprehend?'

'Yes, Monsieur, I understand perfectly. I will do my best. I shall be inspired. How magnificent it is!'

'Allow me to congratulate you, sir,' said one of the old gentlemen, advancing. 'Myself and colleagues have been greatly struck by your work. I am empowered to say on their behalf that whatever difference of opinion there may be among us as to the discretion with which you have employed your powers, of the extraordinary nature of those powers there can no longer be a doubt; and we are thoroughly gratified at having chosen for performance a work which displays so much orginality and talent as your fantasia.'

'Ten years ago,' said Jack, looking steadily at him, 'I might have been glad to hear you say so. At present the time for compliments is past, unless you wish to congratulate me on the private interest that has gained my work a hearing. My talent and originality have been my chief obstacles here.'

'Are you not a little hasty?' said the gentleman, disconcerted. 'Success comes late in London; and you are still, if I may say so, a comparatively young man.'

'I am not old enough to harp on being comparatively young. I am thirty-four years old; and if I had adopted any other profession than that of composer of music, I should have been earning a respectable livelihood by this time. As it is, I have never made a farthing by my compositions. I don't blame those who have stood between me and the public: their ignorance is their misfortune, and not their fault. But now that I have come to light by a chance in spite of their teeth, I am not in the humour to exchange pretty speeches with them. Understand, sir: I do not mean to rebuff you personally. But as for your colleagues, tell them that it does not become them to pretend to acknowledge spontaneously what I have just, after many hard years, forced them to admit. Look at those friends of yours shaking their heads over my score there. They have *heard* my music; but they do not know what to say until they *see* it. Would you like me to believe that they are admiring it?'

'I am confident that they cannot help doing so.'

'They are showing one another why it ought not to have been written – hunting out my consecutive fifths and sevenths, and my false relations – looking for my first subject, my second subject, my working out; and the rest of the childishness that could be taught to a poodle. Don't they wish they may find them?'

The gentleman seemed at a loss how to continue the conversation. 'I hope you are satisfied with the orchestra,' he said after a pause.

'No, I am not,' said Jack. 'They are overcivilized. They are as much afraid of showing their individuality as if they were common gentlemen. You cannot handle a musical instrument with kid gloves on. However, they did better than I hoped. They are at least not coarse. That young woman is a genius.'

'Ye-es. Almost a genius. She is young, of course. She has not the – I should call it the *gigantic* power and energy of such a player, for instance, as – '

'Pshaw!' said Jack, interrupting him. 'I, or anybody else, can get excited with the swing of a Chopin's polonaise, and thrash it out of the piano until the room shakes. But she! You talk of making a pianoforte sing – a child that can sing itself can do that. But she can make it speak. She has eloquence, the first and last quality of a great player, as it is of a great man. The finale of the fantasia is too coarse for her: it does violence to her nature. It was written to be played by a savage – like me.'

'Oh, undoubtedly, undoubtedly! She is a remarkable player. I did not for a moment intend to convey – ' Here Manlius rapped his desk; and Jack, with an unceremonious nod to his interlocutor, left the platform. As he passed the door leading to the public part of the hall, he heard the voice of the elder lady.

'My child, they seek to deceive you. This Monsieur Jacques, with whose music you are to make your debut here, is he famous in England? Not at all. My God! he is an unknown man.'

'Be tranquil, Mother. He will not long be unknown.'

Jack opened the door a little way; thrust his face through; and smiled pleasantly at the pianist. Her mother, seeing her start, looked round and saw him grimacing within a yard of her.

'Ah, Lord Jesus!' she exclaimed in German, recoiling from him. He chuckled and abruptly shut himself out of her view as the opening unison of the *Coriolan* overture sounded from the orchestra. The old gentleman who had congratulated him had rejoined the others in the stalls.

'Well,' said one of them, 'is your man delighted with himself?'

'No – no, I cannot say that he is – or rather perhaps he is too much so. I am sorry to say that he appears to be rather morose – soured by his early difficulties, perhaps. He is certainly not an agreeable person to speak to.'

'What did you expect?' said another gentleman coldly. 'A man who degrades music to be the vehicle of his own coarse humour, and shows by his method of doing it an ignorant contempt for those laws by which the great composers established order in the chaos of sounds, is not likely to display a courteous disposition and refined nature in the ordinary business of life.'

'I assure you, Professor,' said a third, who had the score of the fantasia open on his knees, 'this chap must know a devil of a lot. He plays old Harry with the sonata form: but he must do it on purpose, you know, really.'

The gentleman addressed as Professor looked severely and incredulously at the other. 'I really cannot listen to such things whilst they are playing Beethoven,' he said. 'I have protested against Mr. Jack and his like; and my protest has passed unheeded. I wash my hands of the consequences. The Antient Orpheus Society will yet acknowledge that I did well when I counselled it to renounce the devil and all his works.' He turned away; sat down on a stall a little way off; and gave all his attention ostentatiously to *Coriolan*.

The pianist came presently and sat near him. The others quickly surrounded her; but she did not speak to them and showed by her attitude that she did not wish to be spoken to. Her mother, who did not care for *Coriolan* and wanted to go home, knitted and looked appealingly at her from time to time, not venturing to express her impatience before so many members of the Antient Orpheus Society. At last Manlius came down; and the whole party rose and went into the performers' room.

'How do you find our orchestra?' said Manlius to her as she took up her muff.

'It is magnificent,' she replied. 'So refined, so quiet, so convenable! It is like the English gentleman.' Manlius smirked. Jack, who had reappeared on the outskirts of the group with his hat on – a desperately ill-used hat – added, 'A Lithuanian or Hungarian orchestra could not play like that, eh?'

'No, truly,' said the Polish lady, with a little shrug. 'I do not think they could.'

'You flatter us,' said Manlius, bowing. Jack began to laugh. The Polish lady hastily made her adieux and went out into Piccadilly, where a cab was brought for her. Her mother got in; and she was about to follow when she heard Jack's voice again, at her elbow.

'May I send you some music?'

'If you will be so gracious, Monsieur.'

'Good. What direction shall I give your driver?'

'F-f-you call it Feetzroysquerre?'

'Fitzroy Square,' shouted Jack to the cabman. The hansom went off; and he, running recklessly through the mud to a passing Hammersmith omnibus, which was full inside, climbed to the roof, and was borne away in the rain.

Musicians

Thomas Mann

The Infant Prodigy

The infant prodigy entered. The hall became quiet.

It became quiet and then the audience began to clap, because somewhere at the side a leader of mobs, a born organizer, clapped first. The audience had heard nothing yet, but they applauded; for a mighty publicity organization had heralded the prodigy and people were already hypnotized, whether they knew it or not.

The prodigy came from behind a splendid screen embroidered with Empire garlands and great conventionalized flowers, and climbed nimbly up the steps to the platform, diving into the applause as into a bath; a little chilly and shivering, but yet as though into a friendly element. He advanced to the edge of the platform and smiled as though he were about to be photographed; he made a shy, charming gesture of greeting, like a little girl.

He was dressed entirely in white silk, which the audience found enchanting. The little white jacket was fancifully cut, with a sash underneath it, and even his shoes were made of white silk. But against the white socks his bare little legs stood out quite brown, for he was a Greek boy.

He was called Bibi Saccellaphylaccas. And such indeed was his name. No one knew what Bibi was the pet name for, nobody but the impresario, and he regarded it as a trade secret. Bibi had smooth black hair reaching to his shoulders; it was parted on the side and fastened back from the narrow domed forehead by a little silk bow. His was the most harmless childish countenance in the world, with an unfinished nose and guileless mouth. The area beneath his pitch-black mouselike eyes was already a little tired and visibly lined. He looked as though he were nine years old but was really eight and given out for seven. It was hard to tell whether to believe this or not. Probably everybody knew better and still believed it, as happens about so many things. The average man thinks that a little falseness goes with beauty. Where should we get any excitement out of our daily life if we were not willing to pretend a bit? And the average man is quite right, in his average brains!

The prodigy kept on bowing until the applause died down, then he went up to the grand piano, and the audience cast a last look at its programmes. First came a *Marche solonnelle*, then a *Rêverie*, and then *Le Hibou et les Moineaux* – all by Bibi Saccellaphylaccas. The whole programme was by him, they were all his compositions. He could not score them, of course, but he had them all in his extraordinary little head and they possessed real artistic significance, or so it said, seriously and objectively, in the programme. The programme sounded as though the impresario had wrested these concessions from his critical nature after a hard struggle.

The prodigy sat down upon the revolving stool and felt with his feet for the pedals, which were raised by means of a clever device so that Bibi could reach them. It was Bibi's own piano, he took it everywhere with him. It rested upon wooden trestles and its polish was somewhat marred by the constant transportation – but all that only made things more interesting.

Bibi put his silk-shod feet on the pedals; then he made an artful little face, looked straight ahead of him, and lifted his right hand. It was a brown, childish little hand; but the wrist was strong and unlike a child's, with well-developed bones.

Bibi made his face for the audience because he was aware that he had to entertain them a little. But he had his own private enjoyment in the thing too, an enjoyment which he could never convey to anybody. It was that prickling delight, that secret shudder of bliss, which ran through him every time he sat at an open piano – it would always be with him. And here was the keyboard again, these seven black and white octaves, among which he had so often lost himself in abysmal and thrilling adventures – and yet it always looked as clean and untouched as a newly washed blackboard. This was the realm of music that lay before him. It lay spread out like an inviting ocean, where he might plunge in and blissfully swim, where he might let himself be borne and carried away, where he might go under in night and storm, yet keep the mastery: control, ordain – he held his right hand poised in the air.

A breathless stillness reigned in the room – the tense moment before the first note came . . . How would it begin? It began so. And Bibi, with his index finger, fetched the first note out of the piano, a quite unexpectedly powerful first note in the middle register, like a trumpet blast. Others followed, an introduction developed – the audience relaxed.

The concert was held in the palatial hall of a fashionable first-class hotel. The walls were covered with mirrors framed in gilded arabesques, between frescos of the rosy and fleshly school. Ornamental columns supported a ceiling that displayed a whole universe of electric bulbs, in clusters darting a brilliance far brighter than day and filling the whole space with thin, vibrating golden light. Not a seat was unoccupied, people were standing in the side aisles and at the back. The front seats cost twelve marks; for the impresario believed that anything worth having was worth paying for. And they were occupied by the best society, for it was in the upper classes, of course, that the greatest enthusiasm was felt. There were even some children, with their legs hanging down demurely from their chairs and their shining eyes staring at their gifted little white-clad contemporary.

Down in front on the left side sat the prodigy's mother, an extremely obese woman with a powdered double chin and a feather on her head. Beside her was the impresario, a man of oriental appearance with large gold buttons on his conspicuous cuffs. The princess was in the middle of the front row – a wrinkled, shrivelled little old princess but still a patron of the arts, especially everything full of sensibility. She sat in a deep, velvet-upholstered arm-chair, and a Persian carpet was spread before her feet. She held her hands folded over her grey striped-silk breast, put her head on one side, and presented a picture of elegant composure as she sat looking up at the performing prodigy. Next to her sat her lady-in-waiting, in a green striped-silk gown. Being only a lady-in-waiting she had to sit up very straight in her chair.

Bibi ended in a grand climax. With what power this wee manikin belaboured the keyboard! The audience could scarcely trust its ears. The march theme, an infectious, swinging tune, broke out once more, fully harmonized, bold and showy; with every note Bibi flung himself back from the waist as though he were marching in a triumphal procession. He ended *fortissimo*, bent over, slipped sideways off the stool, and stood with a smile awaiting the applause.

And the applause burst forth, unanimously, enthusiastically; the child made his demure little maidenly curtsy and people in the front seat thought: 'Look what slim little hips he has! Clap, clap! Hurrah, bravo, little chap, Saccophylax or whatever your name is! Wait, let me take off my gloves – what a little devil of a chap he is!'

Bibi had to come out three times from behind the screen before they would stop. Some late-comers entered the hall and moved about looking for seats. Then the concert continued. Bibi's *Rêverie* murmured its numbers, consisting almost entirely of arpeggios, above which a bar of melody rose now and then, weak-winged. Then came *Le Hibou et les Moineaux*. This piece was brilliantly successful, it made a strong impression; it was an affective childhood fantasy, remarkably well envisaged. The bass represented the owl, sitting morosely rolling his filmy eyes; while in the treble the impudent, half-frightened sparrows chirped. Bibi received an ovation when he finished, he was called out four times. A hotel page with shiny buttons carried up three great laurel wreaths on to the stage and proffered them from one side while Bibi nodded and expressed his thanks. Even the princess shared in the applause, daintily and noiselessly pressing her palms together.

Ah, the knowing little creature understood how to make people clap! He stopped behind the screen, they had to wait for him; lingered a little on the steps of the platform, admired the long streamers on the wreaths – although actually such things bored him stiff by now. He bowed with the utmost charm, he gave the audience plenty of time to rave itself out, because applause is valuable and must not be cut short. '*Le Hibou* is my drawing card,' he thought – this expression he had learned from the impresario. 'Now I will play the fantasy, it is a lot better than *Le Hibou*, of course, especially the C-sharp passage. But you idiots dote on the *Hibou*, though it is the first and the silliest thing I wrote.' He continued to bow and smile.

Next came a *Méditation* and then an *Etude* – the programme was quite comprehensive. The *Méditation* was very like the *Rêverie* – which was nothing against it – and the *Etude* displayed all of Bibi's virtuosity, which naturally fell a little short of his inventiveness. And then the *Fantaisie*. This was his favourite; he varied it a little each time, giving himself free rein and sometimes surprising even himself, on good evenings, by his own inventiveness.

He sat and played, so little, so white and shining, against the great black grand piano, elect and alone, above that confused sea of faces, above the heavy, insensitive mass soul, upon which he was labouring to work with his individual, differentiated soul. His lock of soft black hair with the white silk bow had fallen over his forehead, his trained and bony little wrists pounded away, the muscles stood out visibly on his brown childish cheeks.

Sitting there he sometimes had moments of oblivion and solitude, when the gaze of his strange little mouselike eyes with the big rings beneath them would lose itself and stare through the painted stage into space that was peopled with strange vague life. Then out of the corner of his eye he would give a quick look back into the hall and be once more with his audience.

'Joy and pain, the heights and the depths – that is my *Fantaisie*,' he thought lovingly. 'Listen, here is the C-sharp passage.' He lingered over the approach, wondering if they would notice anything. But no, of course not, how should they? And he cast his eyes up prettily at the ceiling so that at least they might have something to look at.

All these people sat there in their regular rows, looking at the prodigy and thinking all sorts of things in their regular brains. An old gentleman with a white beard, a seal ring on his finger and a bulbous swelling on his bald spot, a growth if you like, was thinking to himself: 'Really, one ought to be shamed.' He had never got any further than 'Ah, thou dearest Augustin' on the piano, and here he sat now, a grey old man, looking on while this little hop-o'-my-thumb performed miracles. Yes, yes, it is a gift of God, we must remember that. God grants His gifts, or He withholds them, and there is no shame in being an ordinary man. Like with the Christ Child. – Before a child one may kneel without feeling shamed. Strange that thoughts like these should be so satisfying – he would even say so sweet, if it was not too silly, for a tough old man like him to use the word. That was how he felt, anyhow.

Art . . . the business man with the parrot-nose was thinking. 'Yes, it adds something cheerful to life, a little good white silk and a little tumty-ti-ti-tum. Really he does not play so badly. Fully fifty seats, twelve marks apiece, that makes six hundred marks – and everything else besides. Take off the rent of the hall, the lighting and the programmes, you must have fully a thousand marks' profit. That is worth while.'

That was Chopin he was just playing, thought the piano-teacher, a lady with a pointed nose; she was of an age when the understanding sharpens as the hopes decay. 'But not very original – I will say that afterwards, it sounds well. And his hand position is entirely amateur. One must be able to lay a coin on the back of the hand – I would use a ruler on him.'

Then there was a young girl, at that self-conscious and chlorotic time of life when the most ineffable ideas come into the mind. She was thinking to herself: 'What is it he is playing? It is expressive of passion, yet he is a child. If he kissed me it would be as though my little brother kissed me – no kiss at all. Is there such a thing as passion all by itself, without any earthly object, a sort of child's-play of passion? What nonsense! If I were to say such things aloud they would just be at me with some more cod-liver oil. Such is life.'

An officer was leaning against a column. He looked on at Bibi's success and thought: 'Yes, you are something and I am something, each in his own way.' So he clapped his heels together and paid to the prodigy the respect which he felt to be due to all the powers that be.

Then there was a critic, an elderly man in a shiny black coat and turned-up trousers splashed with mud. He sat in his free seat and thought: 'Look at him, this young beggar of a Bibi. As an individual he has still to develop, but as a type he is already quite complete, the artist *par excellence*. He has in himself all the artist's exaltation and his utter worthlessness, his charlatanry and his sacred fire, his burning contempt and his secret raptures. Of course I can't write all that, it is too good. Of course, I should have been an artist myself if I had not seen through the whole business so clearly.'

Then the prodigy stopped playing and a perfect storm arose in the hall. He had to come out again and again from behind his screen. The man with the shiny buttons carried up more wreaths: four laurel wreaths, a lyre made of violets, a bouquet of roses. He had not arms enough to convey all these tributes, the impresario himself mounted the stage to help him. He hung a laurel wreath around Bibi's neck, he tenderly stroked the black hair – and suddenly as though overcome he bent down and gave the prodigy a kiss, a resounding kiss, square on the mouth. And then the storm became a hurricane. That kiss ran through the room like an electric shock, it went direct to people's marrow and made them shiver down their backs. They were carried away by a helpless compulsion of sheer noise. Loud shouts mingled with the hysterical clapping of hands. Some of Bibi's commonplace little friends down there waved their handkerchiefs. But the critic thought: 'Of course that kiss had to come – it's a good old gag. Yes, good Lord, if only one did not see through everything quite so clearly – '

And so the concert drew to a close. It began at half past seven and finished at half past eight. The platform was laden with wreaths and two little pots of flowers stood on the lampstands of the piano. Bibi played as his last number his *Rhapsodie grecque*, which turned into the Greek national hymn at the end. His fellow-countrymen in the audience would gladly have sung it with him if the company had not been so august. They made up for it with a powerful noise and hullabaloo, a hot-blooded national demonstration. And the ageing critic was thinking: 'Yes, the hymn had to come too. They have to exploit every vein – publicity cannot afford to neglect any means to its end. I think I'll criticize that as inartistic. But perhaps I am wrong, perhaps that is the most artistic thing of all. What is the artist? A jack-in-the-box. Criticism is on a higher plane. But I can't say that.' And away he went in his muddy trousers.

After being called out nine or ten times the prodigy did not come any more from behind the screen but went to his mother and the impresario down in the hall. The audience stood about among the chairs and applauded and pressed forward to see Bibi close at hand. Some of them wanted to see the princess too. Two dense circles formed, one round the prodigy, the other round the princess, and you could actually not tell which of them was receiving more homage. But the court lady was commanded to go over to Bibi; she smoothed down his silk jacket a bit to make it look suitable for a court function, led him by the arm to the princess, and solemnly indicated to him that he was to kiss the royal hand. 'How do you do it, child?' asked the princess. 'Does it come into your head of itself when you sit down?' '*Oui, madame*,' answered Bibi. To himself he thought: 'Oh, what a stupid old princess!' Then he turned round shyly and uncourtier-like and went back to his family.

Outside in the cloakroom there was a crowd. People held up their numbers and received with open arms furs, shawls, and galoshes. Somewhere among her acquaintances the piano-teacher stood making her critique. 'He is not very original,' she said audibly and looked about her.

In front of one of the great mirrors an elegant young lady was being arrayed in her evening cloak and fur shoes by her brothers, two lieutenants. She was exquisitely beautiful, with her steel-blue eyes and her clean-cut, well-bred face. A really noble dame. When she was ready she stood waiting for her brothers. 'Don't stand so long in front of the glass, Adolf,' she said softly to one of them, who could not tear himself away from the sight of his simple, good-looking young features. But Lieutenant Adolf thinks: What cheek! He would button his overcoat in front of the glass, just the same. Then they went out on the street where the arc-lights gleamed cloudily through the white mist. Lieutenant Adolf struck up a little nigger-dance on the frozen snow to keep warm, with his hands in his slanting overcoat pockets and his collar turned up.

A girl with untidy hair and swinging arms, accompanied by a gloomy-faced youth, came out just behind them. A child! she thought. A charming child. But in there he was an awe-inspiring . . . and aloud in a toneless voice she said: 'We are all infant prodigies, we artists.'

'Well, bless my soul!' thought the old gentleman who had never got further than Augustin on the piano, and whose boil was now concealed by a top hat. 'What does all that mean? She sounds very oracular.' But the gloomy youth understood. He nodded his head slowly.

Then they were silent and the untidy-haired girl gazed after the brothers and sister. She rather despised them but she looked after them until they had turned the corner.

Frank O'Connor

The Cornet-Player Who Betrayed Ireland

At this hour of my life I don't profess to remember what we inhabitants of Blarney Lane were patriotic about: all I remember is that we were very patriotic, that our main principles were something called 'Conciliation and Consent,' and that our great national leader, William O'Brien, once referred to us as 'The Old Guard.' Myself and other kids of the Old Guard used to parade the street with tin cans and toy trumpets, singing 'We'll hang Johnnie Redmond on a sour apple tree.' (John Redmond, I need hardly say, was the leader of the other side.)

Unfortunately, our neighbourhood was bounded to the south by a long ugly street leading uphill to the cathedral, and the lanes off it were infested with the most wretched specimens of humanity who took the Redmondite side for whatever could be got from it in the way of drink. My personal view at the time was that the Redmondite faction was maintained by a conspiracy of publicans and brewers. It always saddened me, coming through this street on my way from school, and seeing the poor misguided children, barefoot and in rags, parading with tin cans and toy trumpets and singing 'We'll hang William O'Brien on a sour apple tree.' It left me with very little hope for Ireland.

Of course, my father was a strong supporter of 'Conciliation and Consent.' The parish priest who had come to solicit his vote for Redmond had told him he would go straight to Hell, but my father had replied quite respectfully that if Mr O'Brien was an agent of the devil, as Father Murphy said, he would go gladly.

I admired my father as a rock of principle. As well as being a house-painter (a regrettable trade which left him for six months 'under the ivy', as we called it), he was a musician. He had been a bandsman in the British Army, played the cornet extremely well, and had been a member of the Irishtown Brass and Reed Band from its foundation. At home we had two big pictures of the band after each of its most famous contests, in Belfast and Dublin. It was after the Dublin contest when Irishtown emerged as the premier brass band that there occurred an unrecorded episode in operatic history. In those days the best band in the city was always invited to perform in the Soldiers' Chorus scene in Gounod's 'Faust'. Of course, they were encored to the echo, and then, ignoring conductor and everything else, they burst into a selection from Moore's Irish Melodies. I am glad my father didn't live to see the day of pipers' bands. Even fife and drum bands he looked on as primitive.

As he had great hopes of turning me into a musician too he frequently brought me with him to practices and promenades. Irishtown was a very poor quarter of the city, a channel of mean houses between breweries and builder's yards with the terraced hill-sides above it on either side, and nothing but the white Restoration spire of Shandon breaking the skyline. You came to a little footbridge over the narrow stream; on one side of it was a redbrick chapel, and when we arrived there were usually some of the bandsmen sitting on the bridge, spitting back over their shoulders into the stream. The bandroom was over an undertaker's shop at the other side of the street. It was a long, dark, barn-like erection overlooking the bridge and decorated with group photos of the band. At this hour of a Sunday morning it was always full of groans, squeaks and bumps.

Then at last came the moment I loved so much. Out in the sunlight, with the bridge filled with staring pedestrians, the band formed up. Dickie Ryan, the bandmaster's son, and myself took our places at either side of the big drummer, Joe Shinkwin. Joe peered over his big drum to right and left to see if all were in place and ready; he raised his right arm and gave the drum three solemn flakes: then, after the third thump the whole narrow channel of the street filled with a roaring torrent of drums and bass, the mere physical impact of which hit me in the belly. Screaming girls in shawls tore along the pavements calling out to the bandsmen, but nothing shook the soldierly solemnity of the men with their eyes almost crossed on the music before them. I've heard Toscanini conduct Beethoven, but compared with Irishtown playing 'Marching Through Georgia' on a Sunday morning it was only like Mozart in a girls' school. The mean little houses, quivering with the shock, gave it back to us: the terraced hillsides that shut out the sky gave it back to us; the interested faces of passers-by in their Sunday clothes from the pavements were like mirrors reflecting the glory of the music. When the band stopped and again you could hear the gapped sound of feet, and people running and chattering, it was like a parachute jump into commonplace.

Sometimes we boarded the paddle-steamer and set up our music stands in some little field by the sea, which all day echoed of Moore's Melodies, Rossini and Gilbert and Sullivan: sometimes we took a train into the country to play at some sports meeting. Whatever it was, I loved it, though I never got a dinner: I was fed on lemonade, biscuits and sweets, and, as my father spent most of the intervals in the pub, I was sometimes half mad with boredom.

One summer day we were playing at a fête in the grounds of Blarney Castle, and, as usual, the band departed to the pub and Dickie Ryan and myself were left behind, ostensibly to take care of the instruments.

A certain hanger-on of the band, one John P., who to my knowledge was never called anything else, was lying on the grass, chewing a straw and shading his eyes from the light with the back of his hand. Dickie and I took a side drum each and began to march about with them. All at once Dickie began to sing to his own accompaniment 'We'll hang William O'Brien on a sour apple tree.' I was so astonished that I stopped drumming and listened to him. For a moment or two I thought he must be mocking the poor uneducated children of the lanes round Shandon Street. Then I suddenly realised that he meant it. Without hesitation I began to rattle my side drum even louder and shouted 'We'll hang Johnnie Redmond on a sour apple tree.' John P. at once started up and gave me an angry glare. 'Stop that now, little boy!' he said threateningly. It was quite plain that he meant me, not Dickie Ryan.

I was completly flabbergasted. It was bad enough hearing the bandmaster's son singing a traitorous song, but then to be told to shut up by a fellow who wasn't even a bandsman; merely a hanger-on who looked after the music stands and carried the big drum in return for free drinks! I realised that I was among enemies. I quietly put aside the drum and went to find my father. I knew that he could have no idea what was going on behind his back in the band.

I found him at the back of the pub, sitting on a barrel and holding forth to a couple of young bandsmen.

'Now, "Brian Boru's March" ' he was saying with one finger raised, 'that's a beautiful march. I heard the Irish Guards do that on Salisbury Plain, and they had the English fellows' eyes popping out. "Paddy," one of them says to me (they all call you Paddy) "wot's the name of the shouting march?" but somehow we don't get the same fire into it at all. Now, listen, and I'll show you how that should go!'

'Dadda,' I said in a whisper, pulling him by the sleeve, 'do you know what Dickie Ryan was singing?'

'Hold on a minute now,' he said, beaming at me affectionately. 'I just want to illustrate a little point.'

'But, dadda,' I went on determinedly, 'he was singing 'We'll hang William O'Brien from a sour apple tree.'' '

'Hah, hah, hah,' laughed my father, and it struck me that he hadn't fully appreciated the implications of what I had said.

'Frank,' he added, 'get a bottle of lemonade for the little fellow.'

'But dadda,' I said despairingly, 'when I sang "We'll hang Johnnie Redmond," John P. told me to shut up.'

'Now, now,' said my father with sudden testiness, 'that's not a nice song to be singing.'

This was a stunning blow. The anthem of 'Conciliation and Consent' – not a nice song to be singing!

'But, dadda,' I wailed, 'aren't we *for* William O'Brien?'

'Yes, yes, yes,' he replied, as if I were goading him, 'but everyone to his own opinion. Now drink your lemonade and run out and play like a good boy.'

I drank my lemonade all right, but I went out not to play but to brood. There was but one fit place for that. I went to the shell of the castle; climbed the stair to the tower and leaning over the battlements watching the landscape like bunting all round me I thought of the heroes who had stood here, defying the might of England. Everyone to his own opinion! What would they have thought of a statement like that? It was the first time that I realised the awful strain of weakness and the lack of strong principle in my father, and understood that the old bandroom by the bridge was in the heart of enemy country and that all round me were enemies of Ireland like Dickie Ryan and John P.

It wasn't until months after that I realised how many these were. It was Sunday morning, but when we reached the bandroom there was no one on the bridge. Upstairs the room was almost full. A big man wearing a bowler hat and a flower in his buttonhole was standing before the fireplace. He had a red face with weak, red-rimmed eyes and a dark moustache. My father, who seemed as surprised as I was, slipped quietly into a seat behind the door and lifted me on to his knee.

'Well, boys,' the big man said in a deep husky voice, 'I suppose ye have a good notion what I'm here for. Ye know that next Sunday night Mr. Redmond is arriving in the city, and I have the honour of being Chairman of the Reception Committee.'

'Well, Alderman Doyle,' said the bandmaster doubtfully, 'you know the way we feel about Mr. Redmond, most of us anyway.'

'I do, Tim, I do,' said the Alderman evenly as it gradually dawned on me that the man I was listening to was the Arch-Traitor, locally known as Scabby Doyle, the builder whose vile orations my father always read aloud to my mother with chagrined comments on Doyle's past history. 'But feeling isn't enough, Tim. Fair Lane Band will be there of course. Watergrasshill will be there. The Butter Exchange will be there. What will the backers of this band, the gentlemen who helped it through so many difficult days, say if we don't put in an appearance?'

'Well, ye see, Alderman,' said Ryan nervously, 'we have our own little difficulties.'

'I know that, Tim,' said Doyle. 'We all have our difficulties in troubled times like these, but we have to face them like men in the interests of the country. What difficulties have you?'

'Well, that's hard to describe, Alderman,' said the bandmaster.

'No, Tim,' said my father quietly, raising and putting me down from his knee, ''tis easy enough to describe. I'm the difficulty, and I know it.'

'Now, Mick,' protested the bandmaster, 'there's nothing personal about it. We're all old friends in this band.'

'We are, Tim,' agreed my father. 'And before ever it was heard of, you and me gave this bandroom its first coat of paint. But every man is entitled to his principles, and I don't want to stand in your light.'

'You see how it is, Mr. Doyle,' said the Bandmaster appealingly. 'We had others in the band that were of Mick Twomey's persuasion, but they left us to join O'Brienite bands. Mick didn't, nor we didn't want him to leave us.'

'Nor don't,' said a mournful voice, and I turned and saw a tall, gaunt, spectacled young man sitting on the window sill. 'I had three men,' said my father earnestly, holding up three fingers in illustration of the fact, 'three men up at the house on different occasions to get me to join other bands. I'm not boasting Tim Ryan knows who they were.'

'I do, I do,' said the bandmaster.

'And I wouldn't,' said my father passionately. 'I'm not boasting, but you can't deny it: there isn't another band in Ireland to touch ours.'

'Nor a cornet-player in Ireland to touch Mick Twomey,' chimed in the gaunt young man, rising to his feet. 'And I'm not saying that to coddle or cock him up.'

'You're not, you're not,' said the bandmaster. 'No one can deny he's a musician.'

'And listen here to me, boys,' said the gaunt young man, with a wild wave of his arm, 'don't leave us be led astray by anyone. What were we before we had the old band? Nobody. We were no better than the poor devils that sit on that bridge outside all day, spitting into the river. Whatever we do, leave us be all agreed. What backers had we when we started, only what we could collect ourselves outside the chapel gates on Sunday, and hard enough to get permission for that itself? I'm as good a party man as anyone here, but what I say is, music is above politics . . . Alderman Doyle,' he begged, 'tell Mr. Redmond whatever he'll do not to break up our little band on us.'

'Jim Ralegh,' said the Alderman, with his red-rimmed eyes growing moist, 'I'd sooner put my hand in the fire than injure this band. I know what ye are, a band of brothers . . . Mick,' he boomed at my father, 'will you desert it in its hour of trial?'

'Ah,' said my father testily, 'is it the way you want me to play against William O'Brien?'

'Play against William O'Brien,' echoed the Alderman. 'No one is asking you to play *against* anyone. As Jim Ralegh here says, music is above politics. What we're asking you to do is to play *for* something: for the band, for the sake of unity. You know what'll happen if the backers withdraw? Can't you pocket your pride and make this sacrifice in the interest of the band?'

My father stood for a few moments, hestitating. I prayed that for once he might see the true light; that he might show this group of misguided men the faith that was in him. Instead he nodded curtly, said 'Very well, I'll play,' and sat down again. The rascally Alderman said a few humbugging words in his praise which didn't take me in. I don't think they even took my father in, for all the way home he never addressed a word to me. I saw then that his conscience was at him. He knew that by supporting the band in the unprincipled step it was taking he was showing himself a traitor to Ireland and our great leader, William O'Brien.

Afterwards, whenever Irishtown played at Redmondite demonstrations, my father accompanied them, but the moment the speeches began he retreated to the edge of the crowd, rather like a pious Catholic compelled to attend a heretical religious service, and stood against the wall with his hands in his pockets, passing slighting and witty comments on the speakers to any O'Brienites he might meet. But he had lost all dignity in my eyes. Even his gibes at Scabby Doyle seemed to me false, and I longed to say to him, 'If that's what you believe, why don't you show it?' Even the seaside lost its attraction when at any moment the beautiful daughter of a decent O'Brienite family might point to me and say: 'There is the son of the cornet-player who betrayed Ireland.'

Then one Sunday we went to play at some idolatrous function in a seaside town called Bantry. While the meeting was on my father and the rest of the band retired to the pub and I with them. Even by my presence in the Square I wasn't prepared to countenance the proceedings. I was looking idly out of the window when I suddenly heard a roar of cheering and people began to scatter in all directions. I was mystified until someone outside started to shout, 'Come on, boys! The O'Brienites are trying to break up the meeting.' The bandsmen rushed for the door. I would have done the same but my father looked hastily over his shoulder and warned me to stay where I was. He was talking to a young clarinet-player of serious appearance.

'Now,' he went on, raising his voice to drown the uproar outside. 'Teddy the Lamb was the finest clarinet-player in the whole British Army.'

There was a fresh storm of cheering, and wild with excitement I saw the patriots begin to drive a deep wedge of whirling sticks through the heart of the enemy, cutting them into two fighting camps.

'Excuse me, Mick,' said the clarinet-player, going white, 'I'll go and see what's up.'

'Now, whatever is up,' my father said appealingly, 'you can't do anything about it.'

'I'm not going to have it said I stopped behind while my friends were fighting for their lives,' said the young fellow hotly.

'There's no one fighting for their lives at all,' said my father irascibly, grabbing him by the arm. 'You have something else to think about. Man alive, you're a musician, not a bloody infantryman.'

'I'd sooner be that than a bloody turncoat, anyway,' said the young fellow, dragging himself off and making for the door.

'Thanks, Phil,' my father called after him in a voice of a man who had to speak before he has collected his wits. 'I well deserved that from you. I well deserved that from all of ye.' He took out his pipe and put it back into his pocket again. Then he joined me at the window and for a few moments he looked unseeingly at the milling crowd outside. 'Come on,' he said shortly.

Though the couples were wrestling in the very gutters no one accosted us on our way up the street; otherwise I feel murder might have been committed. We went to the house of some cousins and had tea, and when we reached the railway station my father led me to a compartment near the engine; not the carriage reserved for the band. Though we had ten minutes to wait it wasn't until just before the whistle went that Tim Ryan, the bandmaster, spotted us through the window.

'Mick!' he shouted in astonishment. 'Where the hell were you? I had men out all over the town looking for you? Is it anything wrong?'

'Nothing, Tim,' replied my father, leaning out of the window to him. 'I wanted to be alone, that's all.'

'But we'll see you at the other end?' bawled Tim as the train began to move.

'I don't know will you,' replied my father grimly. 'I think ye saw too much of me.'

When the band formed up outside the station we stood on the pavement and watched them. He had a tight hold of my hand. First Tim Ryan and then Jim Ralegh came rushing over to him. With an intensity of hatred I watched those enemies of Ireland again bait their traps for my father, but now I knew they would bait them in vain.

'No, no, Tim,' said my father, shaking his head, 'I went too far before for the sake of the band, and I paid dear for it. None of my family was ever called a turncoat before today, Tim.'

'Ah, it is a young fool like that?' bawled Jim Ralegh with tears in his wild eyes. 'What need a man like you care about him?'

'A man have his pride, Jim,' said my father gloomily.

'He have,' cried Ralegh despairingly, 'and a fat lot any of us has to be proud of. The band was all we ever had, and if that goes the whole thing goes. For the love of the Almighty God, Mick Twomey, come back with us to the bandroom anyway.'

'No, no, no,' shouted my father angrily. 'I tell you after today I'm finished with music.'

'Music is finished with us you mean,' bawled Jim. 'The curse of God on the day we ever heard of Redmond or O'Brien! We were happy men before it . . . All right, lads,' he cried, turning away with a wild and whirling motion of his arm. 'Mick Twomey is done with us. Ye can go on without him.'

And again I heard the three solemn thumps on the big drum, and again the street was flooded with a roaring torrent of music, and though it no longer played for me, my heart rose to it and the tears came from my eyes. Still holding my hand, my father followed on the pavement. They were playing 'Brian Boru's March,' his old favourite. We followed them through the ill-lit town and as they turned down the side street to the bridge, my father stood on the kerb and looked after them as though he wished to impress every detail on his memory. It was only when the music stopped and the silence returned to the narrow channel of the street that we resumed our lonely way homeward.

D. J. Enright

Master Kung at the Keyboard

He's Oriental, he's Japanese, he's Chinese
Watch and you'll see him trip over his tail!
He's a child! What can he know of Vienna woods
Of Ludwig's deafness and J. S. B.'s fine ears?

Of tiaras and galas and programmes
Of hussars and cossacks and pogroms
Of Vespers, Valhallas and Wagrams
And the fine old flower of the Vienna woods?

(Wine, beef, pheasant, cheese, thirst, hunger)

Reared on rice and Taoist riddles
Water torture and the Yellow River
Yang Kwei-fei and one-stringed fiddles –
What can he know of the Water Music
Of barges and gondolas
Of emperors and haemophilias
Of the Abbé, the Princess, and her black cigars?

Wer das Dichten will verstehen
Muss ins Land der Dichtung gehen
Seven days with loaded Canon
Snapping prince and priest and peon.

So he went overseas for his studies? –
It is not in his blood.
What is in his blood?
Blood is.

(Rice, tea, pork, fish, hunger, thirst)

Compared with the minimum of 4,000 characters
Required at the finger-tips for near-literacy
And admission into provincial society
88 keys are child's play.

Play, child!

His heart pumps red rivers through his fingers
His hands chop Bechsteins into splinters
His breath ravishes the leaves
His hair never gets in his eyes.

I am down on my knees.

Every second pianist born is a Chinese
Schubert, Chopin, Mozart, Strauss and Liszt –
He'll be playing on
When the old Vienna woods have gone to
chopsticks
Chopsticks every one.

Valerie Gillies

The Piano Tuner

Two hundred miles, he had come
    to tune one piano, the last hereabouts.
Both of them were relics of imperial time:
    the Anglo-Indian and the old upright knock-about.

He peered, and peered again
    into its monsoon-warped bowels.
From the flats of dead sound he'd beckon
    a tune on the bones out to damp vowels.

His own sounds were pidgin.
    The shapeliness of his forearms
lent his body an English configuration,
    but still, sallow as any snakecharmer

he was altogether piebald.
    Far down the bridge of his nose
perched roundrimmed tortoiseshell spectacles;
    his hair, a salt-and-pepper, white foreclosed.

But he rings in the ear yet,
    his interminable tapping of jarring notes:
and, before he left,
    he gave point to those hours of discord.

With a smile heavenly
    because so out of place, cut off from any home there,
he sat down quietly
    to play soft music: that tune of 'Beautiful Dreamer',

a melody seized from yellowed ivories
    and rotting wood. A damper
muffled the pedal point of lost birthright. We eaves-
    dropped on an extinct creature.

Heinrich Heine

Paganini

From *Florentine Nights*

'Do you admire Paganini?' asked Maria.

'I consider him an honour to his country,' answered Maximilian, 'and he certainly deserves a most distinguished position among the musical celebrities of Italy.'

'I have never seen him,' said Maria, 'but, if report speaks truly, his looks would hardly satisfy a fine eye for beauty. I have seen portraits of him.'

'None of which resemble him,' said Maximilian, interrupting her. 'They all either flatter, or do him injustice. I believe there was but one man who ever succeeded in transferring Paganini's features to paper, and he was a deaf painter named Lyser, who, in his genial eccentricity, with a few rough strokes, made so truthful a likeness of Paganini, that the spectator was at once impressed with a double feeling of mirth and fear. "The devil guided my hand" said the deaf painter, while he chuckled mysteriously and shook his head with an air of good-natured irony, as was his wont when he indulged in such madcap flights. Ah! he was a strange fellow. In spite of his deafness, he loved music enthusiastically, and when he could get near enough to the orchestra could, it was said, read the music in the faces of the players, and tell whether the performance was more or less successful by watching the movements of their fingers. He also wrote operatic criticisms for one of the leading journals of Hamburg. But is there anything remarkable in that? The deaf artist could see tones in the visible characters of playing. Are there not human beings to whom tones are as invisible characters in which they hear colours and forms?'

'You are such a one!' exclaimed Maria.

'I am sorry that I no longer possess Lyser's little drawing; it might have given you an idea of Paganini's appearance. Those strange features that seemed to belong to the sulphurous land of shadows rather than to the world of sunshine could only be seized in bold, sharp lines. When we stood in front of the Alster pavilion in Hamburg, on the day of Paganini's first concert, the deaf painter again assured me that Satan had directed his hand. "Yes," he continued, "what all the world says about him, must be true. He sold himself, body and soul, to the devil; and, in return, was to become the greatest of all violinists, to fiddle millions into his pocket, and to be liberated from the accursed galleys in which he had languished for so many years. For, you see, he got to be chapel-master at Lucca, and fell in love with a theatrical princess, of whom, and a little *abbate*, he became jealous, and by whom, in all probability, he was henpecked; whereupon, he stabbed his *amata*, in most approved Italian style, was sent to the galleys at Genoa, and, as I told you before, sold himself, in the end, to Satan in order that he might escape, become the greatest of violinists, and be able to levy a contribution of two *thalers* upon every one of us. But look! Let all good souls praise God! For there he comes through the allée, accompanied by his ambiguous *famulo*!''

'It was, indeed, Paganini who approached. He wore a dark grey overcoat, reaching down to his feet, and making him appear very tall. His long black hair fell upon his shoulders in wild locks, and, like a frame, encompassed his pale, corpse-like face, upon which grief and genius and hell had graven their indestructible characters. A short, self-complacent person in plain attire tripped along at his side. His face, although florid, was full of wrinkles. He wore a light grey coat, with steel buttons, and bowed in every direction, with most ex-cruciating politeness, while he, now and then, cast half-fearful, half-insipid glances at the sombre figure walking at his side, serious and wrapt in meditation. It reminded one of Retsch's picture of Faust and Wagner, walking before the gates of Leipzig. The painter, however, criticised both individuals in his droll, peculiar way, and made me take particular notice of Paganini's long and measured step. ''Does it not,'' he asked, ''seem as if he still had the iron bar between his legs? He will never get rid of that gait. Do you observe with what contemptuous irony he looks down upon his companion whenever the latter annoys him with his dull and prosy questions. He cannot get rid of him. A bloody compact binds him to this servant, who is none other than Satan himself. The ignorant imagine his companion to be the dramatist and anecdotist Harris, of Hanover, and believe that Paganini carries him along in his travels in order that he may attend to the financial management of the concerts. They do not know that Satan has merely borrowed the form of Mr. George Harris, and that, along with other trash, the poor soul of that poor creature will remain locked up in a chest in Hanover, until the devil returns its carnal envelope; when, in the nobler guise of a black poodle, he will accom-pany his master Paganini through the world.''

'But if Paganini looked sufficiently wild and remarkable in broad daylight, when he walked toward me, below the Jungfernstieg, how much more surprising was his terribly bizarre appearance at the concert in the evening! The performance took place in the Hamburg theatre, and the art-loving public had assembled at so early an hour, and in such numbers, that I experienced difficulty in getting a seat near the orchestra. Although it was *post-day*, I saw, in the first tier of boxes, all of the fashionable world – a perfect Olympus of bankers and other millionaires, gods of coffee and sugar, attended by their fat household divinities, the Junos of Wantrum and the Aphrodites of Dreckwall. All eyes were directed towards the stage; every ear prepared to listen. My neighbour, an old fur-broker, removed the dirty cotton from his ears, so that he might the more easily drink in the expensive tones, to hear which he had already paid two thalers. At last, a sombre figure, which seemed to have risen from the dark regions, appeared on the stage. It was Paganini, in full evening dress. His black coat and vest were of such horrible cut as infernal etiquette prescribes at the court of Proserpine. The black pantaloons flapped about his legs most wildly. His long arms seemed still longer when he made his strange obeisance to the audience, and bent so far forward that the bow in one hand and the violin in the other almost touched the floor. There was something so terribly wooden and so foolishly animal in the angular bendings of his body, that his bowing provoked a great desire to laugh outright. But his pale face, rendered still more death-like by the glaring lights, seemed so supplicating and so full of shy timidity, that shuddering compassion suppressed it. Had he learned these salutations from an automaton or a dog? Is his imploring look that of one doomed to death, or does the shrewd miser's scorn lurk behind it? Is it a living being, about to expire, and who in the arena of art, like a dying gladiator, wishes to regale the public with the death-throes? or is it a dead man risen from the grave – a vampire with a violin, who instead of drinking our heart's blood, contents himself with drawing the money out of our pockets?

'Such were the ideas that engaged us while Paganini cut his interminable capers. All such thoughts vanished when the wonderful master placed his violin under his chin and began to play. As for myself – you know all about my musical second-sight, my gift of seeing the corresponding acoustic figure for every tone that I hear. Thus it was that every stroke of his bow displayed, to my eyes, visible scenes and forms; that in tuneful picture writing he told me all sorts of strange stories, and caused gaudy phantoms, in which he, playing, was always the central figure, to stalk before me. As soon as his bow touched the strings, the scene around him suddenly changed. There he stood beside his music-desk, in a cheerful apartment loaded down with bright decorations and filled with scrolled furniture *a la Pompadour*. On every hand there was a profusion of small mirrors, gilt cupids, Chinese porcelain; a charming chaos of books, wreaths, white gloves, torn laces, false pearls, diadems of gold-foil, and other such tinsel-ware as one is apt to find in the sanctum of a prima-donna. In the meanwhile, Paganini's appearance had changed for the better. He now wore short breeeches of violet satin, a white vest embroidered with silver, and a coat of light-blue velvet with gold-covered buttons. His hair was carefully dressed in small locks and played about his blooming and youthful face, which was full of a sweet and tender expression whenever he glanced towards the pretty little woman who stood beside him while he played.

'In truth, at his side, I seemed to behold a young and pretty creature, clad in old-fashioned attire. She wore a dress of white satin slashed below the hips, her waist seeming the more charmingly narrow in consequence. As her powdered hair was brushed back, the round face beamed forth the more freely with its sparkling eyes, rouged cheeks and beauty-patches, and its pretty, saucy little nose. She held a roll of white paper in her hand, and, from the coquettish way in which her body moved to and fro, she seemed as if singing. But not a single note of hers was audible. It was only through the violin-playing, with which young Paganini accompanied the beautiful creature, that I got at what she was singing, and the emotions that filled his heart while she sang. They were melodies such as the nightingale warbles at twilight, when the rose's perfume fills her yearning heart with the promise of spring. O what melting voluptuousness! What blissful languor! There were tones that kissed, and then, pouting, eluded one another – then, laughing, they intertwined, and becoming as one, died away, drunk with joy. Yes, the sounds sported gaily, like butterflies – just as when one mischievously flees from another, hides behind a flower, is at last caught, and then, in thoughtless joy, flutters upward with its pursuer through the golden sunlight. But a mere spider can suddenly prepare a sad fate for such loving butterflies. Had the young heart such dread forebodings? A sad, sighing tone, like a presentiment of stealthily approaching misfortune, softly glided through the most ravishing melodies that radiated from Paganini's violin . . . His eyes became moist . . . He knelt in prayer at the feet of his *amata*. But alas! just as he bent forward to kiss her feet, he espied a little *abbate* under the bed. I do not know what he may have had against the poor fellow, but the Genoese became as pale as death, grasped the little man with hands of rage, administered several slaps in the face, and, after bestowing quite a number of kicks, threw him out of the room; then drawing a long stiletto from his pocket, he plunged it into the lady's heart.

'At the same moment, cries of "Bravo! Bravo!" resounded on all sides. Hamburg's enthusiastic men and women were bestowing their most boisterous plaudits upon the artist who had just finished the first movement of his concerto. He was bowing with even more angles and contortions than before, and his face expressed still greater dejection and humility than it had done in the earlier part of the evening. His eyes glared with terrible fear, like those of a poor sinner.

' "Divine!" exclaimed my neighbour the fur-broker, while he scratched his ears. "That piece alone was worth two thalers."

'When Paganini again began to play, everything seemed dimmed and darkened to my sight. The tones did not, as before, assume distinct form and colour; the body of the master seemed enveloped in dark shadows, from the depths of which his music sent forth a most piercing, sorrowful wail. Only at intervals, when the little lamp that hung above shed its rays upon him, did I behold his pale face from which the traces of youth had not yet departed. His dress was peculiar and was divided off into two colours, yellow and red. At his feet he dragged heavy chains. Behind him there moved a face, which revealed a merry, faun-like disposition; and I could occasionally see the long hand that seemed to belong to it, fingering about the strings of the violin as if to assist Paganini. At times it guided the hand in which he held his bow, and a bleating laugh accompanied the tones that flowed from the instrument as though they had cost pain and blood. Those tones were like the songs of the fallen angels who descended to the earth, their faces blushing with shame because they had been banished from the realm of the immortals on account of their having wooed the daughters of the earth. There was not one ray of hope or consolation in the abysmal depths of those tones . . .

'But, suddenly, the tormented violinist drew his bow with such energy of frantic despair that his chains rattled and broke, when his forbidding assistant and the mocking furies vanished.

'That very moment my neighbour the fur-broker said: "Pity! what a pity! His string has broken – and that comes of his everlasting *pizzicato*!"

'Had the string really broken? I do not know. I only observed the transfiguration of the tones, and Paganini and his surroundings seemed to have undergone another sudden change. I could hardly recognise him in the brown monk's dress that hid, rather than clothed, him. With his bewildered face half hidden by his hood, a rope around his hips, and barefooted, Paganini, alone and defiant, stood on a rocky promontory by the ocean, playing on his violin; methought it was twilight. The glow of evening was reflected on the broad expanse of waters that gradually became redder, and roared more awfully in mysterious harmony with the tones of the violin; while the sea gained in ruddiness, the heavens grew paler, and when at last the angry waters seemed like so much red blood, the sky became ghastly and livid as a corpse, and large threatening stars came forth – and the stars were black – as black as shining coals. But the tones of the violin continued to grow bolder and more boisterous; the eyes of the terrible player sparkled with a horrid desire to destroy, and his thin lips moved so rapidly and fearfully that it seemed as if he were muttering some wicked old charm to lay the storm, and unfetter the evil spirits imprisoned in the depths of the ocean. He would sometimes stretch forth his bare arm, so long and haggard from the wide sleeve of his gown, and move his fiddle-bow through the air. Then, more than ever, did he seem a wizard, who with magic wand rules the elements . . .

'The whole scene so confounded me that I held my ears and closed my eyes, for fear of becoming crazed. When I opened them again, the phantom had vanished, and the poor Genoese, looking as usual, was making his accustomed obeisance, while the audience applauded most energetically.

' "Ah!" said my neighbour, "that was the renowned performance on the G string. I play the violin myself, and I know what it takes to acquire the command of that instrument."

'Fortunately, the intermission was not a long one, or else the musical judge of furs had muffled me up in a long art discussion. Paganini quietly placed the violin against his chin and, with the first stroke of his bow, the transfiguration of tones began again. The shapes they now assumed were less bright and corporeal than before. They arose in peaceful, majestic waves, swelling like the notes of an organ choral in a cathedral, and around me everything had extended in width and increased height, until the space was so colossal that the eye of the soul alone could grasp it. A sphere of light floated in the centre of the space; on it stood a man of giant stature and proud mien, who was playing on a violin. Was the sphere the sun? I know not. But in the man's features I recognised those of Paganini, beautifully idealised, serenely clear, and wearing a smile of forgiveness. His form glowed with manly strength, a light blue garment covered his noble form and his black hair fell in curls upon his shoulders. And when, like some great god, he stood there playing the violin, it seemed as if the whole universe were listening to him. . . . Such tones the ear never hears, but the heart may dream them when at night it rests against the heart it loves. Perhaps, too, the heart can understand them, even by day, when, rapturously admiring some Grecian work of art, it loses itself in the beautiful lines and curves – '

'Or when one has taken a bottle too much of champagne!' suddenly exclaimed a laughing voice that startled our storyteller as from a dream. When he turned around he beheld the doctor who had softly entered the room.

Maximilian, who had been too much absorbed by his fancies to notice that Maria had fallen asleep, bit his lip with vexation. . . .

'Whither?' said Maximilian, as the doctor seized his arm and led him out of the room.

Sholom Aleichem

The Fiddle

Today I'll play you something on the fiddle.

I don't know how you feel, but as for me, there is nothing more wonderful than to be able to play a fiddle. As far back as I can remember my heart has gone out to the fiddle. In fact, I loved everything about music. Whenever there was a wedding in our town I was the first one on hand to greet the musicians. I would steal up behind the bass violin, pluck a string – boom! – and run off. Boom – and run off again. For doing this I once caught the devil from Berel Bass. Berel Bass, a fierce-looking man with a flat nose and a sharp eye, pretended not to see me as I stole up behind his bass violin. But just as I was stretching my hand out to pull at the string he caught me by the ear and led me to the door with a great show of courtesy.

'Don't forget to kiss the *mazuza* on your way out,' he said.

But that experience taught me nothing. I couldn't stay away from musicians. I was in love with every one of them, from Shaike Fiddele, with his fine black beard and slim white fingers to round-shouldered Getzie Peikler with the big bald spot that reached down to his ears. Many a time when they chased me away, I hid myself under a bench and listened to them playing. From under the bench I watched Shaike's nimble fingers dancing over the strings and listened to the sweet tones that he so skilfully drew out of his little fiddle.

After that I would go around for days in a trance with Shaike and his fiddle constantly before my eyes and moving through my dreams at night. Pretending that I was Shaike, I would crook my left arm, move my fingers, and draw the right arm across as though I held a bow. All this while I threw my head to one side and dreamily shut my eyes. Just like Shaike. Exactly like him.

When the rabbi caught me – this was in *cheder* – drumming my fingers in the air, throwing my head back and rolling my eyes, he gave me a loud smack. 'You rascal, you are supposed to be learning something, and here you are – fooling around – catching flies!'

I vowed to myself, 'Let the world come to an end, I must have a fiddle. No matter what it cost, I must have one.' But how do you make a fiddle? Naturally, of cedarwood. It is easy to say – cedarwood. But where do you get this wood that is supposed to grow only in the Holy Land? So what does God do? He gives me this idea: we had an old sofa at our house, an inheritance from my grandfather, Reb Anshel, over which my two uncles and my father had quarreled for a long time. My uncle Ben argued that he was the oldest son, therefore the sofa was his.

Uncle Sender argued that he was the youngest, therefore the sofa belonged to him. My father admitted that he, being only a son-in-law, had no claim to the sofa, but since his wife, my mother, was my grandfather's only daughter , the sofa rightfully belonged to her. All this time the sofa remained at our house. But my two aunts, Aunt Itke and Aunt Zlatke, entered the feud. They carried their bickerings back and forth between them. The sofa this, the sofa that. Your sofa, my sofa. The whole town rocked with it. Meanwhile, the sofa remained our sofa.

This sofa of which I speak had a wooden frame with a thin veneer, which was loose and puffed out in several places. Now this veneer, which was loose in spots, was the real cedarwood that fiddles are made of. That was what I had heard in *cheder*. The sofa had one drawback which was really a virtue. When you sat down on it you couldn't get up, because it sloped—there was a bulge on one end and a depression in the middle. This meant that no one wanted to sit on it. So it was put away in a corner and was pensioned off.

But now I began to cast an eye at this sofa. I had already arranged for a bow a long time ago. I had a friend, Yudel the teamster's Shimeleh, and he promised me as many hairs as I would need from the tail of his father's horse. And a piece of resin, to rub the bow with, I had all my own. I hated to rely on miracles. I got it in a trade with another friend of mine – Maier, Lippe-Sarah's boy—for a small piece of steel from my mother's old crinoline that had been lying up in the attic. Later, out of this piece of steel, Maier made himself a knife sharpened at both ends, and I was even ready to trade back with him, but he wouldn't think of it. He shouted at me:

'You think you're smart! You and your father, too! Here I go and work for three nights, sharpening and sharpening, and cut all my fingers, and you come around and want it back again!'

Well, I had everything. There was only one thing to do—to pick off enough of the cedar veneer from the sofa. And for that I chose a very good time—when my mother was out shopping and my father lay down for his afternoon nap. I crept into the corner with a big nail and began clawing away with real energy. In his sleep my father heard someone burrowing, and apparently thought it was a mouse. He began to hiss: 'Shhh shhhhh.' I didn't move, I didn't breathe.

My father turned over on his other side and when I heard that he was snoring again I went back to my work. Suddenly I looked up— there stood my father, watching me with a puzzled look. At first he didn't seem to know what was going on, but when he saw the gouged-out sofa he dragged me out by the ear and shook me till I rattled. I thought I was going to faint.

'God help you – what are you doing to the child?' my mother screamed from the threshold.

'Your pride and joy! He's driving me into my grave!' gasped my father, pale as the white-washed wall, as he clasped at his heart and went into a coughing spell.

'Why do you eat yourself up like that?' asked my mother. 'You're sick enough without that. Just take a look at yourself, just look!'

The desire to play the fiddle grew as I grew. The older I grew, the more anxious I was to be able to play, and as if in spite I had to listen to music every day. Just about halfway between home and *cheder* there was a small sod-covered shack, and whenever you passed that shack you heard all sorts of sounds, the strains of all kinds of instruments, and especially the sound of a fiddle. It was the home of a musician, Naftaltzi Bezborodka, a Jew with a shortened coat, with clipped earlocks and with a starched collar. His nose was large and looked almost as if it were pasted on, his lips were thick, his teeth black, his face was pockmarked and without the trace of a beard. And that was why they called him Bezborodka, the beardless one. His wife was a crone who was known as Mother Eve, and they had at least a dozen and a half children – tattered, half-naked, barefoot, and every one of them, from the oldest to the youngest, played on some instrument – this one the fiddle, that one the cello, the other the bass, one the trumpet, another the flute, the bassoon, the harp, the cymbal, the balalaika, the drum. Some of them could whistle the most complicated melody with their lips, or through their teeth, on glass tumblers or pots, or on pieces of wood. They were magicians – or devils of some sort!

With this family I became acquainted in a most unexpected way. I was standing under their window one day, drinking in the music, when one of the boys caught sight of me and came out. He was Pinny, the flutist, a boy about fifteen, but barefoot like the rest.

'What do you think of the music?' he asked.

'I wish I could play that well in ten years,' I told him.

'You can,' he said, and explained that for two *rubles* a month his father would teach me to play. Or, if I wanted, he himself would teach me.

'What instrument would you like to play?' he asked. 'The fiddle?'

'The fiddle,' I said.

'The fiddle,' he repeated. 'Could you pay a *ruble* and a half a month – or are you as penniless as I am?'

'I can pay,' I told him. 'But there is one thing. Neither my father nor my mother nor my rabbi must know a thing about it.'

'God forbid!' he exclaimed. 'Why should anyone find out?' He
moved up closer to me and whispered, 'Have you got a cigar butt – or
a cigarette?' I shook my head. 'No? You don't smoke? Well, then,
lend me a few *groschen* so I can buy some cigarettes. But don't tell
anybody. My father doesn't know that I smoke, and if my mother
found out she'd take the money away and buy some bread.'

He took the money and said in a friendly voice, 'Come on in. You'll
get nothing done standing out here.'

With great fear, my heart pounding and my legs trembling, I
crossed the threshold of this small paradise.

My new friend Pinny introduced me to his father. 'This is Sholom
– Nochem-Vevik's. A rich man's son . . . He wants to learn to play
the fiddle.'

Naftaltzi Bezborodka pulled at his earlock, straightened his collar,
and buttoned up his coat. Then he began a long and detailed lecture on
the subject of music in general and fiddle playing in particular. He
gave me to understand that the fiddle was the best and finest of all
instruments – there was no instrument that ranked higher. Else why
is the fiddle the chief instrument in an orchestra, and not the trombone
or the flute? Because the fiddle is the mother of all instruments . . .

Thus Naftaltzi spoke, accompanying his words with motions of his
hands and large nose. I stood gaping at him, swallowing every word
that came out.

'The fiddle,' Naftaltzi continued, apparently pleased with his
lecture, 'the fiddle, you understand, is an instrument that is older than
all other instruments. The first fiddler in the world was Tubal Cain or
Methuselah, I am not sure which. You may know, you study such
things in *cheder*. The second fiddler was King David. The third, a man
named Paganini, also a Jew. The best fiddlers have always been Jews.
I can name you a dozen. Not to mention myself . . . They say I don't
play badly, but how can I compare myself to Paganini? Paganini, we
are told, sold his soul to the devil for a fiddle. He never would play for
the great of the world – the kings and the princes – no matter how
much they gave him. He preferred to play for the common people in
the taverns and the villages, or even in the woods for the beasts and
birds. Ah, what a fiddler Paganini was!'

Suddenly he turned around: 'Fellow artists – to your
instruments!'

Thus Naftaltzi called out to his band of children, who gathered
about him immediately, each with his own instrument. Naftaltzi
himself struck the table with his bow, threw a sharp look at each child
separately and at all of them at once, and the concert began. They
went at it with such fury that I was almost knocked off my feet. Each

one tried to outdo the other, but loudest of all played a little boy named Chemeleh, a thin child with a running nose and bare spindly legs. Chemeleh played a strange instrument – some sort of a sack – and when he blew, it gave out an unearthly shriek, like a cat when its tail is stepped on. With his bare foot Chemeleh marked time and all the while watched me out of his small impish eyes and winked at me as if to say, 'I am doing well, ain't I?' . . . But hardest of all worked Naftaltzi himself. He both played and conducted, working with his hands, his feet, his nose, his eyes, his whole body; and if anyone made a mistake, he gritted his teeth and yelled out:

'*Forte*, you fool! *Forte, fortissimo!* Count, stupid – count! One, two, three! One, two, three!'

I arranged with Naftaltzi Bezborodka to take three lessons a week, an hour and a half each time, for two *rubles* a month. I begged him over and over to keep this a secret, or I would get into trouble. He gave me his word of honor that he would breathe it to no one.

'We are people,' he said gravely, adjusting his collar, 'of small means, but when it comes to honor and integrity, we have more than the richest of the rich. By the way – can you spare me a few *groschen*?'

I pulled a *ruble* out of my pocket. Naftaltzi took it from me like a professor – very refined – with the tips of his fingers. Then he called Mother Eve, and hardly looking at her, said, 'Here, get something for dinner.'

Mother Eve took the money from him with both hands and every one of her fingers, inspected it carefully, and said, 'What shall I buy?'

'Anything you want,' he said with a show of indifference. 'Get a few rolls – two or three herring – a sausage. And don't forget – an onion, some vinegar and oil – and, maybe, a bottle of brandy . . .'

When the food was laid out on the table the crowd fell on it with such gusto as after a fast. Watching them made me so ravenous that when they asked me to join them I couldn't refuse. And I don't know when I enjoyed any food as much as I did that meal.

When we were through, Bezborodka winked at the crowd, signaled for them to reach for their instruments, and I was treated to another concert, this time an 'original composition.' This they played with such verve and spirit that my ears rang and my head swam and I left the house drunk with Naftaltzi Bezborodka's 'composition.'

All that day in *cheder* the rabbi, the boys and the books all danced before my eyes and the music rang incessantly in my ears. At night I dreamed of Paganini riding the devil. He hit me over the head with his fiddle. I woke screaming, my head splitting, and I began to babble – I don't know what. Later my older sister Pessel told me that I was out of my head. What I said made no sense – crazy words like 'composition,' 'Paganini,' 'the devil' . . . Another thing my sister told me was that while I was sick someone came to ask about me – somebody from Naftaltzi the musician – a barefoot boy. He was chased away and told never to come back.

'What did that fiddler's boy want from you?' my sister nagged, but I held my tongue.

'I don't know. I don't know a thing. What are you talking about?'

'How does it look?' my mother said. 'You are a grown boy already – we are trying to arrange a match for you – and you pick yourself friends like these. Barefoot fiddlers! What have you got to do with musicians anyway? What did Naftaltzi's boy want of you?'

'Which Naftaltzi?' I asked innocently. 'What musicians?'

'Look at him!' my father broke in. 'He doesn't know a thing. Poor little fellow! At your age I was engaged a long time already, and you are still playing games with children. Get dressed and go to *cheder*. And if you meet Hershel Beltax on the way and he asks what was the matter with you, tell him you had a fever. Do you hear what I said? A fever.'

I didn't begin to understand. What did I have to do with Hershel Beltax? And why did I have to tell him about a fever? In a few weeks my question was answered.

Hershel Beltax (he was called that because he and his father and his grandfather had all worked for the tax collector) was a man with a round little belly, a short red beard, small moist eyes and a broad white forehead – the mark of a wise man. He had the reputation in town of being an intelligent man, accomplished and learned – up to a certain point – in the *Torah*. He was a fine writer – that is, he had a clear handwriting. It was said that at one time his writings were known all over the countryside. And besides that he had money and a daughter, an only daughter, with red hair and moist eyes – the exact image of him. Her name was Esther, she was called by a nickname – Flesterl. She was timid and delicate, and terribly afraid of us schoolboys because we teased her all the time. When we met her we sang this song:

> Esther, Flester,
> Where is your sister?

What was so terrible about that? Nothing, it seemed to me, and yet when Esther heard it she covered her ears and ran off crying. She would hide in her room and not go out on the street for days.

But that was a long time ago when she was a child. Now she was a grown girl with long red braids and went about dressed in the latest fashion. My mother was very fond of her. 'Gentle as a dove,' she used to say. Sometimes on Saturday Esther used to come to visit my sister and when she saw me she would turn even redder than she was and drop her eyes. And my sister would call me over and start asking me questions – and watch us both to see how we acted.

One day – into the *cheder* walked my father with Hershel Beltax, and behind them trailed Reb Sholom-Shachne, the matchmaker, a man with a curly black beard, a man with six fingers, as people used to say. Seeing such guests, the rabbi, Reb Zorach, grabbed his coat and put on his hat in such a hurry that one of his earlocks was caught behind his ear, and his skullcap stuck out from under his hat, and his cheeks began to flame. We could see that something unusual was about to happen. Lately Reb Sholom-Shachne the matchmaker had been coming to the *cheder* frequently and each time he came he called the rabbi out of the room and there through the doorway we could see them whispering together, shrugging their shoulders, gesturing with their hands – ending up with a sigh.

'Well, it's the same old story. If it's to be, it will be. Regardless.'

Now when these guests came in, the rabbi, Reb Zorach, was so confused he didn't know what to do or where to seat them. He grabbed hold of a low bench on which his wife used to salt the meat, and carried it around the room with him, till he finally put it down and sat on it himself. But he quickly jumped up and said to his guests, 'Here is a bench. Won't you sit down?'

'That's all right, Reb Zorach,' said my father. 'We just came in for a minute. We'd like to hear my son recite something – out of the Bible.' And he inclined his head toward Hershel Beltax.

'Surely, why not?' said the rabbi, and picking up the Bible he handed it to Hershel Beltax, with a look that said, 'Here – do what you can with it.'

Hershel Beltax took the Bible like a man who knew what he was doing, bent his head sideways, shut one eye, shuffled the pages and handed it to me open at the first paragraph of the *Song of Songs*.

'The *Song of Songs*?' said Reb Zorach with a smile, as though to say, 'You couldn't find something harder?' 'The *Song of Songs*,' says Hershel Beltax, 'is not as easy as you think. One has to understand it.'

'That's not a lie,' said Reb Sholom-Shachne, the matchmaker, with a laugh.

The rabbi beckons to me. I walk up to the table, and begin to chant in a loud voice, with a fine rhythm:

'The *Song of Songs!* A song above all other songs. Other songs have been sung by a prophet, but this song was sung by a prophet who was the son of a prophet. Other songs have been sung by a sage, but this was sung by a sage who was the son of a sage. Other songs have been sung by a king. This was sung by a king who was the son of a king.'

While I sang I watched my examiners and saw on the face of each of them a different expression. On my father's face I saw great pride and joy. On the rabbi's face was fear lest I make a mistake. His lips silently repeated each word. Hershel Beltax sat with his head bent sideways, his beard between his lips, one eye shut, and the other raised aloft, listening with a very knowing look. Reb Sholom-Schachne the matchmaker did not take his eyes off Hershel Beltax the whole time. He sat with his body bent forward, swaying back and forth along with me, interrupting me with a sound that was part exclamation, part laugh, part a cough, pointing his fingers at me:

'When I said he knew it I really meant he knew it.'

A few weeks later plates were broken, and I became engaged to Hershel Beltax's daughter, Flesterl.

Sometimes it happens that a person ages more in one day than in ten years. When I became engaged I suddenly felt grown up – seemingly the same boy and yet not the same. From the smallest boy to the rabbi himself they all treated me with respect. After all, I was a young man engaged to be married – and I had a watch! No longer did my father scold me – and as for whippings – that was out of the question. How could you whip a young man who wore a gold watch? It would be a shame and a disgrace. Once a boy named Eli who, like me, was engaged to be married, received a whipping in *cheder* because he was caught skating on the ice with some peasant boys. The whole town talked about it, and when his fiancée learned of the scandal she cried so long that her parents broke the engagement. And the young man, Eli, was so heartbroken and so ashamed that he wanted to throw himself into the river. Fortunately, the water was frozen over . . .

Such a calamity befell me, too, but not over a whipping, and not over skating on ice, but over a fiddle. And here is the story:

In our tavern we had a frequent guest, Tchetchek, the band leader, whom we called Colonel. He was a strapping fellow, tall, with a large, round beard and sinister eyebrows. His speech was a mixture of several languages, and when he spoke he moved his eyebrows up and down. When he lowered his eyebrows his face became black as night, and when he raised them, his face glowed like the sun, because under those thick eyebrows were a pair of eyes that were bright blue and full of laughter. He wore a uniform with gold buttons and that was why we called him Colonel. He came to our tavern frequently – not because he was a heavy drinker, but because my father used to make a raisin wine – 'the best – and rarest – Hungarian wine' – that Tchetchek could hardly praise enough. He would put his enormous hand on my father's thin shoulder and roar in his queer mixed language:

'Herr Kellermeister, you have the best Hungarian wine in the world. There is no such wine even in Budapest, *predbozhe.*'

Tchetchek was very friendly with me. He praised me for my stories and liked to ask questions like: 'Who was Adam? Who was Isaac? Who was Joseph?'

'You mean – *Yosef?*' I would say.

'I mean Joseph.'

'*Yosef,*' I corrected him again.

'To us he is Joseph, to you he is *Yosef,*' he would say and pinch my cheek. 'Joseph or *Yosef, Yosef* or Joseph, it's all the same, all equal – *wszystko yedno.*'

But when I became engaged Tchetchek's attitude also changed. Instead of treating me like a child he began to talk to me as to an equal, to tell me stories of the army and of musicians. (The Colonel had wonderful stories to tell but no one had time to listen except me.) Once, when he was talking about music, I questioned him, 'What instrument does the Colonel play?'

'All instruments,' he said, and raised his eyebrows.

'The fiddle too?' I asked, and his face became in my eyes the face of an angel.

'Come to my house some day,' he said, 'and I will play for you.'

'I can only come on the Sabbath. But please, Colonel, no one must know.' '*Przed bohem,*' he said fervently and raised his eyebrows.

Tchetchek lived far off beyond the town in a small white cottage with small windows and brightly painted shutters, surrounded by a garden full of bright, yellow sunflowers that carried themselves as proudly as lilies or roses. They bent their heads a little, swayed in the breeze and beckoned to me, 'Come to us, young man, come to us. Here is space, here is freedom, here it is bright and fresh, warm and cheerful.' And after the stench and heat and dust of the town, the noise and turmoil of the crowded *cheder*, I was glad to come, for here was space and freedom, here it was bright and fresh, warm and cheerful. I felt like running, leaping, yelling, singing, or like throwing myself on the ground with my face deep in the fragrant grass. But that is not for you, Jewish children. Yellow sunflowers, green grass, fresh air, the clean earth, the clear sky, these are not for you . . .

When I came to the gate the first time, I was met by a shaggy, black dog with fiery, red eyes, who jumped at me with such force that I was almost knocked over. Luckily he was tied to a rope. When Tchetchek heard me yell he came running out of the house, without his uniform on, and told the dog to be quiet. Then he took me by the hand and led me up to the black dog. He told me not to be afraid. 'Here, pat him – he won't hurt you.' And taking my hand he passed it over the dog's fur, calling him odd names in a kindly voice. The dog dropped his tail, licked himself all over and gave me a look that said, 'Lucky for you my master is standing here, or you would be leaving without a hand.'

Having recovered from my fright, I entered the house with the Colonel and there I was struck dumb: all the walls were covered with guns, and on the floor lay a skin with the head of a lion – or maybe a leopard – with fierce teeth. The lion didn't bother me so much – he was dead. But those guns – all those guns! I didn't enjoy the fresh plums and juicy apples with which my host treated me. I couldn't keep my eyes away from the walls. But later, when Tchetchek took out of its red case a small round fiddle with an odd belly, spread over it his large round beard and placed on it his huge powerful hand and passed the bow over it a few times, and the first melody poured out, I forgot in one instant the black dog, the fierce lion and the loaded guns. I saw only Tchetchek's spreading beard, his overhanging eyebrows, I saw only a round fiddle with an odd belly, and fingers which danced over the strings with such speed that it was hard to imagine where so many fingers came from.

Then Tchetchek himself disappeared – with his spreading beard, his thick eyebrows, and his wonderful fingers – and I saw nothing in front of me. I only heard a singing, a sighing, a weeping, a sobbing, a talking, a roaring – all sorts of strange sounds that I had never heard in my life before. Sounds sweet as honey, smooth as oil, kept pouring without end straight into my heart, and my soul soared far far away into another world, into a paradise of pure sound.

'Would you like some tea?' calls out Tchetchek, putting down the fiddle and slapping me on the back.

I felt as though I had fallen from the seventh heaven down to earth again.

After that I visited Tchetchek every Saturday to listen to his playing. I went straight to the house, not afraid of anyone, and I even became so familiar with the black dog that he would wag his tail when he saw me, and try to lick my hand. But I wouldn't allow that. 'Let's be friends at a distance,' I said.

At home no one knew where I spent my Saturdays. No one stopped me. After all, I was not a child any more.

And they wouldn't have known until now if a fresh calamity had not occurred – a great calamity which I shall now describe.

Who should care if a young fellow takes a Sabbath walk by himself a short distance out of town? Whose business is it? Apparently there are people who care, and one such person was Ephraim Klotz, a busybody who knew what was cooking in every pot. He made it his business to know. This man watched me closely, followed me, found out where I was going, and later swore with many pious oaths that he had seen me at the Colonel's house eating pork and smoking cigarettes on the Sabbath.

Every Saturday when I was in my way to Tchetchek's I would meet him on the bridge, walking along in a sleeveless, patched, summer coat that reached to his ankles. He walked with his arms folded behind him, his overcoat flapping, humming to himself in a thin voice.

'A good Sabbath,' I would say to him.

'Good Sabbath,' he would reply. 'Where is the young man going?'

'Just for a walk,' I said.

'For a walk? Alone?' he repeated, with a meaningful smile . . .

One afternoon when I was sitting with Tchetchek and drinking tea, we heard the dog barking and tearing at his rope. Looking out of the window, I thought I saw someone small and dark with short legs running out of sight. From his way of running I could swear it was Ephraim Klotz.

That night, when I got home, I saw Ephraim Klotz sitting at the table. He was talking with great animation and laughing his odd little laugh that sounded like dried peas pouring out of a dish. Seeing me, he fell silent and began to drum with his short fingers on the table. Opposite him sat my father, his face pale, twisting his beard and tearing hairs out one by one – a sign that he was angry.

'Where are you coming from?' asked my father, with a glance at Ephraim Klotz.

'Where should I be coming from?' I said.

'Where have you been all day?' said my father.

'Where should I be all day? In *shul*.'

'What did you do there all day?'

'What should I be doing there? Studying . . .'

'What were you studying?' said my father.

'What should I be studying? The *Gamorah* . . .'

'Which *Gamorah*?' said my father.

At this point Ephraim Klotz laughed his shrill laugh and my father could stand it no more. He rose from his seat and leaning over, gave me two resounding, fiery slaps in the face. My mother heard the commotion from the next room and came running in . . .

'Nochem,' she cried, 'God be with you! What are you doing? The boy is engaged to be married. Suppose his father-in-law hears of this?'

My mother was right. My future father-in-law heard the whole story. Ephraim repeated it to him himself. It was too good to keep.

The next day the engagement was broken and I was a privileged person no more. My father was so upset that he became ill and stayed in bed for days. He would not let me come near him, no matter how much my mother pleaded for me.

'The shame of it,' he said. 'The disgrace. That is worst of all.'

'Forget about it,' my mother begged. 'God will send us another match. Our lives won't be ruined by this. Perhaps it was not his lot.'

Among those who came to visit my father while he was ill was the bandmaster. When my father saw him, he took off his skullcap, sat up in bed, and extending an emaciated hand, said to him:

'Ah, Colonel, Colonel . . .'

More he could not say because his voice became choked with tears and he was seized with a fit of coughing. This was the first time in my life that I had seen my father cry. My heart ached and my soul went out to him. I stood staring out of the window, swallowing tears. How I regretted the trouble I had caused!

Silently I swore to myself never, never, to disobey my father again, never to cause him such grief, never in this world.

No more fiddles.

Translated by Frances and Julius Butwin

John Ormond

Organist

Sole village master of the yellowing manual,
And market gardener: his sense of perfect pitch
Took in the cracks between the keys.
He was equipped to hear the tiny discord struck
By any weed which innocently mistook
His garden for a place to grow in.

Five days a week John Owen dug and planted,
Potted and weeded, worried
About Saturday's price in Swansea Market
For his green co-productions with God.

Walking to town at dawn, five miles
With Mary Ann his wife fluting beside him
(She, as they said, would laugh at her own shadow)
With creaking baskets laden, he nearly deafened
Himself with the noise of his own boots.

Sabbath, inside the spade-sharp starch
Of his crippling collar, he husbanded
On the harmonium aged couplers
And celestes into a grave, reluctant
Order; took no heed in the hymns
Of the congregation trailing a phrase behind,
Being intent and lost in the absolute beat.

But, with the years, philosopher as he was,
A Benthamite of music, he set more store
By the greatest harmony of the greatest number.
When, pentecostal, guilts were flung away
Fortissimo from pinnacles of fervour,
When all were cleansed of sin in wild
Inaccurate crescendoes of Calvary,
Uncaring, born again, dazzled by diadems
In words of a Jerusalem beyond their lives,
The choristers would stray from the safe fold
Of the true notes. John Owen would transpose
By half a tone in the middle of the hymn
To disguise the collective error,
But sure of the keys of his own kingdom.

He lies long since in counterpoint
With a few stones of earth; is beyond any doubt
The one angel of the village cloud
Who sings from old notation;
The only gardener there whose cocked ear
Can discern the transgression, the trespass
Of a weed into the holy fields,
If there are weeds in heaven.

Anne Ridler

Beecham Concert

A lifetime goes to make this music.
The old body, bundle of bones
Wired together, barely flickers:
Least gestures, costliest pains –
And the sound burns alive from the stick.

Cellini hurled in table, chair,
All that would burn, to cast his metal.
The bronze was flawed despite his care.
But the will itself is inflammable here –
This furnace takes the soul for fuel.

So an old man beats time.
When young men beat, we have in mind
The visible world, and love, and fame;
Here nothing is real but sound,
And death is merely the music's end.

Life is a straw bridging a torrent.
Based on a straw the old man stands.
His style, classical: his dress, elegant;
(On either side the gulf is silent)
Darts of lightning in his hands.

Elias Canetti

The Orchestral Conductor

From *Crowds and Power*

There is no more obvious expression of power than the performance of a conductor. Every detail of his public behaviour throws light on the nature of power. Someone who knew nothing about power could discover all its attributes, one after another, by careful observation of a conductor. The reason why this has never been done is obvious: the music the conductor evokes is thought to be the only thing that counts; people take it for granted that they go to concerts to hear symphonies and no one is more convinced of this than the conductor himself. He believes that his business is to serve music and to interpret it faithfully.

A conductor ranks himself first among the servants of music. He is so full of it that the idea of his activity having another, non-musical meaning never enters his head. No one would be more astonished than he at the following interpretation of it.

The conductor *stands*: ancient memories of what it meant when man first stood upright still play an important part in any representations of power. Then, he is the only person who stands. In front of him sits the orchestra and behind him the audience. He stands on a dais and can be seen both from in front and from behind. In front his movements act on the orchestra and behind on the audience. In giving his actual directions he uses only his hands, or his hands and a baton. Quite small movements are all he needs to wake this or that instrument to life or to silence it at will. He has the power of life and death over the voices of the instruments; one long silent will speak again at his command. Their diversity stands for the diversity of mankind; an orchestra is like an assemblage of different types of men. The willingness of its members to obey him makes it possible for the conductor to transform them into a unit, which he then embodies.

The complexity of the work he performs means that he must be alert. Presence of mind is among his essential attributes; law-breakers must be curbed instantly. The code of laws, in the form of the score, is in his hands. There are others who have it too and can check the way it is carried out, but the conductor alone decides what the law is and summarily punishes any breach of it. That all this happens in public and is visible in every detail gives the conductor a special kind of self-assurance. He grows accustomed to being seen and becomes less and less able to do without it.

The immobility of the audience is as much part of the conductor's design as the obedience of the orchestra. They are under a compulsion to keep still. Until he appears they move about and talk freely among themselves. The presence of the players disturbs no one; indeed they are scarcely noticed. Then the conductor appears and everyone becomes still. He mounts the rostrum, clears his throat and raises his baton; silence falls. While he is conducting no one may move and as soon as he finishes they must applaud. All their desire for movement, stimulated and heightened by the music, must be banked up until the end of the work and must then break loose. The conductor bows to the clapping hands; for them he returns to the rostrum again and again, as often as they want him to. To them, and to them alone, he surrenders; it is for them that he really lives. The applause he receives is the ancient salute to the victor, and the magnitude of his victory is measured by its volume. Victory and defeat become the framework within which his spiritual economy is ordered. Apart from these nothing counts; everything that the lives of other men contain is for him transformed into victory or defeat.

During a concert, and for the people gathered together in the hall, the conductor is a leader. He stands at their head with his back to them. It is him they follow, for it is he who goes first. But, instead of his feet, it is his hands which lead them. The movement of the music, which his hands bring about, represents the path his feet would be the first to tread. The crowd in the hall is carried forward by him. During the whole performance of a work they never see his face. He is merciless; there are no intervals for rest. They see his back always in front of them, as though it were their goal. If he turned round even once the spell would be broken. The road they were travelling would suddenly cease to exist and there would be nothing but a hall full of disillusioned people without movement or impetus. But the conductor can be relied on not to turn round, for, while the audience follows him behind, in front he is faced by a small army of professional players, which he must control. For this purpose, too, he uses his hands, but here they not only point the way, as they do for those behind him, but they also give orders.

His eyes hold the whole orchestra. Every player feels that the conductor sees him personally, and, still more, hears him. The voices of the instruments are opinions and convictions on which he keeps a close watch. He is omniscient, for, while the players have only their own parts in front of them, he has the whole score in his head, or on his desk. At any given moment he knows precisely what each player should be doing. His attention is everywhere at once, and it is to this that he owes a large part of his authority. He is inside the mind of every player. He knows not only what each *should* be doing, but also what he *is* doing. He is the living embodiment of law, both positive and negative. His hands decree and prohibit. His ears search out profanation.

Thus for the orchestra the conductor literally embodies the work they are playing, the simultaneity of the sounds as well as their sequence; and since, during the performance, nothing is supposed to exist except this work, for so long is the conductor the ruler of the world.

Translated by Carol Stewart

Jeremy Robson

Words to a Conductor

for David Atherton

I

The notes are there to start
though the art you give to them
brings pulse-beat, texture, voice
where silence was: the voice
admittedly not yours, but not

his either, quite, who wrote
them down. Your energies involve
themselves at will: tensions, doubts
compound. Last night's row, this
morning's tiff, the dash through

traffic in failing light, a
shirt too stiff, bow too tight –
all crowd, line up for the attack,
are stifled by the disciplines imposed
yet show. Words work less liberally.

Write 'black', the speaker's voice
says 'black'. You have a colour and
a social cause, Othello, riots, cool
Chicago jazz, must choose. Besides,
before you lift your pen you've scanned

the morning mail, stared headlines
out, answered four calls, switched on
switched off the news, a man from the
Electricity Board has called, you've
traded words, are bored, go out.

II

Hard hours later, and our set's
ablaze. You're 'live' from the Albert
Hall, and the announcer's giving way.
Above the instruments' tense scrawl
a vibrant hush is rising to applause.

Outside snow drifts mysteriously;
a tree, raped of its branches,
stares vulnerably back, deposed.
The journey home today by British
Rail has been a babbling Hell

everything means something else.
The Overture breaks through, my tree
takes wings; the snow is somewhere
vast, Siberia perhaps, unrolls.
To tie this with a language that's exact

that *means*, is tone, is colour, shape
is all the things that you and painters
talk about, and more, is what we
try, and still you wonder why
there's 'nothing new' this week.

I envy you your abstract world, and all
that's caught in the music's swell;
a tempest or a nuclear war,
Napoleon's campaigns, a reveller's
sigh, pauper's curse, patron's snore

all there, or less, or more,
removed from the dictionary's stare,
the word worn thin by use, islanded,
abused, there on its own terms, refined
undefined, a baton's beat away.

Eudora Welty

Powerhouse

Powerhouse is playing!

He's here on tour from the city – 'Powerhouse and His Keyboard' – 'Powerhouse and His Tasmanians' – think of the things he calls himself! There's no one in the world like him. You can't tell what he is. 'Nigger man'? – he looks more Asiatic, monkey, Jewish, Babylonian, Peruvian, fanatic, devil. He has pale gray eyes, heavy lids, maybe horny like a lizard's, but big glowing eyes when they're open. He has African feet of the greatest size, stomping, both together, on each side of the pedals. He's not coal-black – beverage colored – looks like a preacher when his mouth is shut, but then it opens – vast and obscene. And his mouth is going every minute: like a monkey's when it looks for something. Improvising, coming on a light and childish melody – *smooch* – he loves it with his mouth.

Is it possible that he could be this! When you have him there performing for you, that's what you feel. You know people on a stage – and people of a darker race – so likely to be marvelous, frightening.

This is a white dance. Powerhouse is not a show-off like the Harlem boys, not drunk, not crazy – he's in a trance; he's a person of joy, a fanatic. He listens as much as he performs, a look of hideous, powerful rapture on his face. Big arched eyebrows that never stop traveling, like a Jew's – wandering-Jew eyebrows. When he plays he beats down piano and seat and wears them away. He is in motion every moment – what could be more obscene? There he is with his great head, fat stomach, and little round piston legs, and long yellow-sectioned strong big fingers, at rest about the size of bananas. Of course you know how he sounds – you've heard him on records – but still you need to see him. He's going all the time, like skating around the skating rink or rowing a boat. It makes everybody crowd around, here in this shadowless steel-trussed hall with the rose-like posters of Nelson Eddy and the testimonial for the mind-reading horse in handwriting magnified five hundred times. Then all quietly he lays his finger on a key with the promise and serenity of a sibyl touching the book.

Powerhouse is so monstrous he sends everybody into oblivion. When any group, any performers, come to town, don't people always come out and hover near, leaning inward about them, to learn what it is? What is it? Listen. Remember how it was with the acrobats. Watch them carefully, hear the least word, especially what they say to one another, in another language – don't let them escape you; it's the only time for hallucination, the last time. They can't stay. They'll be somewhere else this time tomorrow.

Powerhouse has as much as possible done by signals. Everybody, laughing as if to hide a weakness, will sooner or later hand him up a written request. Powerhouse reads each one, studying with a secret face: that is the face which looks like a mask – anybody's; there is a moment when he makes a decision. Then a light slides under his eyelids, and he says '92!' or some combination of figures – never a name. Before a number the band is all frantic, misbehaving, pushing, like children in a schoolroom, and he is the teacher getting silence. His hands over the keys, he says sternly, 'You-all ready? You-all ready to do some serious walking?' – waits – then, STAMP. Quiet. STAMP, for the second time. This is absolute. Then a set of rhythmic kicks against the floor to communicate the tempo. Then, O Lord! say the distended eyes from beyond the boundary of the trumpets, Hello and good-by, and they are all down the first note like a waterfall.

This note marks the end of any known discipline. Powerhouse seems to abandon them all – he himself seems lost – down in the song, yelling up like somebody in a whirlpool – not guiding them – hailing them only. But he knows, really. He cries out, but he must know exactly. 'Mercy! . . . What I say! . . . Yeah!' And then drifting, listening – 'Where that skin beater?' – wanting drums, and starting up and pouring it out in the greatest delight and brutality. On the sweet pieces such a leer for everybody! He looks down so benevolently upon all our faces and whispers the lyrics to us. And if you could hear him at this moment on 'Marie, the Dawn is Breaking'! He's going up the keyboard with a few fingers in some very derogatory triplet-routine, he gets higher and higher, and then he looks over the end of the piano, as if over a cliff. But not in a show-off way – the song makes him do it.

He loves the way they all play, too – all those next to him. The far section of the band is all studious, wearing glasses, every one – they don't count. Only those playing around Powerhouse are the real ones. He has a bass fiddler from Vicksburg, black as pitch, named Valentine, who plays with his eyes shut and talking to himself, very young: Powerhouse has to keep encouraging him. 'Go on, go on, give it up, bring it on out there!' When you heard him like that on records, did you know he was really pleading?

He calls Valentine out to take a solo.

'What you going to play?' Powerhouse looks out kindly from behind the piano; he opens his mouth and shows his tongue, listening.

Valentine looks down, drawing against his instrument, and says without a lip movement, ' "Honeysuckle Rose." '

He has a clarinet player named Little Brother, and loves to listen to anything he does. He'll smile and say, 'Beautiful!' Little Brother takes a step forward when he plays and stands at the very front, with the whites of his eyes like fishes swimming. Once when he played a low note, Powerhouse muttered in dirty praise, 'He went clear downstairs to get that one!'

After a long time, he holds up the number of fingers to tell the band how many choruses still to go – usually five. He keeps his directions down to signals.

It's a bad night outside. It's a white dance, and nobody dances, except a few straggling jitterbugs and two elderly couples. Everybody just stands around the band and watches Powerhouse. Sometimes they steal glances at one another, as if to say, Of course, you know how it is with *them* – Negroes – band leaders – they would play the same way, giving all they've got, for an audience of one.... When somebody, no matter who, gives everything, it makes people feel ashamed for him.

Late at night they play the one waltz they will ever consent to play – by request, 'Pagan Love Song.' Powerhouse's head rolls and sinks like a weight between his waving shoulders. He groans, and his fingers drag into the keys heavily, holding on to the notes, retrieving. It is a sad song.

'You know what happened to me?' says Powerhouse.

Valentine hums a response, dreaming at the bass.

'I got a telegram my wife is dead,' says Powerhouse, with wandering fingers.

'Uh-huh?'

His mouth gathers and forms a barbarous O while his fingers walk up straight, unwillingly, three octaves.

'Gypsy? Why how come her to die, didn't you just phone her up in the night last night long distance?'

'Telegram say – here the words: Your wife is dead.' He puts 4/4 over the 3/4.

'Not but four words?' This is the drummer, an unpopular boy named Scoot, a disbelieving maniac.

Powerhouse is shaking his vast cheeks. 'What the hell was she trying to do? What was she up to?'

'What name has it got signed, if you got a telegram?' Scoot is spitting away with those wire brushes.

Little Brother, the clarinet player, who cannot now speak, glares and tilts back.

'Uranus Knockwood is the name signed.' Powerhouse lifts his eyes open. 'Ever heard of him?' A bubble shoots out on his lip like a plate on a counter.

Valentine is beating slowly on with his palm and scratching the strings with his long blue nails. He is fond of a waltz, Powerhouse interrupts him.

'I don't know him. Don't know who he is.' Valentine shakes his head with the closed eyes.

'Say it agin.'

'Uranus Knockwood.'

'That ain't Lenox Avenue.'

'It ain't Broadway.'

'Ain't ever seen it wrote out in any print, even for horse racing.'

'Hell, that's on a star, boy, ain't it?' Crash of the cymbals.

'What the hell was she up to?' Powerhouse shudders. 'Tell me, tell me, tell me.' He makes triplets, and begins a new chorus. He holds three fingers up.

'You say you got a telegram.' This is Valentine, patient and sleepy, beginning again.

Powerhouse is elaborate. 'Yas, the time I go out, go way downstairs along a long cor-ri-dor to where they puts us: coming back along the cor-ri-dor: steps out and hands me a telegram: Your wife is dead.'

'Gypsy?' The drummer like a spider over his drums.

'Aaaaaaaaa!' shouts Powerhouse, flinging out both powerful arms for three whole beats to flex his muscles, then kneading a dough of bass notes. His eyes glitter. He plays the piano like a drum sometimes – why not?

'Gypsy? Such a dancer?'

'Why you don't hear it straight from your agent? Why it ain't come from headquarters? What you been doing, getting telegrams in the *corridor*, signed nobody?'

They all laugh. End of that chorus.

'What time is it?' Powerhouse calls. 'What the hell place is this? Where is my watch and chain?'

'I hang it on you,' whimpers Valentine. 'It still there.'

There it rides on Powerhouse's great stomach, down where he can never see it.

'Sure did hear some clock striking twelve while ago. Must be *midnight*.'

'It going to be intermission,' Powerhouse declares, lifting up his finger with the signet ring.

He draws the chorus to an end. He pulls a big Northern hotel towel out of the deep pocket in his vast, special cut tux pants and pushes his forehead into it.

'If she went and killed herself!' he says with a hidden face. 'If she up and jumped out that window!' He gets to his feet, turning vaguely, wearing the towel on his head.

'Ha, ha!'

'Sheik, sheik!'

'She wouldn't do that.' Little Brother sets down his clarinet like a precious vase, and speaks. He still looks like an East Indian queen, implacable, divine, and full of snakes. 'You ain't going to expect people doing what they says over long distance.'

'Come on!' roars Powerhouse. He is already at the back door, he has pulled it wide open, and with a wild, gathered-up face is smelling the terrible night.

Powerhouse, Valentine, Scoot and Little Brother step outside into the drenching rain.

'Well, they emptying buckets,' says Powerhouse in a mollified voice. On the street he holds his hands out and turns up the blanched palms like sieves.

A hundred dark, ragged, silent, delighted Negroes have come around from under the eaves of the hall, and follow wherever they go.

'Watch out Little Brother don't shrink,' says Powerhouse. 'You just the right size now, clarinet don't suck you in. You got a dry throat, Little Brother, you in the desert?' He reaches into the pocket and pulls out a paper of mints. 'Now hold 'em in your mouth – don't chew 'em. I don't carry around nothing without limit.'

'Go in that joint and have beer,' says Scoot, who walks ahead.

'Beer? Beer? You know what beer is? What do they say is beer? What's beer? Where I been?'

'Down yonder where it say World Café – that do?' They are in Negrotown now.

Valentine patters over and holds open a screen door warped like a sea shell, bitter in the wet, and they walk in, stained darker with the rain and leaving footprints. Inside, sheltered dry smells stand like screens around a table covered with a red-checkered cloth, in the center of which flies hang onto an obelisk-shaped ketchup bottle. The midnight walls are checkered again with admonishing 'Not Responsible' signs and black-figured, smoky calendars. It is a waiting, silent, limp room. There is a burned-out-looking nickelodeon and right beside it a long-necked wall instrument labeled 'Business Phone, Don't Keep Talking.' Circled phone numbers are written up everywhere. There is a worn-out peacock feather hanging by a thread to an old, thin, pink, exposed light bulb, where it slowly turns around and around, whoever breathes.

A waitress watches.

'Come here, living statue, and get all this big order of beer we fixing to give.'

'Never seen you before anywhere.' The waitress moves and comes forward and slowly shows little gold leaves and tendrils over her teeth. She shoves up her shoulders and breasts. 'How I going to know who you might be? Robbers? Coming in out of the black of night right at midnight, setting down so big at my table?'

'Boogers,' says Powerhouse, his eyes opening lazily as in a cave.

The girl screams delicately with pleasure. O Lord, she likes talk and scares.

'Where you going to find enough beer to put out on this here table?'

She runs to the kitchen with bent elbows and sliding steps.

'Here's a million nickels,' says Powerhouse, pulling his hand out of his pocket and sprinkling coins out, all but the last one, which he makes vanish like a magician.

Valentine and Scoot take the money over to the nickelodeon, which looks as battered as a slot machine, and read all the names of the records out loud.

'Whose "Tuxedo Junction?" ' asks Powerhouse.

'You know whose.'

'Nickelodeon, I request you please to play "Empty Bed Blues" and let Bessie Smith sing.'

Silence: they hold it like a measure.

'Bring me all those nickels on back here,' says Powerhouse. 'Look at that! What you tell me the name of this place?'

'White dance, week night, raining, Alligator, Mississippi, long ways from home.'

'Uh-huh.'

"Sent for You Yesterday and Here You Come Today" plays.

The waitress, setting the tray of beer down on a back table, comes up taut and apprehensive as a hen. 'Says in the kitchen, back there putting their eyes to little hole peeping out, that you is Mr Powerhouse . . . They knows from a picture they seen.'

'They seeing right tonight, that is him,' says Little Brother.

'You him?'

'That is him in the flesh,' says Scoot.

'Does you wish to touch him?' asks Valentine. 'Because he don't bite.'

'You passing through?'

'Now you got everything right.'

She waits like a drop, hands languishing together in front.

'Little-Bit, ain't you going to bring the beer?'

She brings it, and goes behind the cash register and smiles, turning different ways. The little fillet of gold in her mouth is gleaming.

'The Mississippi River's here,' she says once.

Now all the watching Negroes press in gently and bright-eyed through the door, as many as can get in. One is a little boy in a straw sombrero which has been coated with aluminium paint all over.

Powerhouse, Valentine, Scoot and Little Brother drink beer, and their eyelids come together like curtains. The wall and the rain and the humble beautiful waitress waiting on them and the other Negroes watching enclose them.

'Listen!' whispers Powerhouse, looking into the ketchup bottle and slowly spreading his performer's hands over the damp, wrinkling cloth with the red squares. 'Listen how it is. My wife gets missing me. Gypsy. She goes to the window. She looks out and sees you know what. Street. Sign saying Hotel. People walking. Somebody looks up. Old man. She looks down, out the window. Well? . . . *Sssst! Plooey!* What she do? Jump out and bust her brains all over the world.'

He opens his eyes.

'That's it,' agrees Valentine. 'You gets a telegram.'

'Sure she misses you,' Little Brother adds.

'No, it's night time.' How softly he tells them! 'Sure. It's the night time. She say, What do I hear? Footsteps walking up the hall? That him? Footsteps go on off. It's not me. I'm in Alligator, Mississippi, she's crazy. Shaking all over. Listens till her ears and all grow out like old music-box horns but still she can't hear a thing. She says, All right! I'll jump out the window then. Got on her nightgown. I know that nightgown, and her thinking there. Says, Ho hum, all right, and jumps out the window. Is she mad at me! Is she crazy! She don't leave *nothing* behind her!'

'Ya! Ha!'

'Brains and insides everywhere, Lord, Lord.'

All the watching Negroes stir in their delight, and to their higher delight he says affectionately, 'Listen! Rats in here.'

'That must be the way, boss.'

'Only, naw, Powerhouse, that ain't true. That sound too *bad.*'

'Does? I even know who finds her,' cries Powerhouse. 'That no-good pussyfooted crooning creeper, that creeper that follow around after me, coming up like weeds behind me, following around after me everything I do and messing around on the trail I leave. Bets my numbers, sings my songs, gets close to my agent like a Betsy-bug; when I going out he just coming in. I got him now! I got my eye on him.'

'Know who he is?'

'Why it's that old Uranus Knockwood!'

'Ya! Ha!'

'Yeah, and he coming now, he going to find Gypsy. There he is, coming around that corner, and Gypsy kadoodling down, oh-oh, watch out! *Ssssst! Plooey!* See, there she is in her little old nightgown, and her insides and brains all scattered round.'

A sigh fills the room.

'Hush about her brains. Hush about her insides.'

'Ya! Ha! You talking about her brains and insides – old Uranus Knockwood,' says Powerhouse, 'look down and say Jesus! He say, Look here what I'm walking round in!'

They all burst into halloos of laughter. Powerhouse's face looks like a big hot stove.

'Why, he picks her up and carries her off!' he says.

'Ya! Ha!'

'Carries her *back* around the corner . . .'

'Oh, Powerhouse!'

'You know him.'

'Uranus Knockwood!'

'Yeahhh!'

'He take our wives when we gone!'

'He come in when we goes out!'

'Uh-huh!'

'He go out when we comes in!'

'Yeahh!'

'He standing behind the door!'

'Old Uranus Knockwood.'

'You know him.'

'Middle-size man.'

'Wears a hat.'

'That's him.'

Everybody in the room moans with pleasure. The little boy in the fine silver hat opens a paper and divides out a jelly roll among his followers.

And out of the breathless ring somebody moves forward like a slave, leading a great logy Negro with bursting eyes, and says, 'This here is Sugar-Stick Thompson, that drove down to the bottom of July Creek and pulled up all those drownded white people fall out of a boat. Last summer, pulled up fourteen.'

'Hello,' says Powerhouse, turning and looking around at them all with his great daring face until they nearly suffocate.

Sugar-Stick, their instrument, cannot speak; he can only look back at the others.

'Can't even swim. Done it by holding his breath,' says the fellow with the hero.

Powerhouse looks at him seekingly.

'I his half brother,' the fellow puts in.

They step back.

'Gypsy say,' Powerhouse rumbles gently again, looking at *them*, ' "What is the use? I'm gonna jump out so far – so far . . ." Ssssst – !'

'Don't, boss, don't do it agin,' says Little Brother.

'It's awful,' says the waitress. 'I hates that Mr Knockwoods. All that the truth?'

'Want to see the telegram I got from him?' Powerhouse's hand goes to the vast pocket.

'Now wait, now wait, boss.' They all watch him.

'It must be the real truth,' says the waitress, sucking in her lower lip, her luminous eyes turning sadly, seeking the windows.

'No, babe, it ain't the truth.' His eyebrows fly up, and he begins to whisper to her out of his vast oven mouth. His hand stays in his pocket. 'Truth is something worse, I ain't said what, yet. It's something hasn't come to me, but I ain't saying it won't. And when it does, then want me to tell you?' He sniffs all at once, his eyes come open and turn up, almost too far. He is dreamily smiling.

'Don't, boss, don't, Powerhouse!'

'Oh!' the waitress screams.

'Go on git out of here!' bellows Powerhouse, taking his hand out of his pocket and clapping after her red dress.

The ring of watchers breaks and falls away.

'*Look* at that! Intermission is up,' says Powerhouse.

He folds money under a glass, and after they go out, Valentine leans back in and drops a nickel in the nickelodeon behind them, and it lights up and begins to play 'The Goona Goo.' The feather dangles still.

'Take a telegram!' Powerhouse shouts suddenly up into the rain over the street. 'Take a answer. Now what was that name?'

They get a little tired.

'Uranus Knockwood.'

'You ought to know.'

'Yas? Spell it to me.'

They spell it all the ways it could be spelled. It puts them in a wonderful humor.

'Here's the answer. I got it right here. "What in the hell you talking about? Don't make any difference: I gotcha." Name signed: Powerhouse.'

'That going to reach him, Powerhouse?' Valentine speaks in a maternal voice.

'Yas, yas.'

All hushing, following him up the dark street at a distance, like old rained-on black ghosts, the Negroes are afraid they will die laughing.

Powerhouse throws back his vast head into the steaming rain, and a look of hopeful desire seems to blow somehow like a vapor from his own dilated nostrils over his face and bring a mist to his eyes.

'Reach him and come out the other side.'

'That's it, Powerhouse, that's it. You got him now.'

Powerhouse lets out a long sigh.

'But ain't you going back there to call up Gypsy long distance, the way you did last night in that other place? I seen a telephone . . . Just to see if she there at home?'

There is a measure of silence. That is one crazy drummer that's going to get his neck broken some day.

'No,' growls Powerhouse. 'No! How many thousand times tonight I got to say No?'

He holds up his arm in the rain.

'You sure-enough unroll your voice some night, it about reach up yonder to her,' says Little Brother, dismayed.

They go on up the street, shaking the rain off and on them like birds.

Back in the dance hall, they play 'San' (99). The jitterbugs start up like windmills stationed over the floor, and in their orbits – one circle, another, a long stretch and a zigzag – dance the elderly couples with old smoothness, undisturbed and stately.

When Powerhouse first came back from intermission, no doubt full of beer, they said, he got the band tuned up again in his own way. He didn't strike the piano keys for pitch – he simply opened his mouth and gave falsetto howls – in A, D and so on – they tuned by him. Then he took hold of the piano, as if he saw it for the first time in his life, and tested it for strength, hit it down in the bass, played an octave with his elbow, lifted the top, looked inside, and leaned against it with all his might. He sat down and played it for a few minutes with outrageous force and got it under his power – a bass deep and coarse as a sea net – then produced something glimmering and fragile, and smiled. And who could ever remember any of the things he says? They are just inspired remarks that roll out of his mouth like smoke.

They've requested 'Somebody Loves Me,' and he's already done twelve or fourteen choruses, piling them up nobody knows how, and it will be a wonder if he ever gets through. Now and then he calls and shouts, ' "Somebody loves me! Somebody loves me, I wonder who!" ' His mouth gets to be nothing but a volcano. 'I wonder who!'

'Maybe . . .' He uses all his right hand on a trill.

'Maybe . . .' He pulls back his spread fingers, and looks out upon the place where he is. A vast, impersonal and yet furious grimace transfigures his wet face.

'... Maybe it's you!'

Performances

Paul Zimmer

The Duke Ellington Dream

Of course Zimmer was late for the gig.
Duke was pissed and growling at the piano,
But Jeep, Brute, Rex, Cat and Cootie
All moved down on the chairs
As Zimmer walked in with his tenor.
Everyone knew that the boss had arrived.

Duke slammed out the downbeat for Caravan
And Zimmer stood up to take his solo.
The whole joint suddenly started jiving,
Chicks came up by the bandstand
To hang their lovelies over the rail.
Duke was sweating but wouldn't smile
Through chorus after chorus after chorus.

It was the same with Warm Valley,
Do Nothing Till You Hear From Me,
Satin Doll, In A Sentimental Mood;
Zimmer blew them so they would stay played.

After the final set he packed
His horn and was heading out
When Duke came up and collared him.
'Zimmer,' he said, 'You most astonishing ofay!
You have shat upon my charts,
But I love you madly.'

S. T. Coleridge

Lines Composed in a Concert-Room

Nor cold, nor stern, my soul; yet I detest
    These scented rooms, where, to a gaudy throng,
Heaves the proud harlot her distended breast
    In intricacies of laborious song.

These feel not Music's genuine power, nor deign
    To melt at Nature's passion-warbled plaint;
But when the long-breathed singer's uptrilled strain
    Bursts in a squall – they gape for wonderment.

Hark! the deep buzz of vanity and hate!
    Scornful, yet envious, with self-torturing sneer
My lady eyes some maid of humbler state,
    While the pert captain, or the primmer priest,
Prattles accordant scandal in her ear.

O give me, from this heartless scene released,
    To hear our old musician, blind and gray,
(Whom stretching from my nurse's arms I kissed,)
    His Scottish tunes and warlike marches play,
By moonshine, on the balmy summer night.
    The while I dance amid the tedded hay
With merry maids, whose ringlets toss in light.

Or lies the purple evening on the bay
Of the calm glassy lake, O let me hide
    Unheard, unseen, behind the alder-trees,
For round their roots the fisher's boat is tied,
    On whose trim seat doth Edmund stretch at
    ease,
And while the lazy boat sways to and fro,
    Breathes in his flute sad airs, so wild and slow,
That his own cheek is wet with quiet tears.

But O, dear Anne! when midnight wind careers,
And the gust pelting on the out-house shed
Makes the cock shrilly on the rain-storm crow,
To hear thee sing some ballad full of woe,
Ballad of shipwrecked sailor floating dead,
    Whom his own true-love buried in the sands!
Thee, gentle woman, for thy voice remeasures
Whatever tones and melancholy pleasures
    The things of Nature utter; birds or trees
Or moan of ocean-gale in weedy caves,
Or where the stiff grass 'mid the heath-plant waves,
    Murmur and music thin of sudden breeze.

Robert Browning

A Toccata of Galuppi's

Oh, Galuppi, Baldassaro, this is very sad to find!
I can hardly misconceive you; it would prove me deaf and blind;
But although I take your meaning, 'tis with such a heavy mind!

Here you come with your old music, and here's all the good it
    brings.
What, they lived once thus at Venice where the merchants were the
    kings,
Where Saint Mark's is, where the Doges used to wed the sea with
    rings?

Aye, because the sea's the street there; and 'tis arched by . . . what
    you call
. . . Shylock's bridge with houses on it where they kept the carnival:
I was never out of England – it's as if I saw it all.

Did young people take their pleasure when the sea was warm in
    May?
Balls and masks begun at midnight, burning ever to midday,
When they made up fresh adventures for the morrow, do you say?

Was a lady such a lady, cheeks so round and lips so red –
On her neck the small face buoyant, like a bellflower on its bed,
O'er the breast's superb abundance where a man might base his
    head?

Well, and it was graceful of them – they'd break talk off and afford
– She, to bite her mask's black velvet – he, to finger on his sword,
While you sat and played toccatas, stately at the clavichord?

What? Those lesser thirds so plaintive, sixths diminished, sigh on
    sigh,
Told them something? Those suspensions, those solutions – 'Must
    we die?'
Those commiserating sevenths – 'Life might last! We can but try!'

'Were you happy?' – 'Yes.' – 'And are you still as happy?' –
    'Yes. And you?'

– 'Then, more kisses!' – Did I stop them, when a million seemed
    so few?'
Hark, the dominant's persistence till it must be answered to!

So, an octave struck the answer. Oh, they praised you, I dare say!
'Brave Galuppi! That was music; good alike at grave and gay!
I can always leave off talking when I hear a master play!'

Then they left you for their pleasure: till in due time, one by one,
Some with lives that came to nothing, some with deeds as well
    undone,
Death stepped tacitly and took them where they never see the sun.

But when I sit down to reason, think to take my stand nor swerve,
While I triumph o'er a secret wrung from nature's close reserve,
In you come with your cold music till I creep through every nerve.

Yes, you, like a ghostly cricket, creaking where a house was burned:
'Dust and ashes, dead and done with, Venice spent what Venice
    earned.
The soul, doubtless, is immortal – where a soul can be
    discerned.

Yours for instance: you know physics, something of geology,
Mathematics are your pastime; souls shall rise in their degree;
Butterflies may dread extinction – you'll not die, it cannot be!

As for Venice and her people, merely born to bloom and drop,
Here on earth they bore their fruitage, mirth and folly were the
    crop:
What of soul was left, I wonder, when the kissing had to stop?

Dust and ashes!' So you creak it, and I want the heart to scold.
Dear dead women, with such hair, too – what's become of all the
    gold
Used to hang and brush their bosoms? I feel chilly and grown old.

Marcel Proust

From *Remembrance of Things Past*

Ever since, more than a year before, discovering to him many of the riches of his own soul, the love of music had been born, and for a time at least had dwelt in him, Swann had regarded musical *motifs* as actual ideas, of another world, of another order, ideas veiled in shadows, unknown, impenetrable by the human mind, which none the less were perfectly distinct one from another, unequal among themselves in value and in significance. When, after that first evening at the Verdurins', he had had the little phrase played over to him again, and had sought to disentangle from his confused impressions how it was that, like a perfume or a caress, it swept over and enveloped him, he had observed that it was to the closeness of the intervals between the five notes which composed it and to the constant repetition of two of them that was due that impression of a frigid, a contracted sweetness; but in reality he knew that he was basing this conclusion not upon the phrase itself, but merely upon certain equivalents, substituted (for his mind's convenience) for the mysterious entity of which he had become aware, before ever he knew the Verdurins, at that earlier party, when for the first time he had heard the sonata played. He knew that his memory of the piano falsified still further the perspective in which he saw the music, that the field open to the musician is not a miserable stave of seven notes, but an immeasurable keyboard (still, almost all of it, unknown), on which, here and there only, separated by the gross darkness of its unexplored tracts, some few among the millions of keys, keys of tenderness, of passion, of courage, of serenity, which compose it, each one differing from all the rest as one universe differs from another, have been discovered by certain great artists who do us the service, when they awaken in us the emotion corresponding to the theme which they have found, of shewing us what richness, what variety lies hidden, unknown to us, in that great black impenetrable night, discouraging exploration, of our soul, which we have been content to regard as valueless and waste and void. Vinteuil had been one of those musicians. In his little phrase, albeit it presented to the mind's eye a clouded surface, there was contained, one felt, a matter so consistent, so explicit, to which the phrase gave so new, so original a force, that those who had once heard it preserved the memory of it in the treasure chamber of their minds. Swann would repair to it as to a conception of love and happiness, of which at once he knew as well in what respects it was peculiar as he would know of the *Princesse de Clèves*, or of *René*, should either of those titles occur to him. Even when he was not thinking of the little phrase, it existed, latent, in his mind, in the same way as certain other conceptions without material equivalent, such as our notions of light, of sound, of perspective, of bodily desire, the rich possessions wherewith our inner temple is diversified and adorned. Perhaps we shall lose them, perhaps they will be obliterated, if we return to nothing in the dust. But so long as we are alive, we can no more bring ourselves to a state in which we shall not have known them than we can with regard to any material object, than we can, for example, doubt the luminosity of a lamp that has just been lighted, in view of the changed aspect of everything in the room, from which has vanished even the memory of the darkness. In that way Vinteuil's phrase, like some theme, say, in *Tristan*, which represents to us also a certain acquisition of sentiment, had espoused our mortal state, had endued a vesture of humanity that was affecting enough. Its destiny was linked, for the future, with that of the human soul, of which it was one of the special, the most distinctive ornaments. Perhaps it is not-being that is the true state, and all our dream of life is without existence; but, if so, we feel that it must be that these phrases of music, these conceptions which exist in relation to our dream, are nothing either. We shall perish, but we have for our hostages these divine captives who shall follow and share our fate. And death in their company is something less bitter, less inglorious, perhaps even less certain.

So Swann was not mistaken in believing that the phrase of the sonata did, really, exist. Human as it was from this point of view, it belonged, none the less, to an order of supernatural creatures whom we have never seen, but whom, in spite of that, we recognise and acclaim with rapture when some explorer of the unseen contrives to coax one forth, to bring it down from that divine world to which he has access to shine for a brief moment in the firmament of ours. This was what Vinteuil had done for the little phrase. Swann felt that the composer had been content (with the musical instruments at his disposal) to draw aside its veil, to make it visible, following and respecting its outlines with a hand so loving, so prudent, so delicate and so sure, that the sound altered at every moment, blunting itself to indicate a shadow, springing back into life when it must follow the curve of some more bold projection. And one proof that Swann was not mistaken when he believed in the real existence of this phrase, was that anyone with an ear at all delicate for music would at once have detected the imposture had Vinteuil, endowed with less power to see and to render its forms, sought to dissemble (by adding a line, here and there, of his own invention) the dimness of his vision or the feebleness of his hand.

The phrase had disappeared. Swann knew that it would come again at the end of the last movement, after a long passage which Mme. Verdurin's pianist always 'skipped'. There were in this passage some admirable ideas which Swann had not distinguished on first hearing the sonata, and which he now perceived, as if they had, in the cloak-room of his memory, divested themselves of their uniform disguise of novelty. Swann listened to all the scattered themes which entered into the composition of the phrase, as its premisses enter into the inevitable conclusion of a syllogism; he was assisting at the mystery of its birth. 'Audacity,' he exclaimed to himself, 'as inspired, perhaps, as a Lavoisier's or an Ampère's, the audacity of a Vinteuil making experiment, discovering the secret laws that govern an unknown force, driving across a region unexplored towards the one possible goal the invisible team in which he has placed his trust and which he never may discern!' How charming the dialogue which Swann now heard between piano and violin, at the beginning of the last passage. The suppression of human speech, so far from letting fancy reign there uncontrolled (as one might have thought), had eliminated it altogether. Never was spoken language of such inflexible necessity, never had it known questions so pertinent, such obvious replies. At first the piano complained alone, like a bird deserted by its mate; the violin heard and answered it, as from a neighbouring tree. It was as at the first beginning of the world, as if there were not yet but these twain upon the earth, or rather in this world closed against all the rest, so fashioned by the logic of its creator than in it there should never be any but themselves; the world of this sonata. Was it a bird, was it the soul, not yet made perfect, of the little phrase, was it a fairy, invisibly somewhere lamenting, whose plaint the piano heard and tenderly repeated? Its cries were so sudden that the violinist must snatch up his bow and race to catch them as they came. Marvellous bird! The violinist seemed to wish to charm, to tame, to woo, to win it. Already it had passed into his soul, already the little phrase which it evoked shook like a medium's the body of the violinist, 'possessed' indeed. Swann knew that the phrase was going to speak to him once again. And his personality was now so divided that the strain of waiting for the imminent moment when he would find himself face to face, once more, with the phrase, convulsed him in one of those sobs which a fine line of poetry or a piece of alarming news will wring from us, not when we are alone, but when we repeat one or the other to a friend, in whom we see ourselves reflected, like a third person, whose probable emotion softens him. It reappeared, but this time to remain poised in the air, and to sport there for a moment only, as though immobile, and shortly to expire. And so Swann lost nothing of the precious time for which it lingered. It was still there, like an iridescent bubble that floats for a while unbroken. As a rainbow, when its brightness fades, seems to subside, then soars again and, before it is extinguished, is glorified with greater splendour than it has ever shewn; so to the two colours which the phrase had hitherto allowed to appear it added others now, chords shot with every hue in the prism, and made them sing. Swann dared not move, and would have liked to compel all the other people in the room to remain still also, as if the slightest movement might embarrass the magic presence, supernatural, delicious, frail, that would so easily vanish. But no one, as it happened, dreamed of speaking. The ineffable utterance of one solitary man, absent, perhaps dead (Swann did not know whether Vinteuil were still alive), breathed out above the rites of those two hierophants, sufficed to arrest the attention of three hundred minds, and made of that stage on which a soul was thus called into being one of the noblest altars on which a supernatural ceremony could be performed. It followed that, when the phrase at last was finished, and only its fragmentary echoes floated among the subsequent themes which had already taken its place, if Swann at first was annoyed to see the Comtesse de Monteriender, famed for her imbecilities, lean over towards him to confide in him her impressions, before even the sonata had come to an end; he could not refrain from smiling, and perhaps also found an underlying sense, which she was incapable of perceiving, in the words that she used. Dazzled by the virtuosity of the performers, the Comtesse exclaimed to Swann: 'It's astonishing! I have never seen anything to beat it . . .' But a scrupulous regard for accuracy making her correct her first assertion, she added the reservation, 'anything to beat it . . . since the table-turning!'

Translated by C. K. Scott Moncrieff

Gjertrud Schnackenberg

The Living Room

From *19 Hadley Street*

We've hung David's *La Vierge et les Saintes*
Near the piano. The companionable blessed
Surround the Virgin, her eyes are tolerant,
Dull with fulfillment. She is perfectly dressed,
Silk sleeves, green velvet gown, and jeweled cap;
Waves cascade down her back. Her Book of Hours,
Unlatched and lying open on her lap,
Reveals white, distant, miniature towers
Against a sky of pure, medieval blue,
Rude peasants worshipping, broad fields of wheat
Beneath the sun, moon, stars. A courtly zoo
Feeds in the letters, magnified, ornate,
The lion, monkey, fox, and snakes twining
Around the words amuse her. She chooses not
To read just now, but touches her wedding ring,
And round her waist a gold rope in a knot.
From where she sits, her eyes rest on the keys,
Watching my hands at practice. She enjoys
Bach in Heaven, his sacred Fantasies
For her alone spin like fabulous toys.
Lines shift and break, she finds it rich and right,
Such music out of black dots on the page,
Symbols, the world a symbol from her height,
Great voices rising like smoke from time's wreckage.

Bach, like an epoch, at his clavichord,
Paused, listening, and shaking the great head
He watched his mind revolve. He pressed a chord.
He would compose tonight. Upstairs in bed
Anna Magdalyn worried, one o'clock
And him so tired, straining the clouded eyes to
Blindness; blindly for hours the master shook
The notes like legible blood drops onto
The page, Europe a small book in his palm,
Players in history's pages saying, 'Not brook
But rather Ocean should be his name.' At dawn
His wife awoke the first on earth to hear
These silver lines beginning, plucked, revolved,
Unearthly trills spiraling up the stair,
The night dispelled, Leipzig itself dissolved,
And Paradise a figuring of air.

Giles Gordon

Maestro

The pianist walked on to the platform to only a smattering of applause, the odd left hand banging the palm of the odd right hand, perhaps to keep warm in the cold hall, and keep the blood circulating in the body. Then the clapping stopped, the last pair of palms ceasing to beat, vibrate, echo in the mind. He sat on the stool, pulled it and himself a little towards the instrument, then pushed the stool and himself back, slightly. It may have ended up in precisely the position where it began. The gesture may have been less for physical comfort than for psychological reasons. How could I know? I neither knew the pianist from Adam nor was I sitting close enough to the platform to be able to observe the minutest movement. He shook his fingers, his hands, a few times, holding them above the keyboard as if shaking water off them and on to the instrument, anointing it with some essential lotion. His face, in so far as the profile was representative of the three dimensional visage, was motionless, rapt. It was reassuring to observe such childlike concentration in the expression of a man aged between thirty and forty.

He tilted his head a bit, towards the audience. Not to look at individual members of it, to meet eyes with eyes, but to indicate that he was ready to commence when they were ready for him to begin. His ear was cupped towards us, as if to catch any stray and unwelcome sounds, to absorb them silently before he began. Someone coughed, as if nervously challenged to do so by the angle of the pianist's ear and head, and the aggression implied. He waited for the man to get it over with, to cease coughing (no woman would cough in such an abandoned manner). Though the man who coughed had paid for his ticket, had paid to hear the man on the platform play, there was no question as to which of them – pianist or member of the audience – was in command. The coughing fell away. There was a splutter, a stutter of coughing a few rows from the front but it was smothered nearly as soon as it began.

Once more the fingers were poised above the keyboard. The five hundred, six hundred people in the hall held their breath – all that indrawing of breath at the same time – their lives, for a second, a moment of time, a few seconds. How long in clock time is unimportant. Their identities were suspended, missing, in limbo. They ceased, individually and collectively, to exist because they had brought so much intensity to bear on the situation. Then in the silence, into the silence rather than against it, his hand, his left hand, came down, his fingers then his right hand, the two hands, both of them, and music, the notes, the sounds, floated away as I tried to listen, I was there to listen, in advance of listening I had paid to listen, I tried to listen, I concentrated on listening, the note, notes, sound, sounds – stop full stop, full point before I, after both of them, the first two notes, finger tips touching the keyboard, stop, oh Christ, this is, was, too much, relax, relax, back to the beginning, please, the fingers above the keyboard, the concentration, withdraw.

Look, he played the first note, with a finger – one of ten – on a key, white or black, no white, definitely white, of that I am certain. How do I know, sitting where I was, as far back as row M? I just know. But as I was relishing that note, mouthing it in the air, feeling its flavour, he played a second note. I didn't, at that time, want to hear it. My life, the chemicals contained within my body, my head – emotions, desires and intellect – couldn't at that moment accommodate the second note. The first still lived, had its being. The second note was neither more nor less significant in itself than the first but it followed so quickly upon the first that I couldn't think about it, in actuality, in the physical world, and in my mind's eye, I couldn't listen to it in its solitary glory. Yet the combination of the first two notes, the one after the other, the second immediately after the first, the two together to all intents and . . . was, simply, devastating. Will that suffice, an adequate word to try to signify the exquisiteness of the sound produced?

If those two notes had been all, I might have grown to know them, to absorb them into my being, my knowledge and understanding of life, art. Mentally, I would have built an open space around me and I would have listened to them, heard them again and again. They would have given me sustenance, fulfilled me. I would have listened, and heard. But, but, but, but, and more quickly than the first of those buts can be spoken, a third note followed the second, and a fourth the third, and the fingers were above the keyboard and they came down, kept coming down, and a fifth note and a sixth, seventh, eighth – stop, please, stop – and a ninth – stop, stop, stop – and a tenth – you're destroying it, the creation – eleventh, thirty-eighth, seventy-third, one hundred and – stop – first. Heavy, heavy, breathing. Stop. Oh God. The waste. Stop. Maestro. Please. *Please.*

I was standing up in the hall, holding out my right hand and arm as if I were a traffic policeman. I was facing the pianist from thirteen rows back, and my companion was tugging at the hem of my jacket, pulling it with absurd force, trying to make me sit down, but neither her strength nor anyone else's would have been able to restrain me. And the hands, the fingers went on playing, the keys were touched, the notes oozed out, soared up and away, a confusion of sweetness and clarity, intensity and indistinctness emanating from the hands, the keyboard, the instrument. And in the hall, six hundred faces in serious, pedantic rows looked round and focused upon my face, and those behind me had to make do with the back of my head. They were, I could tell (my companion kept pulling, tugging my jacket), shocked, appalled, outraged at my behaviour but I could not concern myself with that, I could not care, I could not have the music ruined – nothing less – in this way.

My companion, with her hitherto free hand, seized one of the sleeves of my jacket and I wriggled out of the garment, then in my shirt sleeves thrust out my right hand in front of me again, begging the pianist to take notice of me, of my protest, begging him to stop and I was shouting at him, at least my mouth was open wide, opening and closing as if I were shouting, the lips parting and coming together slowly, as if the words were being projected across a great distance. And when I brought my lips together after expelling the words, the notes which hung in the air, about the hall, were not finding their way into my mouth, my head and my being. They were not concerned with me, and I wanted them to be. I needed them, they had to become mine.

The audience was increasingly menacing, between clenched teeth they told me to shush, be quiet, shut up, desist, piss off, get out. One or two individuals were standing up, leaning in my direction as if they wished to do me physical harm. They made grotesque sounds, contorted and twisted their faces into ugly, improbable shapes. The ferocity, the venom, the near hysteria was frightening. Had I not been concentrating upon the pianist's fingers, the ravishment at the front of the hall, on the platform, very likely I would have been more alarmed and concerned than I was. No, I won't shush, I can't shush. Maestro, maestro, stop. My hands were now both over my ears, I couldn't bear to listen to another note, not one, I couldn't bear to have it forced into my hearing, have it waft through the air so that I couldn't avoid it. And he went on playing, as if unaware of my discontent, my unhappiness and despair, as if he alone was both making the music and listening to it. My appealing to him, the urgency and importance of my action, had somehow not penetrated to his person, though everyone else in the hall seemed aware of my presence.

Stop, I shouted, as if the veil of the temple was being rent, which in every sense it was. Around me, five, six hundred faces drew in breath, gasped, were aghast, understanding that the decline of the second Roman Empire was nigh, that the end of the world might well be at hand. Involuntarily I began to cry – certainly did more than snivel – a proper weep, not the way a grown-up is supposed to behave in public or even, ducky, in private, but I was in public and the notes were still being played, oh God, oh God, they were still being played, I had long, long ago, ages ago at the beginning of the world, lost count of how many notes there had been, and the pianist's hands, those ten fingers now surely beginning to become a little sticky, were still producing those sounds, that surfeit of beauty. Those notes that hung in the air for an instant, then soared, filled the room, the hall, as if birds each more beautiful than any previously created were – invisible to the human eye – flying around the hall yet reaching to their own heaven oblivious of our, my response. As soon as one was created it was snuffed out, softly smothered, even in the memory extinguished by another, and another, and on and on and. And there were, of course – *of course* – too many, it was intolerable, all this beauty being taken for granted, tastefully absorbed.

I shouted at the pianist (what more could I do?), but he played on. The notes, the bloody notes. I besought him to stop, to let me listen, even if no one else wanted to, to hear again those two, twenty, two hundred, two thousand notes, however many there were and had been, however few there were, to let me hear them individually, one by one. First one. Then another: after I had heard the first for as long as I needed to hear it, allowing my mind to obtain from it all it had to give, to feed upon it until I was replete, content. I wanted them, one by one, enshrined in marble – but no, I wanted them liquid, as notes, sounds, as themselves, not as replicas, oh no, no, no. They existed out of time, away from solidity. I couldn't listen to the next notes, the subsequent ones as I was still mourning the earlier ones, the first ones, the first one.

My companion, white with rage and embarrassment, was pulling at my shirt tail, whispering noisily to me, asking me what the hell I thought I was doing. If it wasn't clear to her, if she didn't feel at least something of what I felt, I doubted whether she was the girl for me. Five hundred, six hundred faces were looking at me – if looks could kill I was dead five hundred, six hundred times, ha – and I was standing there, tears pouring down my face, and if my mouth and ears could have cried, and my nostrils, they'd have cried as well. I was shaking my head, over and over again, all the time now, backwards and forwards like a metronome but not in time to the music, far, far too slow for that, and my sex was disappearing into my arse or through my navel, I wasn't clear of the direction or the purpose, it was unimportant. My spirit was endeavouring to leave my body. Stop, stop, maestro. The notes went on, spilled out. That my body was still in one piece, that I still understood that I had a mind, should not be held against me, should not be laid at my door. And the fingers, the two hands, were still – always – making the notes, the sounds, they were touching the keyboard;-weren't they?

Did I then have my first moment of doubt? The fingers were moving up and down, touching the keys, black and white, striking them, yet I no longer, if I ever had, heard a sound, the faces were no longer looking at me, they were looking towards the front of the hall, to the piano and the pianist there. And his body, his movements were in control, his discipline was impeccable, yes, impeccable. Between pieces he would stand up, bow, leave the platform, return, sit down again at the stool, play another piece, more notes. Wipe the sweat off his brow and fingers with a huge white handkerchief. Smile and bow a lot, and play again. The notes had undermined my equilibrium, destroyed my self.

They began again, I could hear them. *Could* hear them? Did hear them. Couldn't block them out. Stop, stop, stop, I shouted, shaking my head (shaking my head again, yes? I'd done it before?), crying, crying again, crying still. There's a limit to the amount of beauty the human frame can stand, once it begins to accept that what it is experiencing is, in its way, perfect. And the tears were pouring in streams down my cheeks, my naked body. For my clothes were shed without my having been aware of removing them, or of having had them removed by my companion or by anyone else. Not a button could I remember loosening. And I was crawling on the floor, I had adopted a crawling position that is, akin to a beast of the field or of the jungle, siren seduced by the notes, ravished from afar, and my genitals were beneath me, hanging down, dissolving, dissolved, they too affected by the shrinking of the universe. And the audience faced the front, the platform, appreciating the music. Appreciating it, I ask you. There were smiles, even of ecstasy, on some of their faces, and some had musical scores on their laps. My companion listened with a rapt, glazed expression. Neither she nor anyone else in the hall seemed aware of where I was, the state I enjoyed, Which was as well. Which was right; and said something, more than something, for the pianist and the music played.

And the bugger played on (he took another bow, applause, and played on), my torturer. The exquisiteness, the perfection, the expansion of human potential was intolerable. He was immaculate in evening dress, none of your jeans and tee-shirt. His face was expressionless, vapid; didn't he care? And I crawled towards him on my hands (the floor was dusty) and knees (the boards were splintery) and I was getting nowhere, no nearer, and the notes kept coming – stop, stop, stop – and I realised that I wasn't moving or if I was the platform was moving away from me at the same speed at which I was approaching it and that to say the least was unlikely or at any rate I gave it the benefit of the doubt.

I acknowledged that I was too overcome to progress backwards or forwards and I remained in my monkey run position, a beast in an alien land trying and failing to understand the code of the place. And the music squeezed out, sensuously, filled the air precisely, and I lowered my thighs and arms towards the ground without being aware of doing so, I lay flat on the boards, reaching down to their level. I didn't want to feel any more. I wanted to become inanimate. I beat the boards with my knuckles, my fists, but there was no sound, I made no effect. The music from the platform smothered and stifled my ludicrous gesture. My head shook, and I was no longer myself, I was no longer anyone, let alone someone. But as I could think so far, as I could rationalise the situation to that extent, was I in fact still myself, the self I had been or had become? Who was I? I must have become more than I was, entirely because of the notes, those sounds.

The music stopped. Again, or for the first time: I no longer knew or cared. The fingers, the hands were removed from the keyboard, the instrument. No new notes filled the air though all those which had sounded, had happened, packed my head, a jumble and jaggle of allusive noises, kaleidoscopically seen and experienced through a prism. Every left palm in the hall, except for mine and the pianist's, seemed to be striking every right palm. The man at the piano stood up, pushed back a little the stool upon which he had sat. He turned slightly to face the audience, bowed stiffly, as if it wasn't something he was accustomed to doing. The applause continued, there was the odd idiotic shout of 'Bravo' and 'Hurrah'. He bowed again, then nipped off the platform as if he were a mouse escaping to its hole. Almost as soon as he was away he was back, the applause continued as if it was being regulated for radio transmission. Hurrah, Bravo and Hurrah again. He left the platform for the last time (being unable to take it with him, huh?) and the lights in the hall were dimmed. The audience began to leave, those of it which hadn't already shuffled away to catch trains, buses or in some cases taxis. The hall emptied.

A man, probably the caretaker, walked on to the platform in his shirt sleeves. He closed the top of the piano, banged down the lid. I was left in the hall, lying on the floor, on my belly at one with the dust. My companion hadn't even, before she departed, said good-bye, wished me well – or ill. If I had embarrassed her, I was sorry about that. But there's more to life than minor embarrassments. The caretaker turned off the remaining lights in the hall, and went out. He hadn't noticed me, there on the floor, below the chairs, nor my clothes on one of the seats.

I was alone with the notes, every one that had been played. They had come to me, to envelop me. Or if that was asking too much, one of them, just one. I needed to concentrate upon it to my dying day. I began to cry again. Was it hopeless? Was it too much to ask? Couldn't I hear one note? Couldn't it become me, and me it? I heard a door bang shut, then there was silence again. Silence. Not a sound, no noise. Certainly no notes, no music. I had even stopped crying.

Thomas Hardy

Lines to a Movement in Mozart's E Flat Symphony

Show me again the time
When in the Junetide's prime
We flew by meads and mountains northerly! –
Yea, to such freshness, fairness, fulness, fineness, freeness,
    Love lures life on.

Show me again the day
When from the sandy bay
We looked together upon the pestered sea! –
Yea, to such surging, swaying, sighing, swelling, shrinking,
    Love lures life on.

Show me again the hour
When by the pinnacled tower
We eyed each other and feared futurity! –
Yea, to such bodings, broodings, beatings, blanchings, blessings,
    Love lures life on.

Show me again just this:
The moment of that kiss
Away from the prancing folk, by the strawberry-tree! –
Yea, to such rashness, ratheness, rareness, ripeness, richness,
    Love lures life on.

Ivan Turgenev

The Singers

It was an insufferably hot day in July when, slowly dragging my feet along, I went up alongside the Kolotovka ravine with my dog towards the 'Welcome Resort.' The sun blazed, as it were, fiercely in the sky, baking the parched earth relentlessly; the air was thick with stifling dust. Glossy crows and ravens with gaping beaks looked plaintively at the passers-by, as though asking for sympathy; only the sparrows did not droop, but, pluming their feathers, twittered more vigorously than ever as they quarrelled among the hedges, or flew up all together from the dusty road, and hovered in grey clouds over the green hemp-fields. I was tormented by thirst. There was no water near: in Kolotovka, as in many other villages of the steppes, the peasants, having no spring or well, drink a sort of thin mud out of the pond . . . For no one could call that repulsive beverage water. I wanted to ask for a glass of beer or kvas at Nikolai Ivanitch's.

When I went into the 'Welcome Resort,' a fairly large party were already assembled there.

In his usual place behind the bar, almost filling up the entire opening in the partition, stood Nikolai Ivanitch in a striped print shirt; with a lazy smile on his full face, he poured out with his plump white hand two glasses of spirits for the Blinkard and the Gabbler as they came in; behind him, in a corner near the window, could be seen his sharp-eyed wife. In the middle of the room was standing Yashka the Turk; a thin, graceful fellow of three-and-twenty, dressed in a long-skirted coat of blue nankeen. He looked a smart factory hand, and could not, to judge by his appearance, boast of very good health. His hollow cheeks, his large, restless grey eyes, his straight nose, with its delicate mobile nostrils, his pale brown curls brushed back over the sloping white brow, his full but beautiful, expressive lips, and his whole face betrayed a passionate and sensitive nature. He was in a state of great excitement; he blinked, his breathing was hurried, his hands shook, as though in fever, and he was really in a fever – that sudden fever of excitement which is so well known to all who have to speak and sing before an audience. Near him stood a man of about forty, with broad shoulders and broad jaws, with a low forehead, narrow Tartar eyes, a short flat nose, a square chin, and shining black hair coarse as bristles. The expression of his face – a swarthy face, with a sort of leaden hue in it – and especially of his pale lips, might almost have been called savage, if it had not been so still and dreamy. He hardly stirred a muscle; he only looked slowly about him like a bull under the yoke. He was dressed in a sort of surtout, not over-new, with smooth brass buttons; an old black silk handkerchief was twisted round his immense neck. He was called the Wild Master. Right opposite him, on a bench under the holy pictures, was sitting Yashka's rival, the booth-keeper from Zhizdry; he was a short, stoutly-built man about thirty, pock-marked and curly-headed, with a blunt, turn-up nose, lively brown eyes, and a scanty beard. He looked keenly about him, and, sitting with his hands under him, he kept carelessly swinging his legs and tapping with his feet, which were encased in stylish top-boots with a coloured edging. He wore a new thin coat of grey cloth, with a plush collar, in sharp contrast with the crimson shirt below, buttoned close across the chest. In the opposite corner, to the right of the door, a peasant sat at the table in a shabby smock-frock, with a huge rent on the shoulder. The sunlight fell in a narrow, yellow-ish streak through the dusty panes of the two small windows , but it seemed as if it struggled in vain with the habitual darkness of the room; all the objects in it were dimly, as it were patchily, lighted up. On the other hand, it was almost cool in the room, and the sense of stifling heat dropped off me like a weary load directly I crossed the threshold.

My entrance, I could see, was at first somewhat disconcerting to Nikolai Ivanitch's customers; but observing that he greeted me as a friend, they were reassured, and took no more notice of me. I asked for some beer and sat down in the corner, near the peasant in the ragged smock.

'Well, well,' piped the Gabbler, suddenly draining a glass of spirits at one gulp, and accompanying his exclamation with the strange gesticulations without which he seemed unable to utter a single word; 'what are we waiting for? If we're going to begin, then begin. Hey, Yashka?'

'Begin, begin,' chimed in Nikolai Ivanitch approvingly.

'Let's begin, by all means,' observed the booth-keeper coolly, with a self-confident smile; 'I'm ready.'

'And I'm ready,' Yakov pronounced in a voice that thrilled with excitement.

'Well, begin, lads,' whined the Blinkard. But, in spite of the unanimously expressed desire, neither began; the booth-keeper did not even get up from the bench – they all seemed to be waiting for something.

'Begin!' said the Wild Master sharply and sullenly. Yashka started. The booth-keeper pulled down his girdle and cleared his throat.

'But who's to begin?' he inquired in a slightly changed voice of the Wild Master, who still stood motionless in the middle of the room, his stalwart legs wide apart and his powerful arms thrust up to the elbows into his breeches pockets.

'You, you, booth-keeper,' stammered the Gabbler: 'you, to be sure, brother.'

The Wild Master looked at him from under his brows. The Gabbler gave a faint squeak, in confusion looked away at the ceiling, twitched his shoulder, and said no more.

'Cast lots,' the Wild Master pronounced emphatically; 'and the pot on the table.'

Nikolai Ivanitch bent down, and with a gasp picked up the pot of beer from the floor and set it on the table.

The Wild Master glanced at Yakov, and said, 'Come!'

Yakov fumbled in his pockets, took out a half penny, and marked it with his teeth. The booth-keeper pulled from under the skirts of his long coat a new leather purse, deliberately untied the string, and shaking out a quantity of small change into his hand, picked out a new halfpenny. The Gabbler held out his dirty cap, with its broken peak hanging loose; Yakov dropped his halfpenny in, and the booth-keeper his.

'You must pick out one,' said the Wild Master, turning to the Blinkard.

The Blinkard smiled complacently, took the cap in both hands, and began shaking it.

For an instant a profound silence reigned; the halfpennies clinked faintly, jingling against each other. I looked round attentively; every-face wore an expression of intense expectation; the Wild Master himself showed signs of uneasiness; my neighbour, even, the peasant in the tattered smock, craned his neck inquisitively. The Blinkard put his hand into the cap and took out the booth-keeper's halfpenny; every-one drew a long breath. Yakov flushed, and the booth-keeper passed his hand over his hair.

'There, I said you'd begin,' cried the Gabbler; 'didn't I say so?'

'There, there, don't cluck,' remarked the Wild Master contemptu-ously. 'Begin,' he went on, with a nod to the booth-keeper.

'What song am I to sing?' asked the booth-keeper, beginning to be nervous.

'What you choose,' answered the Blinkard; 'sing what you think best.'

'What you choose, to be sure,' Nikolai Ivanitch chimed in, slowly smoothing his hand on his breast, 'you're quite at liberty about that. Sing what you like; only sing well; and we'll give a fair decision afterwards.'

'A fair decision, of course,' put in the Gabbler, licking the edge of his empty glass.

'Let me clear my throat a bit, mates,' said the booth-keeper, fingering the collar of his coat.

'Come, come, no nonsense – begin!' protested the Wild Master, and he looked down . . .

And so the booth-keeper stepped forward, and, half shutting his eyes, began singing in high falsetto. He had a fairly sweet and pleasant voice, though rather hoarse: he played with his voice like a woodlark, twisting and turning it in incessant roulades and trills up and down the scale, continually returning to the highest notes, which he held and prolonged with special care. Then he would break off, and again suddenly take up the first motif with a sort of go-ahead daring. His modulations were at times rather bold, at times rather comical; they would have given a connoisseur great satisfaction, and have made a German furiously indignant. He was a Russian *tenore di grazia, ténor léger.* He sang a song to a lively dance-tune, the words of which, all that I could catch through the endless maze of variations, ejaculations, and repetitions, were as follows:

> A tiny patch of land, young lass,
>   I'll plough for thee,
> And tiny crimson flowers, young lass,
>   I'll sow for thee.

He sang; all listened to him with great attention. He seemed to feel that he had to do with really musical people, and therefore was exerting himself to do his best. And they really are musical in our part of the country; the village of Sergievskoe on the Orel high road is deservedly noted throughout Russia for its harmonious chorus-singing. The booth-keeper sang for a long while without evoking much enthusiasm in his audience; he lacked the support of a chorus; but at last, after one particularly bold flourish, which set even the Wild Master smiling, the Gabbler could not refrain from a shout of delight. Every one was roused. The Gabbler and the Blinkard began joining in in an undertone, and exclaiming: 'Bravely done! . . . Take it, you rogue! . . . Sing it out, you serpent! Hold it! That shake again, you dog, you! . . . May Herod confound your soul!' and so on. Nikolai Ivanitch behind the bar was nodding his head from side to side approvingly. The Gabbler at last was swinging his legs, tapping with his feet and twitching his shoulder, while Yashka's eyes fairly glowed like coal and he trembled all over like a leaf, and smiled nervously. The Wild Master alone did not change countenance, and stood motionless as before; but his eyes, fastened on the booth-keeper, looked somewhat softened, though the expression of his lips was still scornful. Emboldened by the signs of general approbation, the booth-keeper went off into a whirl of flourishes, and began to round off such trills, to turn such shakes of his tongue, and to make such furious play with his throat, that when at last, pale, exhausted, and bathed in hot perspiration, he uttered the last dying note, his whole body flung back, a general united shout greeted him in a violent outburst. The Gabbler threw himself on his neck and began strangling him in his long, bony arms; a flush came out on Nikolai Ivanitch's oily face, and he seemed to have grown younger; Yashka shouted like mad: 'Capital, capital!' – even my neighbour, the peasant in the torn smock, could not restrain himself, and with a blow of his fist on the table he cried: 'Aha! well done, damn my soul, well done!' And he spat on one side with an air of decision.

'Well, brother, you've given us a treat!' bawled the Gabbler, not releasing the exhausted booth-keeper from his embraces; 'you've given us a treat, there's no denying ! You've won, brother, you've won! I congratulate you – the quart's yours! Yashka's miles behind you . . . I tell you: miles . . . take my word for it.' (And again he hugged the booth-keeper to his breast.)

'There, let him alone, let him alone; there's no being rid of you . . . ' said the Blinkard with vexation; 'let him sit down on the bench; he's tired, see . . . You're a ninny, brother, a perfect ninny! What are you sticking to him like a wet leaf for? . . . '

'Well, then, let him sit down, and I'll drink to his health,' said the Gabbler, and he went up to the bar. 'At your expense, brother,' he added, addressing the booth-keeper.

The latter nodded, sat down on the bench, pulled a piece of cloth out of his cap, and began wiping his face, while the Gabbler, with greedy haste, emptied his glass, and, with a grunt, assumed, after the manner of confirmed drinkers, an expression of careworn melancholy.

'You sing beautifully, brother, beautifully,' Nikolai Ivanitch observed caressingly. 'And now it's your turn, Yashka; mind, now, don't be afraid. We shall see who's who; we shall see. The booth-keeper sings beautifully, though; 'pon my soul, he does.'

'Very beautifully,' observed Nikolai Ivanitch's wife, and she looked with a smile at Yakov.

'Beautifully, ha!' repeated my neighbour in an undertone.

'Ah, a wild man of the woods!' the Gabbler vociferated suddenly, and going up to the peasant with the rent on his shoulder, he pointed at him with his finger, while he pranced about and went off into an insulting guffaw. 'Ha! ha! get along! wild man of the woods! Here's a ragamuffin from Woodland village! What brought you here?' he bawled amidst laughter.

The poor peasant was abashed, and was just about to get up and make off as fast as he could, when suddenly the Wild Master's iron voice was heard:

'What does the insufferable brute mean?' he articulated, grinding his teeth.

'I wasn't doing nothing,' muttered the Gabbler. 'I didn't . . . I only . . .'

'There, all right, shut up!' retorted the Wild Master. 'Yakov, begin!'

Yakov took himself by his throat:

'Well, really, brothers . . . something . . . Hm, I don't know, on my word, what . . .'

'Come, that's enough; don't be timid. For shame! . . . why go back? . . . Sing the best you can, by God's gift.'

And the Wild Master looked down expectant. Yakov was silent for a minute; he glanced round, and covered his face with his hand. All had their eyes simply fastened upon him, especially the booth-keeper, on whose face a faint, involuntary uneasiness could be seen through his habitual expression of self-confidence and the triumph of his success. He leant back against the wall, and again put both hands under him, but did not swing his legs as before. When at last Yakov uncovered his face it was pale as a dead man's; his eyes gleamed faintly under their drooping lashes. He gave a deep sigh, and began to sing . . . The first sound of his voice was faint and unequal and seemed not to come from his chest, but to be wafted from somewhere afar off, as though it had floated by chance into the room. A strange effect was produced on all of us by this trembling, resonant note; we glanced at one another, and Nikolai Ivanitch's wife seemed to draw herself up. This first note was followed by another, bolder and prolonged, but still obviously quivering, like a harpstring when suddenly struck by a stray finger it throbs in a last, swiftly dying tremble; the second was followed by a third, and gradually gaining fire and breadth, the strains swelled into a pathetic melody. 'Not one little path ran into the field,' he sang, and sweet and mournful it was in our ears. I have seldom, I must confess, heard a voice like it; it was slightly hoarse, and not perfectly true; there was even something morbid about it at first; but it had genuine depth of passion, and youth and sweetness and a sort of fascinating, careless, pathetic melancholy. A spirit of truth and fire, a Russian spirit, was sounding and breathing in that voice, and it seemed to go straight to your heart, to go straight to all that was Russian in it. The song swelled and flowed. Yakov was clearly carried away by enthusiasm; he was not timid now; he surrendered himself wholly to the rapture of his art; his voice no longer trembled; it quivered, but with the scarce perceptible inward quiver of passion,

which pierces like an arrow to the very soul of the listeners; and he
steadily gained strength and firmness and breadth. I remember I once
saw at sunset on a flat sandy shore, when the tide was low and the sea's
roar came weighty and menacing from the distance, a great white sea-
gull; it sat motionless, its silky bosom facing the crimson glow of the
setting sun, and only now and then opening wide its great wings to
greet the well-known sea, to greet the sinking lurid sun; I recalled it, as
I heard Yakov. He sang, utterly forgetful of his rival and all of us; he
seemed supported, as a bold swimmer by the waves, by our silent,
passionate sympathy. He sang, and in every sound of his voice one
seemed to feel something dear and akin to us, something of breadth
and space, as though the familiar steppes were unfolding before our
eyes and stretching away into endless distance. I felt the tears
gathering in my bosom and rising to my eyes; suddenly I was struck by
dull, smothered sobs . . . I looked round – the inn-keeper's wife was
weeping, her bosom pressed close to the window. Yakov threw a quick
glance at her, and he sang more sweetly, more melodiously than ever;
Nikolai Ivanitch looked down; the Blinkard turned away; the
Gabbler, quite touched, stood, his gaping mouth stupidly open; the
humble peasant was sobbing softly in the corner, and shaking his head
with a plaintive murmur; and on the iron visage of the Wild Master,
from under his overhanging brows, there slowly rolled a heavy tear;
the booth-keeper raised his clenched fist to his brow, and did not stir
. . . I don't know how the general emotion would have ended, if Yakov
had not suddenly come to a full stop on a high, exceptionally shrill note
– as though his voice had broken. No one called out, or even stirred;
everyone seemed to be waiting to see whether he was not going to sing
more; but he opened his eyes as though wondering at our silence,
looked round at all of us with a face of inquiry, and saw that the victory
was his . . .

'Yasha,' said the Wild Master, laying his hand on his shoulder, and
he could say no more.

We all stood, as it were, petrified. The booth-keeper softly rose and
went up to Yakov.

'You . . . yours . . . you've won!' he articulated at last with an
effort, and rushed out of the room. His rapid, decided action, as it
were, broke the spell; we all suddenly fell into noisy, delighted talk.
The Gabbler bounded up and down, stammered and brandished his
arms like mill-sails; the Blinkard limped up to Yakov and began
kissing him; Nikolai Ivanitch got up and solemnly announced that he
would add a second pot of beer from himself. The Wild Master
laughed a sort of kind, simple laugh, with an expression which I should
never have expected to see on his face; the humble peasant, as he

wiped his eyes, cheeks, nose, and beard on his sleeves, kept repeating in his corner: 'Ah, beautiful it was, by God! blast me for the son of a dog, but it was fine!' while Nikolai Ivanitch's wife, her face red with weeping, got up quickly and went away. Yakov was enjoying his triumph like a child; his whole face was transformed, his eyes especially fairly glowed with happiness. They dragged him to the bar; he beckoned the weeping peasant up to it, and sent the innkeeper's little son to look after the booth-keeper, who was not found, however; and the festivities began. 'You'll sing to us again: you're going to sing to us till evening,' the Gabbler declared, flourishing his hands in the air.

I took one more look at Yakov and went out. I did not want to stay – I was afraid of spoiling the impression I had received. But the heat was as insupportable as before. It seemed hanging in a thick, heavy layer right over the earth; over the dark-blue sky, tiny bright fires seemed whisking through the finest, almost black dust. Everything was still; and there was something hopeless and oppressive in this profound hush of exhausted nature. I made my way to a hay-loft, and lay down on the fresh-cut, but already almost dry grass. For a long while I could not go to sleep; for a long while Yakov's irresistible voice was ringing in my ears. . . . At last the heat and fatigue regained their sway, however, and I fell into a dead sleep. When I waked up, everything was in darkness; the hay scattered around smelt strong and was slightly damp; through the slender rafters of the half-open roof pale stars were faintly twinkling. I went out. The glow of sunset had long died away, and its last trace showed in a faint light on the horizon; but above the freshness of the night there was still a feeling of heat in the atmosphere, lately baked through by the sun, and the breast still craved for a draught of cool air. There was no wind, nor were there any clouds; the sky all round was clear, and transparently dark, softly glimmering with innumerable but scarcely visible stars. There were lights twinkling about the village; from the flaring tavern close by rose a confused, discordant din, amid which I fancied I recognized the voice of Yakov. Bursts of violent laughter came from there at times. I went up to the little window and pressed my face against the pane. I saw a cheerless though varied and animated scene; all were drunk – all from Yakov upwards. With breast bared, he sat on a bench, and singing in a thick voice a street song to a dance-tune, he lazily fingered and strummed on the strings of a guitar. His moist hair hung in tufts over his fearfully pale face. In the middle of the room, the Gabbler, completely 'screwed' and without his coat, was hopping about in a dance before the peasant in the grey smock; the peasant, on his side, was with difficulty stamping and scraping with his feet, and grinning meaninglessly over his dishevelled beard; he waved one hand from time to time, as much as to say, 'Here goes!' Nothing could be more ludicrous than his face; however much he twitched up his eyebrows, his heavy lids would hardly rise, but seemed lying upon his scarcely visible, dim, and mawkish eyes. He was in that amiable frame of mind of a perfectly intoxicated man, when every passer-by, directly he looks him in the face, is sure to say 'Bless you, brother, bless you!' The Blinkard, as red as a lobster, and his nostrils dilated wide, was laughing malignantly in a corner; only Nikolai Ivanitch, as befits a good tavern-keeper, preserved his composure unchanged. The room was thronged with many new faces; but the Wild Master I did not see in it.

I turned away with rapid steps and began descending the hill on which Kolotovka lies. At the foot of this hill stretches a wide plain; plunged in the misty waves of the evening haze, it seemed more immense, and was, as it were, merged in the darkening sky. I walked with long strides along the road by the ravine, when all at once from somewhere far away in the plain came a boy's clear voice: 'Antropka! Antropka-a-a! . . . ' He shouted in obstinate and tearful desperation, with long, long drawing out of the last syllable.

He was silent for a few instants, and started shouting again. His voice rang out clear in the still, lightly slumbering air. Thirty times at least he had called the name, Antropka, when suddenly, from the farthest end of the plain, as though from another world, there floated a scarcely audible reply:

'Wha-a-at?'

The boy's voice shouted back at once with gleeful exasperation:

'Come here, devil! woo-ood imp!'

'What fo-or?' replied the other, after a long interval.

'Because dad wants to thrash you!' the first voice shouted back hurriedly.

The second voice did not call back again, and the boy fell to shouting 'Antropka' once more. His cries, fainter and less and less frequent, still floated up to my ears, when it had grown completely dark, and I had turned the corner of the wood which skirts my village and lies over three miles from Kolotovka . . . 'Antropka-a-a!' was still audible in the air, filled with the shadows of night.

Philip Larkin

Broadcast

Giant whispering and coughing from
Vast Sunday-full and organ-frowned-on spaces
Precede a sudden scuttle on the drum,
'The Queen', and huge resettling. Then begins
A snivel on the violins:
I think of your face among all those faces,

Beautiful and devout before
Cascades of monumental slithering,
One of your gloves unnoticed on the floor
Beside those new, slightly-outmoded shoes.
Here it goes quickly dark. I lose
All but the outline of the still and withering

Leaves on half-emptied trees. Behind
The glowing wavebands, rabid storms of chording
By being distant overpower my mind
All the more shamelessly, their cut-off shout
Leaving me desperate to pick out
Your hands, tiny in all that air, applauding.

Opera

William Meredith

About Opera

It's not the tunes, although as I get older
Arias are what I hum and whistle.
It's not the plots – they continue to bewilder
In the tongue I speak and in several that I wrestle.

An image of articulateness is what it is:
Isn't this how we've always longed to talk?
Words as they fall are monotone and bloodless
But they yearn to take the risk these noises take.

What dancing is to the slightly spastic way
Most of us teeter through our bodily life
Are these measured cries to the clumsy things we say,
In the heart's duresses, on the heart's behalf.

Bernard Levin

The Year of the Missing Lemon Juice

From *Conducted Tour*

This must be the fourteenth time I have been to Wexford. The thirteenth? The fifteenth? Just as, at Wexford itself, the days and nights blur into each other with less distinction made between them than at any other place on earth with the exception of Las Vegas, so memories of my annual visits have become one extended memory. It is not just a matter of assigning particular moments to particular years, like Americans, back home after doing Europe in three weeks, unable to agree whether the place with the Eiffel Tower was Brussels or London; I have long since stopped trying to remember which was The Year of the Grape-Lady, The Year of the Police Raid, The Year of the Disastrous *Oberon*, The Year There Was No Boat.

But I can remember at once that 1979 was The Year of the Missing Lemon Juice. The Theatre Royal in Wexford holds 440; it was completely full that night, so there are, allowing for a few who have already died (it is not true, though it might well have been, that some died of laughter at the time), hardly more than four hundred people who now share, to the end of their lives, an experience from which the rest of the world, now and for ever, is excluded. When the last of us dies, the experience will die with us, for although it is already enshrined in legend, no one who was not an eye witness will ever really understand what we felt. Certainly I am aware that these words cannot convey more than the facts, and the facts, as so often and most particularly in this case, are only part, and a small part, too, of the whole truth. But I must try.

The opera that night was *La Vestale*, by Spontini. It has been described as 'a poor man's *Norma*', since it tells, in music and drama much inferior to Bellini's, of a vestal virgin who betrays her charge for love. It was revived for Maria Callas, but otherwise figures rarely in the repertoire of the world's leading opera houses. But it is part of Wexford's business to revive operas which other opera houses and festivals unjustly neglect, and I have been repeatedly surprised in a most pleasant manner to discover much of interest and pleasure in some of them; Lalo's *Le Roi d'Ys*, for instance, or Prokoviev's *The Gambler*, or Bizet's *Les Pêcheurs des Perles* ... Well, in 1979 it was *La Vestale*. The set for Act 1 of the opera consisted of a platform laid over the stage, raised about a foot at the back and sloping evenly to the footlights. This was meant to represent the interior of the Temple where burned the sacred flame, and had therefore to look like marble;

the designer had achieved a convincing alternative by covering the raised stage in Formica. But the Formica was slippery; to avoid the risk of a performer taking a tumble, designer and stage manager had between them discovered that an ample sprinkling of lemon juice would make the surface sufficiently sticky to provide a secure foothold. The story now forks; down one road, there lies the belief that the member of the stage staff whose duty it was to sprinkle the lifesaving liquid, and who had done so without fail at rehearsal and at the earlier performances (this was the last one of the Festival), had simply forgotten. Down the other branch in the road is a much more attractive rumour: that the theatre charlady, inspecting the premises in the afternoon, had seen to her horror and indignation that the stage was covered in the remains of some spilt liquid, and, inspired by professional pride, had thereupon set to and given it a good scrub and polish all over.

The roads now join again, for apart from the superior charm of the second version, it makes no difference what the explanation was. What matters is what happened.

What happened began to happen very early. The hero of the opera strides on to the stage immediately after the curtain has gone up. The hero strode; and instantly fell flat on his back. There was a murmur of sympathy and concern from the audience for his embarrassment and for the possibility that he might have been hurt; it was the last such sound that was to be heard that night, and it was very soon to be replaced by sounds of a very different nature.

The hero got to his feet, with considerable difficulty, and, having slid some way down the stage in falling, proceeded to stride up-stage to where he should have been in the first place; he had, of course, gone on singing throughout, for the music had not stopped. Striding up-stage, however, was plainly more difficult than he had reckoned on, for every time he took a step and tried to follow it with another, the foot with which he had taken the first proceeded to slide down-stage again, swiftly followed by its companion; he may not have known it, but he was giving a perfect demonstration of what is called *marcher sur place*, a graceful manoeuvre normally used in mime, and seen at its best in the work of Marcel Marceau.

Finding progress uphill difficult, indeed impossible, the hero wisely decided to abandon the attempt and stay where he was, singing bravely on, no doubt calculating that, since the stage was brightly lit, the next character to enter would notice him and adjust his own movements accordingly. So it proved, in a sense at least, for the next character to enter was the hero's trusted friend and confidant, who, seeing his hero further down-stage than he was supposed to be, loyally

decided to join him there. Truth to tell, he had little choice, for from
the moment he had stepped on to the stage he had begun to slide
downhill, arms semaphoring, like Scrooge's clerk on the way home to
his Christmas dinner. His downhill progress was arrested by his
fetching up against his friend with a thud; this, as it happened, was not
altogether inappropriate, as the opera called for them to embrace in
friendly greeting at that point. It did not, however, call for them,
locked in each other's arms and propelled by the impetus of the
friend's descent, to career helplessly further down-stage with the
evident intention of going straight into the the orchestra pit with vocal
accompaniment – for the hero's aria had, on the arrival of his
companion, been transformed into a duet.

On the brink of ultimate disaster they managed to arrest their joint
progress to destruction and, working their way along the edge of the
stage like mountaineers seeking a route round an unbridgeable
crevasse, most gallantly began, with infinite pain and by a form of
progress most aptly described in the title of Lenin's famous pamphlet,
Four Steps Forward, Three Steps Back, to climb up the terrible hill. It
speedily became clear that this hazardous ascent was not being made
simply from a desire to retain dramatic credibility; it had a much more
practical object. The only structure breaking the otherwise all too
smooth surface of the stage was a marble pillar, a yard or so high, on
which there burned the sacred flame of the rite. This pillar was
embedded firmly in the stage, and it had obviously occurred to both
mountaineers at once that if they could only reach it it would provide
a secure base for their subsequent operations, since if they held on to it
for dear life they would at any rate be safe from any further danger of
sliding downhill and/or breaking their necks.

It was soon borne in upon them that they had undertaken a labour of
truly Sisyphean proportions, and would have been most heartily
pardoned by the audience if they had abandoned the librettist's words
at this point, and fitted to the music instead the old moral verse:

> The heights by great men reached and kept,
> Were not attained by sudden flight;
> But they, while their companions slept,
> Were toiling upwards in the night.

By this time the audience – all 440 of us – were in a state of such
abandon with laughter that several of us felt that if this were to
continue a moment longer we would be in danger of doing ourselves a
serious internal mischief; little did we know that the fun was just
beginning, for shortly after Mallory and Irvine reached their longed-

for goal, the chorus entered, and instantly flung themselves *en masse* into a very freely choreographed version of *Les Patineurs*, albeit to the wrong music. The heroine herself, the priestess Giulia, with a survival instinct strong enough to suggest that she would be the one to get close to should any reader of these lines happen to be shipwrecked along with the Wexford opera company, skated into the wings and kicked her shoes off and then, finding on her return that this had hardly improved matters, skated back to the wings and removed her tights as well.

Now, however, the singing never having stopped for a moment, the chorus had come to the same conclusion as had the hero and his friend, namely that holding on to the holy pillar was the only way to remain upright and more or less immobile. The trouble with this conclusion was that there was only one such pillar on the stage, and it was a small one; as the cast crowded round it, it seemed that there would be some very unseemly brawling among those seeking a hand-hold, a foothold, even a bare finger-hold, on this tiny island of security in the terrible sea of impermanence. By an instinctive understanding of the principles of co-operation, however, they decided the matter without bloodshed; those nearest the pillar clutched it, those next nearest clutched the clutchers, those farther away still clutched those, and so on until, in a kind of daisy-chain that snaked across the stage, everybody was accommodated.

The condition of the audience was now one of fully extended hysteria, which was having the most extraordinary effect – itself intensifying the audience's condition – on the orchestra. At Wexford, the orchestra runs under the stage; only a single row of players – those at the edge of the pit nearest the audience, together, of course, with the conductor – could see what was happening on the stage. The rest realized that *something* out of the ordinary was going on up there, and would have been singularly dull of wit if they had not, for many members of the audience were now slumped on the floor weeping helplessly in the agony of their mirth, and although the orchestra at Wexford cannot see the stage, it can certainly see the auditorium.

Theologians tell us that the delights of the next world are eternal. Perhaps; but what is certain is that all earthly ones, alas, are temporary, and duly, after giving us a glimpse of the more enduring joy of Heaven that must have strengthened the devout in their faith and caused instant conversion among many of the unbelievers, the entertainment came to an end when the first act of the opera did so, amid such cheering as I had never before heard in an opera house, and can never hope to hear again. In the interval before Act II, a member of the production staff walked back and forth across the stage, sprinkling it with the precious nectar, and we knew that our happiness was at an end. But he who, after such happiness, would have demanded more, would be greedy indeed, and most of us were content to know that, for one crowded half-hour, we on honeydew had fed, and drunk the milk of Paradise.

Tito Gobbi

Remembering Callas

From *My Life*

It was on this tour [to South America in 1951] that I sang for the first time with Maria Callas, who was to become the greatest of all my colleagues. Tilde and I had already heard her once in *La Gioconda*, with which she had made her first impact on the Italian audience. Now I sang with her myself in *La Traviata*.

Looking back, I cannot believe that anyone else in the whole history of the work ever sang that first act as she sang it then. Later perhaps she looked the part more convincingly, later she may have added certain refinements to her characterization of the role, but I find it impossible to describe the electrifying brilliance of the coloratura, the beauty, the sheer magic of that sound which she poured out then. And with it – perfect diction, color, inflection, and above all feeling. It was something one hears only once in a lifetime. Indeed, one is fortunate to hear it once!

In 1953 I joined her in the recording of *Lucia* under Serafin in Florence and then, later the same year, came the first recording of *Tosca* under De Sabata. This was the beginning of a long professional association in both recording and stage work, an association so complete in its integration and understanding that I think I may claim the right as well as the privilege to write at some length about what was one of the most amazing appearances in all opera.

I think of Maria – and I venture to believe that she thought of me too – as a friend as well as colleague; and, as far as one can say one understands a fellow artist, I came to understand something of her. First and foremost she was a diva, in the sense that she was set apart: not just in the top rank but beyond even that – something unique. This meant that people demanded the impossible of her, so that she forever carried the burden of having to reaffirm her supremacy or else be regarded (by herself as well as by others) as in some sense failing. Such a unique position creates a great loneliness and a sense of responsibility so crushing in its weight that it is almost more than a human being can bear.

For a singer this striving for eternal perfection is particularly cruel, for the singer – unlike every other musical performer – is his or her own instrument. If the singer is sick, so is the voice. If the singer is under a great strain, so is the voice. If the singer is shaking with terror, only the most reliable technique will save the voice from doing the same.

Self-appointed critics tend to say: 'If you have a good, well-trained voice you should be able to sing well.' But it really is not so simple as that. There are so many other factors, particularly in the case of an opera singer who has to act as well as sing. And it is not acting in the sense of straight stage acting. All must be contained within the musical form. You cannot pause on a word for added dramatic effect. The music does not allow you to declaim, 'To be' – pause for effect with hand or brow – 'or not to be.' The integration of acting and singing must be absolute. In Callas this integration became nothing short of miraculous. Her musical and dramatic instincts were faultless, and her dedication to her art was total. In consequence she did not suffer fools gladly, particularly in her earlier, less patient days, and I am bound to say – why should she? For she never demanded from anyone else a standard for which she was not herself prepared to strive.

It would be absurd to pretend there were not times when she behaved badly – when she was, as people loved to say of her, highly temperamental. Sometimes she was undoubtedly in the wrong, sometimes the stories were complete invention, and sometimes she was fully justified in her reaction – as on the much-publicized and photographed occasion in Chicago when some fellow without even the manners to take off his hat tried to serve a writ on her as she came from the stage. She was perfectly justified in thrusting him from her path with words of furious contempt. How dared this oaf lay a hand on someone who had just given 99 percent of everything she had and was in her effort to serve her art and her public? Suppose she did owe money – the matter could have waited for a couple of hours. To attack any artist at such a time is contemptible.

My own single serious brush with Maria also occurred in Chicago, in 1954, and perhaps deserves a full account since I can personally vouch for the truth of it. I also give it as an illustration of what sometimes happened in the highly charged atmosphere in which this controversial figure moved. It was during a performance of *Traviata*. The second act, with its superb duets between Violetta and the elder Germont, had gone splendidly; she had left the stage, the short scene between Alfredo and me had taken place, and I had sung my final aria which practically closes the act. Then, as the curtain fell, something went wrong with the mechanism so that one half of the curtain came down while the other remained up and then vice versa, all to the amusement of the audience. As the technicians struggled to sort things out people back stage were saying desperately: 'Go out and take another call, Mr. Gobbi, until we get this damned thing right.'

I looked around, inquiring once or twice for Maria and the tenor to join me, but was forced to take several solo calls – to considerable applause. Out of the corner of my eye I saw Maria's husband, Battista Meneghini, go off in the direction of her dressing room and presently she joined me for the last call and, the curtain having decided to behave by now, we went off to our respective dressing rooms.

As the interval lengthened out extraordinarily someone came to me to tell me that Madame Callas was very angry with me and wanted to see me in her dressing room. I went along there, passing Meneghini in the doorway.

'They tell me you are angry with me, Maria,' I said. 'What is the matter?'

'Shut the door,' she ordered, as though I were a servant. And then: 'You must understand that I will not allow anyone to interfere with the success of *my Traviata*. If you ever do such a thing again I will ruin your career.'

As will be imagined, I took a deep breath at this. Then I replied very calmly: 'You were right to suggest that we close the door. Now – first I have always understood that it was Verdi's *Traviata*. As for what happened with the curtain, I did what seemed best at the time, with no thought of harming my colleagues. Your saying you will ruin my career is just a piece of nonsense. It is true you are a power in the opera world, but I also have some power and don't forget that I arrived on the scene ten years before you did. I give you three minutes now to go on the stage and continue the performance. Otherwise I go out and explain to the audience exactly what happened – and you know I will do it.'

I left her then. Two minutes later she passed my door on her way to the stage.

The third act went beautifully and just before the last act I went onto the stage to check the layout, as I usually do. Only the work light was on and suddenly from the shadowed bed a rather subdued voice said in Venetian dialect: '*Tito, s'i tu rabià?*' (Tito, are you angry with me?')

'Oh, Maria,' I replied. 'Are you already there?'

'Yes. Are you still angry with me?'

'No, Maria, I'm not angry,' I said more or less truthfully, for there was something so silly and childlike and touching about this tentatively offered little olive branch that it would have taken a harder man than I am to reject it. 'We all have our nervous explosions at times. Now forget about it.'

I never had any real trouble with her again and in later years there were times when she would not take on certain engagements unless she had my support.

This is a rather extreme case of temperamental behaviour, but when I told her that we all have our nervous explosions it was true. I can myself recall a few times when I kicked things around the dressing room. I hope those occasions will never be chronicled but, if they are, may they be recorded with a little charity.

On the subject of Maria's total dedication to her art, of which I have spoken, there were some interesting personal results, none more so than the dramatic change she made in what might be called her public image. It was, I remember, during the 1953 recording of *Lucia* in Florence, when we were all lunching together, that Maestro Serafin ventured to tell Maria she ate too much and was allowing her weight to become a problem. She protested that when she ate well she sang well and, anyway, she was not *so* heavy.

With a lack of gallantry which surprises me now, I remarked that there was a weighing machine just outside the restaurant door and suggested she should put the matter to the test. We went there together and, after the shock of reading what the machine recorded, she gave me her handbag and her coat and kicked off her shoes. All the palliatives that most of us have tried in our time! The result was still somewhat dismaying, and she became rather silent. In one's middle twenties – which was all she was then – it is not pleasant to have to face the hard facts of excessive overweight.

I saw her only briefly later that year, when we recorded *Tosca*. In the following year, when we were to record again, I was coming from the theater one morning when a voice called: 'Tito!' And I turned to see a lovely, tall young woman in a long coat. She flung open the coat and demanded: 'What do you think of me now?' And I realized that it was Maria, completely transformed.

'Maria,' I said with all my heart, 'you – look – beautiful.'

At which she gave me a smiling, sidelong glance from those lovely long eyes of hers and said, with an enchanting touch of coquetry: 'Tito, are you courting me?'

'Of course!' I replied. 'May I join the queue, Maria?'

To myself I said: 'She is really awakened now; she knows she is a woman and a beautiful one at that.'

I think it was her absolute determination to channel everything into becoming a world star which had induced her to make that dramatic change, and for good or ill it made her a world figure overnight. Now she was not only supremely gifted both musically and dramatically – she was a beauty too. And her awareness of this invested with fresh magic every role she undertook. What it eventually did to her vocal and nervous stamina I am not prepared to say. I only assert that she blossomed into an artist unique in her generation and outstanding in the whole range of vocal history.

Later when we frequently partnered each other in *Tosca* we worked marvelously together, deeply respecting and considering each other for the sake of the performance. During the rehearsals we would study and arrange everything together. Then at the performance we threw ourselves into an exciting adventure, in the absolute certainty that each of us would complete successfully any sudden change. This bold and inebriating freedom gave us moments of supreme excitement rarely experienced on stage. We were never Callas and Gobbi. We *were* Tosca and Scarpia. In some indefinable way we would sense exactly what the other was going to do and even if – as is bound to happen from time to time – something went wrong we would not only work it into the action so that no one guessed there was an emergency, we would even sometimes turn it to an advantage.

I remember once, in the second act of Tosca, at the moment when Cavaradossi is dragged away with Tosca clinging to him, one of the men (as the action demands) pushed her away and, as she staggered back, she either forgot or did not notice that there was a small step behind her and she fell heavily. From the other side of the stage I asked her with my eyes, 'Are you hurt?' and with an answering glance she was able to reassure me. But, realizing what a fine piece of stage 'business' we could make of this, I went over to her and disdainfully extended my left hand to her. Immediately, also realizing what could be done, she almost clawed her way up my arm on the pleading word, 'Salvatelo!' ('Save him!') To which I replied ironically, 'Io? – Voi!' ('I – No, you!') and let go of her, whereupon she dropped back despairingly on the ground with such apparent helplessness and pathos that a slight gasp of indignant sympathy ran through the house. She needed no instructions, no hint of what was in my mind theatrically speaking. She *knew* and made the perfect completion of what I had started.

With Maria it was not performing but living. Today I could not say with certainty what happened here or there, at a rehearsal or a performance, so intense was our commitment. But on one occasion at Covent Garden – I think it was at a dress rehearsal before an audience – I suddenly realized that, when she had backed against Scarpia's desk, her head hanging backward, she had put her wig in the flame on one of the candles and smoke was beginning to rise from the back of her head. I went over and took hold of her, putting my hand on the back of her head as though to draw her into an unwanted embrace, and managed to put out the smoldering curls.

Fully confident and relying on me, she never made a false movement. We simply went on acting and singing. She waited for my help and just whispered, '*Grazie, Tito,*' when the chance came. *That* was Callas.

On another occasion, in Paris in 1958, we were invited to take part in a big gala. We were to do the second act of *Tosca* with only one rehearsal. When we arrived for the rehearsal we found no one in charge or with the remotest idea about what was to be done, and the actors for the minor roles were wandering about aimlessly, most of them loaded with irrelevant theatrical props. There was a good deal of talking and no action: whether from inefficiency or sabotage I am not quite sure.

Suddenly Maria stood up and demanded silence and everyone's attention. She flatly declared that the performance must take place and that, in view of the total lack of organization and co-operation, she had arrived at a final decision. Then she turned to me and said: 'Tito, please will you be the producer and try to organize this performance? And from this moment everybody will obey you!'

So authoritative was she that no one queried this decision and, although I had not had any real experience of producing, it never occurred to me to refuse her request. Everything went smoothly from that moment. Everyone obeyed my direction, including Maria herself. At that time she had not yet become a great Tosca of her later years and when in the stabbing scene she raised her hand menacingly with the knife I said: 'No, no Maria! If you lifted the knife as high as that I would be able to see what was coming and would take evasive action.'

She accepted my instruction like the humblest member of the cast; and her perfect example of professionalism and dedication to the work at hand made everyone else give to me the unquestioned obedience they would have given to the most experienced producer. And that was Callas.

In contrast, I remember one day in New York she was alone and I asked her to join us for dinner. She gladly accepted and played like a young girl with Cecilia, but when we took her later to the hotel lift she suddenly turned to us and said: 'I feel so lonely. I haven't even my little dog with me here. Wouldn't you like to offer me just another ice cream?' And that was Maria.

Again, much later – indeed, as late as October 1967, when she was virtually in retirement – Tilde and I were celebrating my birthday in London with a small group of friends at the Savoy Grill when suddenly Maria appeared smiling in the doorway, her beautiful eyes shining. As she made her way toward our table she said, without raising her voice but with that effortless projection of words which was one of her great gifts: 'Tito, I remembered it was your birthday today. I have just flown over from Paris to wish you a happy birthday. May I join the party?'

It can be imagined with what delight we welcomed her. The next morning I wanted to send her flowers but the hotel staff informed me that she had already left for Paris. She had truly come just for my birthday. And that was Maria.

When in January 1964 she made her great comeback in *Tosca* at Covent Garden (after two or three years of semi-retirement) it was an event of worldwide interest. It is impossible to describe the sensation it caused and, to a creature of Maria's sensibility, it must have been sheer torture. I suppose there are few more appalling ordeals than to make a stage comeback when you are headline news; far worse than any debut. Mercilessly caught in the crossfire of public searchlights, you hang there suspended for all to observe and criticize. Triumph or crucifixion? You are battling for the one, but fate may deal you the other.

Everyone at the Royal Opera House was frantically afraid that she would cancel at the last moment. Sander Gorlinsky, her manager, had no time for anything else. The strictest orders were given that no one should be admitted at any rehearsal and the only reports issued were brief ones to the effect that everything was going well.

One charming incident in connection with this secrecy is worth recording. Maria stayed away from a rehearsal of Act II one day because of a slight cold, and John Copley stood in for her. On this occasion it so happened that a distinguished titled lady came to the box office to pick up her tickets and, realizing that a rehearsal was in progress, she implored Sergeant Martin to allow her just one glimpse of the diva: if he would just open the door a single crack . . . The poor man, with all the solemn authority for which he is famed, explained that he simply could not do so, not even for such a distinguished lady. Well, would he just for one moment open the little window connected with the house so that she might at least hear a note or two from that famous voice?

With this request Sergeant Martin complied and at that moment John Copley, lying in my arms with beard and glasses, let out an excruciating shriek: 'Ah piu' non posso, ah che orrore.'

'Ah, the unmistakable voice!' whispered the delighted lady to Sergeant Martin. 'Thank you, thank you.' And she went away quite satisfied.

But there were not many of these lighter moments for any of us as the first night drew near. To some extent David Webster had put Maria in my care – to coax, to reassure, to support her insofar as one colleague can support another; and never, I think, did I prize a trust more highly. We worked very hard, since Maria was always a tremendously disciplined artist, but after the long rehearsals she would phone me at great length to discuss our parts and go over them all again. At the dress rehearsal, looking a mere girl in the beautiful pale pink dress which Zeffirelli had decreed for her, she was scared to death but sang resolutely and acted superbly. The clicking of cameras backstage made the place sound like an office with twenty typists and, in the atmosphere of nervous tension, even David Webster must, I feel sure, have had some difficulty in maintaining his slight customary smile.

January 21, 1964. Here is Tilde's description of that never-to-be forgotten night, written in her diary next morning.

'What a night! A beautiful performance, though for the first time in my life I heard the "Vissi d'arte" go without applause.' (My own view is that the audience was too spellbound by the drama to interrupt with ill-timed applause) 'The second act was unbelievable: two giants, and they bowed to one another before the curtain like two gallant opponents. The stage was invaded after the endless ovation. I have seen for myself the self-controlled English people go mad, take off their coats, scarves, or whatever and wave them in enthusiasm. Tito was great and it was wonderful to see the perfect reactions of the two of them. Maria certainly gave a big shake-up to the character of Tosca, making her much more human and extrovert. But this can be done *only by her*. Others who would try to imitate – beware!'

In spite of her tremendous, unparalleled triumph she remained desperately nervous. On each day of performance she would phone me to say she could not sing – she had no voice left, or else she must change everything in the second act. I would be half an hour on the telephone consoling the poor girl and encouraging her. 'All right,' I would say, 'you don't sing. It is enough for you to appear. You just act and I'll do the singing . . . All right, you change whatever you want. You know we understand each other – ' and so on.

In the evening she would come by my dressing room before going onstage and I would take her to the wings, holding her icy hand and whispering encouragement while rivulets of perspiration would be running down her neck and the edge of her dress. Yet when she came off stage after her exquisitely sung duet with Cioni she would clasp my hand and wish me luck and stand there waiting until my first phrase had been sung. Indeed, there was something utterly touching in the way she would show endearing flashes of concern for others however deeply absorbed she might be in her own ordeal. When Cecilia arrived in London it was Maria, not I, who said to her: 'Tonight your father and I are going to sing for you.'

We gave six performances in London and we repeated the same team-up in Paris and New York. I doubt if anyone who was present at those performances will ever forget them. I know I never shall – not only for the artistic peak which they reached but for the extraordinary rapport and understanding between us.

Probably millions of words have been written about La Callas, and quite a few about the vulnerable, lonely, elusive creature who was Maria. There is little I can add. She shone for all too brief a while in the world of opera, like a vivid flame attracting the attention of the whole world, and she had a strange magic which was all her own.

I always thought she was immortal – and *she* is.

John Smith

Death at the Opera

Is this what death is like? I sit
Dressed elegantly in black and white, in an expensive seat,
Watching Violetta expire in Covent Garden.
How beautiful she is. As her voice lures me toward her death
The strings of the orchestra moisten my eyes with tears,
Though the tenor is too loud. Is this what death is like?
No one moves. Violetta coughs; stumbles toward the bed.
Twenty miles away in the country my father is dying.
Violetta catches at her throat. Let me repeat: my father
Is dying in a semi-detached house on a main road
Twenty miles off in the country. The skull is visible.

I do not want it to end. How exquisitely moving is death,
The approach to it. The lovers sob. Soon they will be wrenched apart.
How romantic it all is. Her hand is a white moth
Fluttering against the coverlet of the bed. The bones
Of my father's hands poke through his dry skin.
His eyes look into a vacancy of space. He spits into a cup.
In a few moments now Violetta will give up the ghost;
The doctor, the maid, the tenor who does not love her, will sob.
Almost, our hearts will stop beating. How refreshed we have been.
My father's clothes, too large for his shrunken frame,
Make him look like a parcel. Ah! The plush curtains are opening.

The applause! The applause! It drowns out the ugly noise
Of my father's choking and spitting. The bright lights
Glitter far more than the hundred watt bulb at home.
Dear Violetta! How she enjoys the flowers, like wreaths,
Showered for her own death. She gathers them to her.
We have avoided the coffin. I think that my father
Would like a box of good plain beech, being a man
From Buckinghamshire, a man of the country, a man of the soil.
I have seen my father, who is fond of animals, kill a cat
That was old and in pain with a blow from the edge of his palm.
He buried it in the garden, but I cannot remember its name.

Now the watchers are dispersing; the taxis drive away
Black in the black night. A huddle of people wait
Like mourners round the stage door. Is this what death is like?
For Violetta died after all. It is merely a ghost,
The voice gone, the beautiful dress removed, who steps in the rain.
Art, I conceive, is not so removed from life; for we look at death
Whether real or imagined, from an impossible distance
And somewhere a final curtain is always descending.
The critics are already phoning their obituaries to the papers.
I do not think God is concerned with such trivial matters
But, father, though there will be no applause, die well.

Thomas Carlyle

The Opera

Music is well said to be the speech of angels; in fact, nothing among the utterances allowed to man is felt to be so divine. It brings us near to the Infinite: we look for moments, across the cloudy elements, into the eternal Sea of Light, when song leads and inspires us. Serious nations, all nations that can still listen to the mandate of Nature, have prized song and music as the highest; as a vehicle for worship, for prophecy, and for whatsoever in them was divine. Their singer was a *vates*, admitted to the council of the universe, friend of the gods, and choicest benefactor to man.

Reader, it was actually so in Greek, in Roman, in Moslem, Christian, most of all in Old-Hebrew times; and if you look how it now is, you will find a change that should astonish you. Good Heavens, from a Psalm of Asaph to a seat at the London Opera in the Haymarket, what a road have men travelled! The waste that is made in music is probably among the saddest of all our squanderings of God's gifts. Music has, for a long time past, been avowedly mad, divorced from sense and the reality of things; and runs about now as an open Bedlamite, for a good many generations back, bragging that she has nothing to do with sense and reality, but with fiction and delirium only; and stares with unaffected amazement, not able to suppress an elegant burst of witty laughter, at my suggesting the old fact to her.

Fact nevertheless it is, forgotten, and fallen ridiculous as it may be. Tyrtæus, who had a little music, did not sing Barbers of Seville, but the need of beating back one's country's enemies; a most true song, to which the hearts of men did burst responsive into fiery melody, followed by fiery strokes before long. Sophocles also sang, and showed in grand dramatic rhythm and melody, not a fable but a fact, the best he could interpret it; the judgments of Eternal Destiny upon the erring sons of men. Æschylus, Sophocles, all noble poets were priests as well; and sang the *truest* (which was also the divinest) they had been privileged to discover here below. To 'sing the praise of God,' that, you will find, if you can interpret old words, and see what new things they mean, was always, and will always be, the business of the singer. He who forsakes that business, and, wasting our divinest gifts, sings the praise of Chaos, what shall we say of him!

David, king of Judah, a soul inspired by divine music and much other heroism, was wont to pour himself in song; he, with seer's eye and heart, discerned the Godlike amid the Human; struck tones that were an echo of the sphere-harmonies, and are still felt to be such. Reader, art thou one of a thousand, able still to *read* a Psalm of David, and catch some echo of it through the old dim centuries; feeling far off, in thy own heart, what it once was to other hearts made as thine? To sing it attempt not, for it is impossible in this late time; only know that it once was sung. Then go to the Opera, and hear, with unspeakable reflections, what things men now sing! . . .

Of the Haymarket Opera my account, in fine, is this. Lustres, candelabras, painting, gilding at discretion; a hall as of the Caliph Alraschid, or him that commanded the slaves of the Lamp; a hall as if fitted-up by the genii, regardless of expense. Upholstery, and the outlay of human capital, could do no more. Artists, too, as they are called, have been got together from the ends of the world, regardless likewise of expense, to do dancing and singing, some of them even geniuses in their craft. One singer in particular, called Coletti or some such name, seemed to me, by the cast of his face, by the tones of his voice, by his general bearing, so far as I could read it, to be a man of deep and ardent sensibilities, of delicate intuitions, just sympathies; originally an almost poetic soul, or man of *genius*, as we term it; stamped by Nature as capable of far other work than squalling here, like a blind Samson, to make the Philistines sport!

Nay, all of them had aptitudes, perhaps of a distinguished kind; and must, by their own and other people's labour, have got a training equal or superior in toilsomeness, earnest assiduity and patient travail to what breeds men to the most arduous trades. I speak not of kings, grandees, or the like show-figures; but few soldiers, judges, men of letters, can have had such pains taken with them. The very ballet-girls, with their muslin saucers round them, were perhaps little short of miraculous; whirling and spinning there in strange mad vortexes, and then suddenly fixing themselves motionless, each upon her left or right great toe, with the other leg stretched out at an angle of ninety degrees, – as if you had suddenly pricked into the floor, by one of their points, a pair, or rather a multitudinous cohort, of mad restlessly jumping and clipping scissors, and so bidden them rest, with opened blades, and stand still, in the Devil's name! A truly notable motion; marvellous, almost miraculous, were not the people there so used to it. Motion peculiar to the Opera; perhaps the ugliest, and surely one of the most difficult, ever taught a female creature in this world. Nature abhors it; but Art does at least admit it to border on the impossible. One little Cerito, or Taglioni the Second, that night when I was there, went bounding from the floor as if she had been made of Indian-rubber, or filled with hydrogen gas, and inclined by positive levity to bolt through the ceiling; perhaps neither Semiramis nor Catherine the Second had bred herself so carefully.

Such talent, and such martyrdom of training, gathered from the four winds, was now here, to do its feat and be paid for it. Regardless of expense, indeed! The purse of Fortunatus seemed to have opened itself, and the divine art of Musical Sound and Rhythmic Motion was welcomed with an explosion of all the magnificences which the other arts, fine and coarse, could achieve. For you to think of some Rossini or Bellini in the rear of it, too: to say nothing of the Stanfields, and hosts of scene-painters, machinists, engineers, enterprisers; – fit to have taken Gibraltar, written the History of England, or reduced Ireland into Industrial Regiments, had they so set their minds to it!

Alas, and of all these notable or noticeable human talents, and excellent perseverances and energies, backed by mountains of wealth, and led by the divine art of Music and Rhythm vouchsafed by Heaven to them and us, what was to be the issue here this evening? An hour's amusement, not amusing either, but wearisome and dreary, to a high-dizened select populace of male and female persons, who seemed to me not much worth amusing! Could anyone have pealed into their hearts once, one true thought, and glimpse of Self-vision: 'High-dizened, most expensive persons, Aristocracy so-called, or *Best* of the World, beware, beware what proofs you are giving here of Betterness and bestness!' And then the salutary pang of conscience in reply: 'A select populace, with money in its purse, and drilled a little by the posture-master: good Heavens! if that were what, here and everywhere in God's Creation, I *am*? And a world all dying because I am, and show myself to be, and to have long been, even that? John, the carriage, the carriage; swift! Let me go home in silence, to reflection, perhaps to sackcloth and ashes!' This, and not amusement, would have profited those high-dizened persons.

Amusement, at any rate, they did not get from Euterpe and Melpomene. These two Muses, sent-for regardless of expense, I could see, were but the vehicle of a kind of service which I judged to be Paphian rather. Young beauties of both sexes used their opera-glasses, you could notice, not entirely for looking at the stage. And, it must be owned, the light, in this explosion of all the upholsteries, and the human fine arts and coarse, was magical; and made your fair one an Armida, – if you liked her better so. Nay, certain old Improper Females (of quality), in their rouge and jewels, even these looked some *reminiscence* of enchantment; and I saw this and the other lean domestic Dandy, with icy smile on his old worn face; this and the other Marquis Chatabagues, Prince Mahogany, or the like foreign Dignitary, tripping into the boxes of said females, grinning there awhile, with dyed moustachios and macassar-oil graciosity, and then tripping-out again; – and, in fact, I perceived that Coletti and Cerito and the

Rhythmic Arts were a mere accompaniment here.

Wonderful to see; and sad, if you had eyes! Do but think of it. Cleopatra threw pearls into her drink, in mere waste; which was reckoned foolish of her. But here had the Modern Aristocracy of men brought the divinest of its Arts, heavenly Music itself; and, piling all the upholsteries and ingenuities that other human art could do, had lighted them into a bonfire to illuminate an hour's flirtation of Chatabagues, Mahogany, and these improper persons! Never in Nature had I seen such waste before. O Coletti, you whose inborn melody, once of kindred, as I judged, to 'the Melodies Eternal,' might have valiantly weeded-out this and the other false thing from the ways of men, and made a bit of God's Creation more melodious, – they have purchased you away from that; chained you to the wheel of Prince Mahogany's chariot, and here you make sport for a macassar Chatabagues and his improper-females past the prime of life! Wretched spiritual Nigger, O, if you *had* some genius, and were not a born Nigger with mere appetite for pumpkin, should you have endured such a lot? I lament for you beyond all other expenses. Other expenses are light; you are the Cleopatra's pearl that should not have been flung into Mahogany's claret-cup. And Rossini, too, and Mozart and Bellini – O Heavens! when I think that Music too is condemned to be mad, and to burn herself, to this end, on such a funeral pile, – your celestial Opera-house grows dark and infernal to me! Behind its glitter stalks the shadow of Eternal Death; through it too, I look not 'up into the divine eye,' as Richter has it, 'but down into the bottomless eyesocket' – not up towards God, Heaven, and the Throne of Truth, but too truly down towards Falsity, Vacuity, and the dwelling-place of Everlasting Despair. . . .

Good sirs, surely I by no means expect the Opera will abolish itself this year or the next. But if you ask me, Why heroes are not born now, why heroisms are not done now? I will answer you: It is a world all calculated for strangling of heroisms. At every ingress into life, the genius of the world lies in wait for heroisms, and by seduction or compulsion unweariedly does its utmost to pervert them or extinguish them. Yes; to its Hells of sweating tailors, distressed needle-women and the like, this Opera of yours is the appropriate Heaven! Of a truth, if you will read a Psalm of Asaph till you understand it, and then come hither and hear the Rossini-and-Coletti Psalm, you will find the ages have altered a good deal. . . .

Nor do I wish all men to become Psalmist Asaphs and fanatic Hebrews. Far other is my wish; far other, and wider, is now my notion of this Universe. Populations of stern faces, stern as any Hebrew, but capable withal of bursting into inextinguishable laughter on occasion:

– do you understand that new and better form of character? Laughter also, if it come from the heart, is a heavenly thing. But, at least and lowest, I would have you a Population abhorring phantasms; – abhorring *unveracity* in all things; and in your 'amusements,' which are voluntary and not compulsory things, abhorring it most impatiently of all.

James Miller

Italian Opera

In Days of Old, when *Englishmen* were – *Men*,
Their Musick, like themselves, was grave and
    plain;
The manly Trumpet, and the simple Reed,
Alike with *Citizen* and *Swain* agreed;
Whose Songs, in lofty Sense, but humble Verse,
Their Loves and Wars alternately rehearse;
Sung by themselves, their homely Cheer to crown,
In Tunes from Sire to Son deliver'd down.
    But now, since *Britains* are become polite,
Since Few can *read*, and Fewer still can *write*;
Since Trav'ling has so much improv'd our *Beaux*,
That each brings home a foreign *Tongue*, or –
    Nose;
And Ladies paint with that amazing Grace,
That their best *Vizard* is their natural *Face;*
Since *South-Sea Schemes* have so inrich'd the Land,
That *Footmen* 'gainst their *Lords* for *Boroughs* stand;

Since *Masquerades* and *Op'ras* made their Entry,
And *Heydegger* reign'd *Guardian* of our Gentry;
A hundred various Instruments combine,
And foreign *Songsters* in the Concert join:
The *Gallick Horn*, whose winding Tube in vain
Pretends to emulate the *Trumpet*'s Strain;
The *shrill-ton'd Fiddle*, and the *warbling Flute*,
The *grave Bassoon, deep Base*, and *tinkling Lute*,
The *jingling Spinnet*, and the *full-mouth'd Drum*,
A *Roman Capon*, and *Venetian Strum*,
All league, melodious Nonsense to dispense,
And give us *Sound*, and *Show*, instead of *Sense;*
In unknown Tongues mysterious Dullness chant,
Make Love in *Tune*, or *thro' the Gamut rant.*

Leo Tolstoy

At the Opera

From *What Is Art?*

When I arrived, the enormous theatre was already filled from top to bottom. There were Grand-Dukes, and the flower of the aristocracy, of the merchant class, of the learned, and of the middle-class official public. Most of them held the libretto, fathoming its meaning. Musicians – some of them elderly, grey-haired men – followed the music score in hand. Evidently the performance of this work was an event of importance.

I was rather late, but I was told that the short prelude with which the act begins was of slight importance and that it did not matter having missed it. When I arrived, an actor sat on the stage amid decorations intended to represent a cave and before something which was meant to represent a smith's forge. He was dressed in tricot tights, with a cloak of skins, wore a wig and an artificial beard, and with white, weak, genteel hands (his easy movements and especially the shape of his stomach and his lack of muscle revealed the actor) beat an impossible sword with an unnatural hammer in a way in which no one ever uses a hammer; and at the same time, opening his mouth in a strange way, he sang something incomprehensible. The music of various instruments accompanied the strange sounds which he emitted. From the libretto one was able to gather that the actor had to represent a powerful dwarf who lived in the cave, and who was forging a sword for Siegfried, whom he had reared. One could tell he was a dwarf by the fact that the actor walked all the time bending the knees of his tricot-covered legs. This dwarf, still opening his mouth in the same strange way, long continued to sing or shout. The music meanwhile runs over something strange, like beginnings which are not continued and never get finished. From the libretto one could learn that the dwarf is telling himself about a ring a giant had obtained, and which the dwarf wishes to procure through Siegfried's aid, while Siegfried wants a good sword, on the forging of which the dwarf is occupied. After this conversation or singing to himself has gone on rather a long time, other sounds are heard in the orchestra, also like something beginning and not finishing, and another actor appears with a horn slung over his shoulder and accompanied by a man running on all fours dressed up as a bear, whom he sets at the smith-dwarf. The latter runs away without unbending the knees of his tricot-covered legs. This actor with the horn represented the hero, Siegfried. The sounds which were emitted in the orchestra on the entrance of this actor were intended to represent Siegfried's character and are called Siegfried's *leit-motiv*. And these sounds are repeated each time Siegfried appears. There is one fixed combination of sounds, or *leit-motiv*, for each character, and this *leit-motiv* is repeated every time the person whom it represents appears; and when any one is mentioned the *motiv* is heard which relates to that person. Moreover each article also has its own *leit-motiv* or chord. There is a *motiv* of the ring, a *motiv* of the helmet, a *motiv* of the apple, a *motiv* of fire, spear, sword, water, etc.; and as soon as the ring, helmet, or apple is mentioned, the *motiv* or chord of the ring, helmet, or apple, is heard. The actor with the horn opens his mouth as unnaturally as the dwarf, and long continues in a chanting voice to shout some words, and in a similar chant Mime (that is the dwarf's name) makes some reply to him. The meaning of this conversation can only be discovered from the libretto; and it is, that Siegfried was brought up by the dwarf and therefore, for some reason, hates him and always wishes to kill him. The dwarf has forged a sword for Siegfried, but Siegfried is dissatisfied with it. From a ten-page conversation (by the libretto), lasting half-an-hour and conducted with the same strange openings of the mouth and chantings, it appears that Siegfried's mother gave birth to him in the wood, and that concerning his father all that is known is that he had a sword which was broken, the pieces of which are in Mime's possession, and that Siegfried does not know fear and wishes to go out of the wood. Mime however does not want to let him go. During the conversation the music never omits, at the mention of father, sword, etc., to sound the *motiv* of these people and things. After these conversations fresh sounds are heard – those of the god Wotan – and a wanderer appears. This wanderer is the god Wotan. Also dressed up in a wig and also in tights, this god Wotan, standing in a stupid pose with a spear, thinks proper to recount what Mime must have known before, but what it is necessary to tell the audience. He does not tell it simply, but in the form of riddles which he orders himself to guess, staking his head (one does not know why) that he will guess right. Moreover, whenever the wanderer strikes his spear on the ground, fire comes out of the ground and in the orchestra the sounds of spear and of fire are heard. The orchestra accompanies the conversation, and the *motivs* of the people and things spoken of are always artfully intermingled. Besides this, the music expresses feelings in the most naïve manner: the terrible by sounds in the bass, the frivolous by rapid touches in the treble, and so forth.

The riddles have no meaning except to tell the audience what the *nibelungs* are, what the giants are, what the gods are, and what has happened before. This conversation also is chanted with strangely opened mouths, and continues for eight libretto pages and a correspondingly long time on the stage. After this the wanderer departs and Siegfried returns and talks with Mime for thirteen pages more. There is not a single melody the whole of this time, but merely intertwinings of the *leit-motivs* of the people and things mentioned. The conversation shows that Mime wishes to teach Siegfried fear and that Siegfried does not know what fear is. Having finished this conversation, Siegfried seizes one of the pieces of what is meant to represent the broken sword, saws it up, puts it on what is meant to represent the forge, melts it, and then forges it and sings: 'Heiho! heiho! heiho! Ho! ho! Aha! oho! aha! Heiaho! heiaho! heiaho! Ho! ho! Hahei! hoho! hahei!' and Act I finishes . . .

From an author who could compose such spurious scenes, outraging all aesthetic feeling, as those which I had witnessed, there was nothing to be hoped; it may safely be decided that all that such an author can write will be bad, because he evidently does not know what a true work of art is. I wished to leave, but the friends I was with asked me to remain, declaring that one could not form an opinion by that one act and that the second would be better. So I stopped for the second act . . .

I somehow managed to sit out the next scene also, in which the monster appears to the accompaniment of his bass notes intermingled with the *motiv* of Siegfried; but after the fight with the monster, and all the roars, fires, and sword-wavings, I could stand no more of it and escaped from the theatre with a feeling of repulsion which even now I cannot forget.

Listening to this opera I involuntarily thought of a respected, wise, educated, country labourer – one, for instance, of the wise and truly religious men whom I know among the peasants – and I pictured to myself the terrible perplexity such a man would be in were he to witness what I was seeing that evening.

What would he think if he knew of all the labour spent on such a performance, and saw that audience, those great ones of the earth – old, bald-headed, grey-bearded men, whom he had been accustomed to respect – sitting silent and attentive, listening to and looking at all these stupidities for five hours on end? Not to speak of an adult labourer, one can hardly imagine even a child of over seven occupying himself with such a stupid, incoherent, fairy tale.

And yet an enormous audience, the cream of the cultured upper classes, sits out five hours of this insane performance, and goes away imagining that by paying tribute to this nonsense it has acquired a fresh right to esteem itself advanced and enlightened.

I speak of the Moscow public. But what is the Moscow public? It is but a hundredth part of that public which, while considering itself most highly enlightened, esteems it a merit so to have lost the capacity of being infected by art that not only can it witness this stupid sham without being revolted, but can even take delight in it.

In Bayreuth, where these performances were first given, people who considered themselves finely cultured assembled from the ends of the earth, spent, say, £100 each to see this performance, and for four days running went to see and hear this nonsensical rubbish, sitting it out for six hours each day.

But why did people go, and why do they still go, to these performances, and why do they admire them? The question naturally presents itself: How is the success of Wagner's works to be explained?

That success I explain to myself in this way: thanks to his exceptional position in having at his disposal the resources of a king, Wagner was able to command all the methods for counterfeiting art which have been developed by long usage, and employing these methods with great ability he produced a model work of counterfeit art. The reason why I have selected his work for my illustration is that in no other counterfeit of art known to me are all the methods by which art is counterfeited – viz., borrowing, imitations, dramatic effects, and interest – so ably and powerfully united.

From the subject borrowed from antiquity, to the clouds and the risings of the sun and moon, Wagner in this work has made use of all that is considered poetic. We have here the sleeping beauty, and nymphs, and subterranean fires, and dwarfs, and battles, and swords, and love, and incest, and a monster, and singing-birds: the whole arsenal of the poetic is brought into action.

Moreover everything is imitative: the decorations are imitated and the costumes are imitated. All is just as it would have been, according to the data supplied by archaeology, in antiquity. The very sounds are imitative, for Wagner, who was not destitute of musical talent, invented just such sounds as imitate the strokes of a hammer, the hissing of molten iron, the singing of birds, etc.

Furthermore in this work everything is in the highest degree striking in its effects and its peculiarities: its monsters, its magic fires, and its scenes under water; the darkness in which the audience sit, the invisibility of the orchestra, and the hitherto unemployed combinations of harmony.

And besides, it is all interesting. The interest lies not only in the question who will kill whom, and who will marry whom, and who is whose son, and what will happen next? – the interest lies also in the relation of the music to the text. The rolling waves of the Rhine – now how is that to be expressed in music? An evil dwarf appears – how is the music to express an evil dwarf? – and how is it to express the sensuality of this dwarf? How will bravery, fire, or apples, be expressed in music? How are the *leit-motivs* of the people speaking to be interwoven with the *leit-motivs* of the people and objects about whom they speak? And the music has a further interest. It diverges from all formerly accepted laws, and most unexpected and totally new modulations crop up (as is not only possible but even easy in music having no inner law of its being); the dissonances are new and are allowed in a new way – and this, too, is interesting.

And it is this poeticality, imitativeness, effectiveness, and interestingness which, thanks to the peculiarities of Wagner's talent and to the advantageous position in which he was placed, are in these productions carried to the highest pitch of perfection, which so act on the spectator, hypnotizing him as one would be hypnotized who listened for several consecutive hours to maniacal ravings pronounced with great oratorical power.

People say, 'You cannot judge without having seen Wagner performed at Bayreuth: in the dark, where the orchestra is out of sight, concealed under the stage, and where the performance is brought to the highest perfection.' And this just proves that we have here no question of art, but one of hypnotism. It is just what the spiritualists say. To convince you of the reality of their apparitions they usually say, 'You cannot judge; you must try it, be present at several séances,' that is, come and sit silent in the dark for hours together in the same room with semi-sane people and repeat this some ten times over, and you shall see all that we see.

Yes, naturally! Only place yourself in such conditions and you may see what you will. But this can be still more quickly attained by getting drunk or smoking opium. It is the same when listening to an opera of Wagner's. Sit in the dark for four days in company with people who are not quite normal, and through the auditory nerves subject your brain to the strongest action of the sounds best adapted to excite it, and you will no doubt be reduced to an abnormal condition and be enchanted by absurdities. But to attain this end you do not even need four days; the five hours during which one 'day' is enacted, as in Moscow, are quite enough. Nor are five hours needed; even one hour is enough for people who have no clear conception of what art should be and who have concluded in advance that what they are going to see is excellent, and that indifference or dissatisfaction with this work will serve as a proof of their inferiority and lack of culture.

I observed the audience present at this representation. The people who led the whole audience and gave the tone to it were those who had previously been hypnotized and who again succumbed to the hypnotic influence to which they were accustomed. These hypnotized people being in an abnormal condition were perfectly enraptured. Moreover all the art critics, who lack the capacity to be infected by art and therefore always especially prize works like Wagner's opera where it is all an affair of the intellect, also with much profundity expressed their approval of a work affording such ample material for ratiocination. And following these two groups went that large city crowd (indifferent to art, with their capacity to be infected by it perverted and partly atrophied), headed by the princes, millionaires, and art patrons, who like sorry harriers keep close to those who most loudly and decidedly express their opinion.

'Oh yes, certainly! What poetry! Marvellous! Especially the birds!' 'Yes, yes! I am quite captivated', exclaim these people, repeating in various tones what they have just heard from men whose opinion appears to them authoritative.

If some people do feel insulted by the absurdity and spuriousness of the whole thing, they are timidly silent as sober men are timid and silent when surrounded by tipsy people.

And thus, thanks to the masterly skill with which it counterfeits art while having nothing in common with it, a meaningless, coarse, spurious production finds acceptance all over the world, costs millions of rubles to produce, and assists more and more to pervert the taste of people of the upper classes and their conception of art.

Mark Twain

From *At the Shrine of St Wagner*

Yesterday the opera was 'Tristan and Isolde.' I have seen all sorts of audiences – at theaters, operas, concerts, lectures, sermons, funerals – but none which was twin to the Wagner audience of Bayreuth for fixed and reverential attention. Absolute attention and petrified retention to the end of the act of the attitude assumed at the beginning of it. You detect no movement in the solid mass of heads and shoulders. You seem to sit with the dead in the gloom of a tomb. You know that they are being stirred to their profoundest depths; that there are times when they want to rise and wave handkerchiefs and shout their approbation, and times when tears are running down their faces, and it would be a relief to free their pent emotions in sobs or screams; yet you hear not one utterance till the curtain swings together and the closing strains have slowly faded out and died; then the dead rise with one impulse and shake the building with their applause. Every seat is full in the first act; there is not a vacant one in the last. If a man would be conspicuous, let him come here and retire from the house in the midst of an act. It would make him celebrated.

This audience reminds me of nothing I have ever seen and of nothing I have read about except the city in the Arabian tale where all the inhabitants have been turned to brass and the traveler finds them after centuries mute, motionless, and still retaining the attitudes which they last knew in life. Here the Wagner audience dress as they please, and sit in the dark and worship in silence. At the Metropolitan in New York they sit in a glare, and wear their showiest harness; they hum airs, they squeak fans, they titter, and they gabble all the time. In some of the boxes the conversation and laughter are so loud as to divide the attention of the house with the stage. In large measure the Metropolitan is a show-case for rich fashionables who are not trained in Wagnerian music and have no reverence for it, but who like to promote art and show their clothes.

Can that be an agreeable atmosphere to persons in whom this music produces a sort of divine ecstasy and to whom its creator is a very deity, his stage a temple, the works of his brain and hands consecrated things, and the partaking of them with eye and ear a sacred solemnity? Manifestly, no. Then, perhaps the temporary expatriation, the tedious traversing of seas and continents, the pilgrimage to Bayreuth stands explained. These devotees would worship in an atmosphere of devotion. It is only here that they can find it without fleck or blemish or any worldly pollution. In this remote village there are no sights to see, there is no newspaper to intrude the worries of the distant world, there is nothing going on, it is always Sunday. The pilgrim wends to his temple out of town, sits out his moving service, returns to his bed with his heart and soul and his body exhausted by long hours of tremendous emotion, and he is in no fit condition to do anything but to lie torpid and slowly gather back life and strength for the next service. This opera of 'Tristan and Isolde' last night broke the hearts of all witnesses who were of the faith, and I know of some who have heard of many who could not sleep after it, but cried the night away. I feel strongly out of place here. Sometimes I feel like the sane person in a community of the mad; sometimes I feel like the one blind man where all others see; the one groping savage in the college of the learned, and always, during service, I feel like a heretic in heaven.

But by no means do I ever overlook or minify the fact that this is one of the most extraordinary experiences of my life. I have never seen anything like this before. I have never seen anything so great and fine and real as this devotion.

D.H. Lawrence

After the Opera

Down the stone stairs
Girls with their large eyes wide with tragedy
Lift looks of shocked and momentous emotion up at me.
And I smile.

Ladies
Stepping like birds with their bright and pointed feet
Peer anxiously forth, as if for a boat to carry them out of the wreckage;
And among the wreck of the theatre crowd
I stand and smile.
They take tragedy so becomingly;
Which pleases me.

But when I meet the weary eyes
The reddened, aching eyes of the bar-man with thin arms,
I am glad to go back to where I came from.

Music Out of Doors

Thomas Hardy

From *Under the Greenwood Tree*

Going the Rounds, Christmas Eve

Shortly after ten o'clock the singing-boys arrived at the tranter's house, which was invariably the place of meeting, and preparations were made for the start. The older men and musicians wore thick coats, with stiff perpendicular collars, and coloured handkerchiefs wound round and round the neck till the end came to hand, over all which they just showed their ears and noses, like people looking over a wall. The remainder, stalwart ruddy men and boys, were dressed mainly in snow-white smock-frocks, embroidered upon the shoulders and breasts in ornamental forms of hearts, diamonds, and zigzags. The cider-mug was emptied for the ninth time, the music-books were arranged, and the pieces finally decided upon. The boys in the meantime put the old horn-lanterns in order, cut candles into short lengths to fit the lanterns, and, a thin fleece of snow having fallen since the early part of the evening, those who had no leggings went to the stable and wound wisps of hay round their ankles to keep the insidious flakes from the interior of their boots.

Mellstock was a parish of considerable acreage, the hamlets composing it lying at a much greater distance from each other than is ordinarily the case. Hence several hours were consumed in playing and singing within hearing of every family, even if but a single air were bestowed on each. There was Lower Mellstock, the main village; half a mile from this were the church and vicarage, and a few other houses, the spot being rather lonely now, though in past centuries it had been the most thickly-populated quarter of the parish. A mile north-east lay the hamlet of Upper Mellstock, where the tranter lived; and at other points knots of cottages, besides solitary farmsteads and dairies.

Old William Dewy, with the violoncello, played the bass; his grandson Dick the treble violin; and Reuben and Michael Mail the tenor and second violins respectively. The singers consisted of four men and seven boys, upon whom devolved the task of carrying and attending to the lanterns, and holding the books open for the players. Directly music was the theme old William ever and instinctively came to the front.

'Now mind, neighbours,' he said, as they all went out one by one at the door, he himself holding it ajar and regarding them with a critical face as they passed, like a shepherd counting out his sheep. 'You two

counter-boys, keep your ears open to Michael's fingering, and don't
ye go straying into the treble part along o'Dick and his set, as ye did
last year; and mind this especially when we be in 'Arise, and hail.'
Billy Chimlen, don't you sing quite so raving mad as you fain would;
and, all o'ye, whatever ye do, keep from making a great scuffle on the
ground when we go in at people's gates; but go quietly, so as to strike
up all of a sudden, like spirits.'

'Farmer Ledlow's first?'

'Farmer Ledlow first; the rest as usual.'

'And, Voss,' said the tranter terminatively, 'you keep house here
till about half-past two; then heat the metheglin and cider in the
warmer you'll find turned up upon the copper; and bring it wi' the
victuals to church-hatch, as th'st know.'

Just before the clock struck twelve they lighted the lanterns and
started. The moon, in her third quarter, had risen since the
snowstorm; but the dense accumulation of snow-cloud weakened her
power to a faint twilight which was rather pervasive of the landscape
than traceable to the sky. The breeze had gone down, and the rustle of
their feet and tones of their speech echoed with an alert rebound from
every post, boundary-stone, and ancient wall they passed, even where
the distance of the echo's origin was less than a few yards. Beyond their
own slight noises nothing was to be heard save the occasional bark of
foxes in the direction of Yalbury Wood, or the brush of a rabbit among
the grass now and then as it scampered out of their way.

Most of the outlying homesteads and hamlets had been visited by
about two o'clock; they then passed across the outskirts of a wooded
park toward the main village, nobody being at home at the Manor.
Pursuing no recognized track, great care was necessary in walking lest
their faces should come in contact with the low-hanging boughs of the
old lime-trees, which in many spots formed dense overgrowths of
interlaced branches.

'Times have changed from the times they used to be,' said Mail,
regarding nobody can tell what interesting old panoramas with an
inward eye, and letting his outward glance rest on the ground because
it was as convenient a position as any. 'People don't care much about
us now! I've been thinking we must be almost the last left in the county
of the old string players? Barrel-organs, and the things next door to
'em that you blow wi' your foot, have come in terribly of late years.'

'Ay!' said Bowman shaking his head; and old William on seeing
him did the same thing.

'More's the pity,' replied another. 'Time was – long and merry
ago now! – when not one of the varmints was to be heard of; but it

served some of the quires right. They should have stuck to strings as we did, and kept out clarinets, and done away with serpents. If you'd thrive in musical religion, stick to strings, says I.'

'Strings be safe soul-lifters, as far as that do go,' said Mr Spinks.

'Yet there's worse things than serpents,' said Mr Penny. 'Old things pass away, 'tis true; but a serpent was a good old note: a deep rich note was the serpent.'

'Clar'nets, however, be bad at all times,' said Michael Mail. 'One Christmas – years agone now, years – I went the rounds wi' the Weatherbury quire. 'Twas a hard frosty night, and the keys of all the clar'nets froze – ah, they did freeze! – so that 'twas like drawing a cork every time a key was opened; and the players o' 'em had to go into a hedger-and-ditcher's chimley-corner, and thaw their clar'nets every now and then. An icicle o' spet hung down from the end of every man's clar'net a span long; and as to fingers – well, there, if ye'll believe me, we had no fingers at all to our knowing.'

'I can well bring back to my mind,' said Mr Penny, 'what I said to poor Joseph Ryme (who took the treble part in Chalk-Newton Church fo two-and-forty year) when they thought of having clar'nets there. 'Joseph,' I said says I, 'depend upon't, if so be you have them tooting clar'nets you'll spoil the whole set-out. Clar'nets were not made for the service of the Lard; you can see it by looking at 'em,' I said. And what came o't? Why, souls, the parson set up a barrel-organ on his own account within two years o' the time I spoke, and the old quire went to nothing.'

'As far as look is concerned,' said the tranter, 'I don't for my part see that a fiddle is much nearer heaven than a clar'net. 'Tis further off. There's always a rakish, scampish twist about a fiddle's looks that seems to say the Wicked One had a hand in making o'en; while angels be supposed to play clar'nets in heaven, or som'at like 'em if ye may believe picters.'

'Robert Penny, you was in the right,' broke in the eldest Dewy. 'They should ha' stuck to strings. Your brass-man is a rafting dog – well and good; your reed-man is a dab at stirring ye – well and good; you drum-man is a rare bowel-shaker – good again. But I don't care who hears me say it, nothing will spak to your heart wi' the sweetness o' the man of strings!'

'Strings for ever!' said little Jimmy.

'Strings alone would have held their ground against all the new comers in creation.' ('True, true!' said Bowman.) 'But clarinets was death.' ('Death they was!' said Mr. Penny.) 'And harmonions,' William continued in a louder voice, and getting excited by these signs of approval, 'harmonions and barrel-organs' ('Ah!' and groans from

Spinks) 'be miserable – what shall I call 'em? – miserable – '

'Sinners,' suggested Jimmy, who made large strides like the men and did not lag behind with the other little boys.

'Miserable dumbledores!'

'Right, William, and so they be – miserable dumbledores!' said the choir with unanimity.

By this time they were crossing to a gate in the direction of the school which, standing on a slight eminence at the junction of three ways, now rose in unvarying and dark flatness against the sky. The instruments were retuned, and all the band entered the school enclosure, enjoined by old William to keep upon the grass.

'Number seventy-eight,' he softly gave out as they formed round in a semicircle, the boys opening the langerns to get a clearer light, and directing their rays on the books.

Then passed forth into the quiet night an ancient and time-worn hymn, embodying a quaint Christianity in words orally transmitted from father to son through several generations down to the present characters, who sang them out right earnestly:

> Remember Adam's fall,
>   O thou Man:
> Remember Adam's fall
>   From Heaven to Hell.
> Remember Adam's fall;
> How he hath condemn'd all
> In Hell perpetual
>   There for to dwell.
>
> Remember God's goodnesse,
>   O thou Man:
> Remember God's goodnesse,
>   His promise made.
> Remember God's goodnesse;
> He sent His Son sinlesse
> Our ails for to redress;
>   Be not afraid!

In Bethlehem He was born,
        O thou Man:
In Bethlehem He was born,
        For mankind's sake.
In Bethlehem He was born,
        Christmas-day i' the morn:
Our Saviour thought no scorn
        Our faults to take.

Give thanks to God alway,
        O thou Man:
Give thanks to God alway
        With heart-most joy.
Give thanks to God alway
On this our joyful day:
Let all men sing and say,
        Holy, Holy!

Having concluded the last note they listened for a minute or two, but found that no sound issued from the schoolhouse.

'Four breaths, and then, "O, what unbounded goodness!" number fifty-nine,' said William.

This was duly gone through, and no notice whatever seemed to be taken of the performance.

'Good guide us, surely 'tisn't a' empty house, as befell us in the year thirty-nine and forty-three!' said old Dewy.

'Perhaps she's jist come from some musical city, and sneers at our doings?' the tranter whispered.

''Od rabbit her!' said Mr Penny, with an annihilating look at a corner of the school chimney, 'I don't quite stomach her, if this is it. Your plain music well done is as worthy as your other sort done bad, a'b'lieve, souls; so say I.'

'Four breaths, and then the last,' said the leader authoritatively. '"Rejoice, ye Tenants of the Earth," number sixty-four.'

At the close, waiting yet another minute, he said in a clear loud voice, as he had said in the village at that hour and season for the previous forty years –

'A merry Christmas to ye!'

The Listeners

When the expectant stillness consequent upon the exclamation had nearly died out of them all, an increasing light made itself visible in one of the windows of the upper floor. It came so close to the blind that the exact position of the flame could be perceived from the outside. Remaining steady for an instant, the blind went upward from before it, revealing to thirty concentrated eyes a young girl framed as a picture by the window architrave, and unconsciously illuminating her countenance to a vivid brightness by a candle she held in her left hand, close to her face, her right hand being extended to the side of the window. She was wrapped in a white robe of some kind, whilst down her shoulders fell a twining profusion of marvellously rich hair, in a wild disorder which proclaimed it to be only during the invisible hours of the night that such a condition was discoverable. Her bright eyes were looking into the grey world outside with an uncertain expression, oscillating between courage and shyness, which, as she recognized the semicircular group of dark forms gathered before her, transformed itself into pleasant resolution.

Opening the window, she said lightly and warmly –

'Thank you, singers, thank you!'

Together went the window quickly and quietly, and the blind started downward on its return to its place. Her fair forehead and eyes vanished; her little mouth; her neck and shoulders; all of her. Then the spot of candlelight shone nebulously as before; then it moved away.

'How pretty!' exclaimed Dick Dewy.

'If she'd been rale wexwork she couldn't ha' been comelier,' said Michael Mail.

'As near a thing to a spiritual vision as ever *I* wish to see!' said tranter Dewy.

'O, sich I never, never see!' said Leaf fervently.

All the rest, after clearing their throats and adjusting their hats, agreed that such a sight was worth singing for.

'Now to Farmer Shiner's, and then replenish our insides, father?' said the tranter.

'Wi' all my heart,' said old William, shouldering his bass-viol.

Farmer Shiner's was a queer lump of a house, standing at the corner of a lane that ran into the principal thoroughfare. The upper windows were much wider than they were high, and this feature, together with a broad bay-window where the door might have been expected, gave it by day the aspect of a human countenance turned askance, and wearing a sly and wicked leer. Tonight nothing was visible but the outline of the roof upon the sky.

The front of this building was reached, and the preliminaries arranged as usual.

'Four breaths, and number thirty-two, "Behold the Morning Star,"' said old William.

They had reached the end of the second verse, and the fiddlers were doing the up bow-stroke previously to pouring forth the opening chord of the third verse, when, without a light appearing or any signal being given a roaring voice exclaimed –

'Shut up, woll 'ee! Don't make your blaring row here! A feller wi' a headache enough to split his skull likes a quiet night!'

Slam went the window.

'Hullo, that's a' ugly blow for we!' said the tranter, in a keenly appreciative voice, and turning to his companions.

'Finish the carrel, all who be friends of harmony!' commanded old William; and they continued to the end.

'Four breaths, and number nineteen!' said William firmly. 'Give it him well; the quire can't be insulted in this manner!'

A light now flashed into existence, the window opened, and the farmer stood revealed as one in a terrific passion.

'Drown en! – drown en!' the tranter cried, fiddling frantically. 'Play fortissimy, and drown his spaking!'

'Fortissimy!' said Michael Mail, and the music and singing waxed so loud that it was impossible to know what Mr Shiner had said, was saying, or was about to say; but wildly flinging his arms and body about in the forms of capital Xs and Ys, he appeared to utter enough invectives to consign the whole parish to perdition.

'Very onseemly – very!' said old William, as they retired. 'Never such a dreadful scene in the whole round o' my carrel practice – never! And he a churchwarden!'

'Only a drap o' drink got into his head,' said the tranter. 'Man's well enough when he's in his religious frame. He's in his worldly frame now. Must ask en to our bit of a party tomorrow night, I suppose, and so put en in humour again. We bear no mortal man ill-will.'

They now crossed Mellstock Bridge, and went along an embowered path beside the Froom towards the church and vicarage, meeting Voss with the hot mead and bread-and-cheese as they were approaching the churchyard. This determined them to eat and drink before proceeding further, and they entered the church and ascended to the gallery. The lanterns were opened, and the whole body sat round against the wall on benches and whatever else was available, and made a hearty meal. In the pauses of conversation there could be heard through the floor overhead a little world of undertones and creaks from the halting clockwork, which never spread further than the tower they were born in, and raised in the more meditative minds a fancy that here lay the direct pathway of Time.

Having done eating and drinking they again tuned the instruments, and once more the party emerged into the night air.

'Where's Dick?' said old Dewy.

Every man looked round upon every other man, as if Dick might have been transmuted into one or the other; and then they said they didn't know.

'Well now, that's what I call very nasty of Master Dicky, that I do,' said Michael Mail.

'He've clinked off home-along, depend upon't,' another suggested, though not quite believing that he had.

'Dick!' exclaimed the tranter, and his voice rolled sonorously forth among the yews.

He suspended his muscles rigid as stone whilst listening for an answer, and finding he listened in vain, turned to the assemblage.

'The treble man too! Now if he'd been a tenor or counter chap, we might ha' contrived the rest o't without en, you see. But for a quire to lose the treble, why, my sonnies, you may so well lose your . . .' The tranter paused, unable to mention an image vast enough for the occasion.

'Your head at once,' suggested Mr Penny.

The tranter moved a pace as if it were puerile of people to complete sentences when there were more pressing things to be done.

'Was ever heard such a thing as a young man leaving his work half done and turning tail like this!'

'Never,' replied Bowman, in a tone signifying that he was the last man in the world to wish to withhold the formal finish required of him.

'I hope no fatal tragedy has overtook the lad!' said his grandfather.

'O no,' replied tranter Dewy placidly. 'Wonder where he's put that there fiddle of his. Why that fiddle cost thirty shillings, and good words besides. Somewhere in the damp, without doubt; that instrument will be unglued and spoilt in ten minutes – ten! ay, two.'

'What in the name o' righteousness can have happened?' said old William, more uneasily. 'Perhaps he's drownded!'

Leaving their lanterns and instruments in the belfry they retraced their steps along the waterside track. 'A strapping lad like Dick d'know better than let anything happen onawares,' Reuben remarked. 'There's sure to be some poor little scram reason for't staring us in the face all the while.' He lowered his voice to a mysterious tone: 'Neighbours, have ye noticed any sign of a scornful woman in his head, or suchlike?'

'Not a glimmer of such a body. He's as clear as water yet.'

'And Dicky said he should never marry,' cried Jimmy, 'but live at home always along wi' mother and we!'

'Ay, ay, my sonny; every lad has said that in his time.'

They had now again reached the precincts of Mr Shiner's, but hearing nobody in that direction, one or two went across to the schoolhouse. A light was still burning in the bedroom, and though the blind was down the window had been slightly opened, as if to admit the distant notes of the carollers to the ears of the occupant of the room.

Opposite the window, leaning motionless against a beech tree, was the lost man, his arms folded, his head thrown back, his eyes fixed upon the illuminated lattice.

'Why, Dick, is that thee? What b'st doing here?'

Dick's body instantly flew into a more rational attitude, and his head was seen to turn east and west in the gloom as if endeavouring to discern some proper answer to that question; and at last he said in rather feeble accents –

'Nothing, father.'

'Th'st take long enough time about it then, upon my body,' said the tranter as they all turned anew towards the vicarage.

'I thought you hadn't done having snap in the gallery,' said Dick.

'Why, we've been traypsing and rambling about, looking everywhere, and thinking you'd done fifty deathly things, and here have you been at nothing at all!'

'The stupidness lies in that point of it being nothing at all,' murmured Mr Spinks.

The vicarage front was their next field of operation, and Mr Maybold, the lately-arrived incumbent, duly received his share of the night's harmonies. It was hoped that by reason of his profession he would have been led to open the window, and an extra carol in quick time was added to draw him forth. But Mr Maybold made no stir.

'A bad sign!' said old William, shaking his head.

However, at that same instant a musical voice was heard exlaiming from inner depths of bedclothes –

'Thanks, villagers!'

'What did he say?' asked Bowman, who was rather dull of hearing. Bowman's voice, being therefore loud, had been heard by the vicar within.

'I said, "Thanks, villagers!" ' cried the vicar again.

'Oh, we didn't hear 'ee the first time!' cried Bowman.

'Now don't for heaven's sake spoil the young man's temper by answering like that!' said the tranter.

'You won't do that, my friends!' the vicar shouted.

'Well to be sure, what ears!' said Mr Penny in a whisper. 'Beats any horse or dog in the parish, and depend upon't that's a sign he's a proper clever chap.'

'We shall see that in time,' said the tranter.

Old William, in his gratitude for such thanks from a comparatively new inhabitant, was anxious to play all the tunes over again; but renounced his desire on being reminded by Reuben that it would be best to leave well alone.

'Now putting two and two together,' the tranter continued, as they went their way over the hill, and across to the last remaining houses; 'that is, in the form of that young female vision we zeed just now, and this young tenor-voiced parson, my belief is she'll wind en round her finger, and twist the pore young feller about like the figure of 8 – that she will, my sonnies.'

William Wordsworth

Power of Music

An Orpheus! an Orpheus! yes, Faith may grow bold,
And take to herself all the wonders of old; –
Near the stately Pantheon you'll meet with the same
In the street that from Oxford hath borrowed its name.

His station is there; and he works on the crowd,
He sways them with harmony merry and loud;
He fills with his power all their hearts to the brim –
Was aught ever heard like his fiddle and him?

What an eager assembly! what an empire is this!
The weary have life, and the hungry have bliss;
The mourner is cheered, and the anxious have rest;
And the guilt-burdened soul is no longer opprest.

As the Moon brightens round her the clouds of the night,
So He, where he stands, is a centre of light;
It gleams on the face, there, of dusky-browed Jack,
And the pale-visaged Baker's, with basket on back.

That errand-bound 'Prentice was passing in haste –
What matter! he's caught – and his time runs to waste;
The Newsman is stopped, though he stops on the fret;
And the half-breathless Lamplighter – he's in the net!

The Porter sits down on the weight which he bore;
The Lass with her barrow wheels hither her store;
If a thief could be here he might pilfer at ease;
She sees the Musician, 'tis all that she sees!

He stands, backed by the wall; – he abates not his din;
His hat gives him vigour, with boons dropping in,
From the old and the young, from the poorest; and
there!
The one-pennied Boy has his penny to spare.

O blest are the hearers, and proud be the hand
Of the pleasure it spreads through so thankful a band;
I am glad for him, blind as he is! – all the while
If they speak 'tis to praise, and they praise with a smile.

That tall Man, a giant in bulk and in height,
Not an inch of his body is free from delight;
Can he keep himself still, if he would? oh, not he!
The music stirs in him like the wind through a tree.

Mark that Cripple who leans on his crutch; like a tower
That long has leaned forward, leans hour after hour! –
That Mother, whose spirit in fetters is bound,
While she dandles the Babe in her arms to the sound.

Now, coaches and chariots! roar on like a stream;
Here are twenty souls happy as souls in a dream:
They are deaf to your murmurs – they care not for you,
Nor what ye are flying, nor what ye pursue!

Louis MacNeice

Street Scene

Between March and April when barrows of daffodils butter
    the pavement,
The colossus of London stretches his gaunt legs, jerking
The smoke of his hair back from his eyes and puffing
Smoke-rings of heavenward pigeons over Saint Paul's,
While in each little city of each individual person
The black tree yearns for green confetti and the black kerb for
    yellow stalls.

Ave Maria! A sluice is suddenly opened
Making Orphan Street a conduit for a fantastic voice;
The Canadian sergeant turns to stone in his swagger,
The painted girls, the lost demobbed, the pinstriped
    accountant listen
As the swan-legged cripple straddled on flightless wings of
    crutches
Hitting her top note holds our own lame hours in equipoise,

Then waddles a yard and switches *Cruising down the river*
Webbed feet hidden, the current smooth *On a Sunday afternoon*
Sunshine fortissimo; some young man from the Desert
Fumbles, new from battle-dress, for his pocket,
Drops a coin in that cap she holds like a handbag,
Then slowly walks out of range of *A sentimental tune*

Which cruising down – repeat – cruises down a river
That has no source nor sea but is each man's private dream
Remote as his listening eyes; repeat for all will listen
Cruising away from thought with *An old accordion playing*
Not that it is, her accompanist plucks a banjo
On a Sunday afternoon. She ends. And the other stream

Of Orphan Street flows back – instead of silence racket,
Brakes gears and sparrows; the passers-by pass by,
The swan goes home on foot, a girl takes out her compact –
Silence instead of song; the Canadian dives for the pub
And a naval officer on the traffic island
Unsees the buses with a mid-ocean eye.

Dannie Abse

Three Street Musicians

Three street musicians in mourning overcoats
worn too long, shake money boxes this morning,
then, afterwards, play their suicide notes.

The violinist in chic, black spectacles, blind,
the stout tenor with a fake Napoleon stance,
and the loony flautist following behind,

they try to importune us, the busy living,
who hear melodic snatches of music hall
above unceasing waterfalls of traffic.

Yet if anything can summon back the dead
it is the old-time sound, old obstinate tunes,
such as they achingly render and suspend:

'The Minstrel Boy', 'Roses of Picardy'.
No wonder cemeteries are full of silences
and stones keep down the dead that they defend.

Stones too light! Airs irresistible!
Even a dog listens, one paw raised, while the stout,
loud man amazes with nostalgic notes – though half boozed

and half clapped out. And, as breadcrumbs thrown
on the ground charm sparrows down from nowhere,
now, suddenly, there are too many ghosts about.

Gwyn Thomas
From *Gazooka*

Somewhere outside my window a child is whistling. He is walking fast down the hill and whistling. The tune on his lips is 'Swanee'. I go to the window and watch him. He is moving through a fan of light from a street lamp. His head is thrown back, his lips protrude strongly and his body moves briskly. 'D.I.X.I. – Even Mamee, How I love you, how I love you, my dear old Swanee . . .' The Mississippi and the Taff kiss with dark humming lubricity under an ashen hood of years. Swanee, my dear old Swanee.

The sound of it promotes a roaring life inside my ears. Whenever I hear it, brave ghosts, in endless procession, march again. My eyes are full of the wonder they knew in the months of that long, idle, beautifully lit summer of 1926.

By the beginning of June the hills were bulging with a clearer loveliness than they had ever known before. No smoke rose from the great chimneys to write messages on the sky that puzzled and saddened the minds of the young. The endless journeys of coal trams on the incline, loaded on the upward run, empty and terrifyingly fast on the down, ceased to rattle through the night and mark our dreams. The parade of nailed boots on the pavements at dawn fell silent. Day after glorious day came up over the hills that had been restored by a quirk of social conflict to the calm they lost a hundred years before.

When the school holidays came we took to the mountain tops, joining the liberated pit-ponies among the ferns on the broad plateaux. That was the picture for us who were young. For our fathers and mothers there was the inclosing fence of hinted fears, fear of hunger, fear of defeat.

And then, out of the quietness and the golden light, partly to ease their fret, a new excitement was born. The carnivals and the jazz bands.

Rapture can sprout in the oddest places and it certainly sprouted then and there. We formed bands by the dozen, great lumps of beauty and precision, a hundred men and more in each, blowing out their songs as they marched up and down the valleys, amazing and deafening us all. Their instruments were gazookas, with a thunderous bringing up of drums in the rear. Gazookas: small tin zeppelins through which you hummed the tune as loudly as possible. Each band was done up in the uniform of some remote character never before seen in Meadow Prospect. Foreign Legionaries, Chinamen, Carabinieri, Grenadiers, Gauchos, Sultans, Pearl-divers, or what we

thought these performers looked like, and there were some very
myopic voters among the designers. There was even one group of lads
living up on the colder slopes of Mynydd Coch, and eager to put in a
word from the world's freezing fringes who did themselves up as
Eskimos, but they were liquidated because even Mathew Sewell the
Sotto, our leading maestro and musical adviser, could not think up a
suitable theme song for boys dressed up as delegates from the Arctic
and chronically out of touch with the carnival spirit . . .

At the carnival's end Gomer and Cynlais said we would go back
over the mountain path, for the macadamed roads would be too hard
after the disappointments of the day. Up the mountain we went.
Everything was plain because the moon was full. The path was narrow
and we walked single file, women, children, Matadors, Sons of Dixie
and Britannias. We reached the mountaintop. We reached the
straight green path that leads past Llangysgod on down to Meadow
Prospect. And across the lovely deep-ferned plateau we walked slowly,
like a little army, most of the men with children hanging on to their
arms, the women walking as best they could in the rear. Then they all
fell quiet. We stood still, I and two or three others, and watched them
pass, listening to the curious quietness that had fallen upon them. Far
away we heard a high crazy laugh from Cynlais Coleman, who was
trying to comfort Moira Hallam in their defeat. Some kind of sadness
seemed to have come down on us. It was not a miserable sadness, for
we could all feel some kind of contentment enriching its dark root. It
may have been the moon making the mountain seem so secure and
serene. We were like an army that had nothing left to cheer about or
cry about, not sure if it was advancing or retreating and not caring.
We had lost. As we watched the weird disguises, the strange, yet
utterly familiar faces, of Britannias, Matadors and Africans, shuffle
past, we knew that the bubble of frivolity, blown with such pathetic
care, had burst for ever and that new and colder winds of danger
would come from all the world's corners to find us on the morrow. But
for that moment we were touched by the moon and the magic of
longing. We sensed some friendliness and forgiveness in the loved and
loving earth we walked on. For minutes the silence must have gone on.
Just the sound of many feet swishing through the summer grass. Then
somebody started playing a gazooka. The tune he played was one of
those sweet, deep things that form as simply as dew upon a mood like
ours. It must have been 'All Through the Night' scored for a million
talking tears and a basic disbelief in the dawn. It had all the golden
softness of an age-long hunger to be at rest. The player, distant from
us now, at the head of the long and formless procession, played it very

quietly, as if he were thinking rather than playing. Thinking about the night, conflict, beauty, the intricate labour of living and the dark little dish of thinking self in which they were all compounded. Then the others joined in and the children began to sing.

Iain Crichton Smith

Two Girls Singing

It neither was the words nor yet the tune.
Any tune would have done and any words.
Any listener or no listener at all.

As nightingales in rocks or a child crooning
in its own world of strange awakening
or larks for no reason but themselves.

So on the bus through late November running
by yellow lights tormented, darkness falling,
the two girls sang for miles and miles together

and it wasn't the words or tune. It was the singing.
It was the human sweetness in that yellow,
the unpredicted voices of our kind.

D.J. Enright

Seaside Sensation

The strains of an elastic band
Waft softly o'er the sandy strand.
The maestro stretches out his hands
To bless the bandiest of bands.

Their instruments are big and heavy –
A glockenspiel for spieling Glock,
A handsome, bandsome cuckoo clock,
For use in Strauss (Johann not Levi),

Deep-throated timpani in rows
For symphonies by Berlioz,
And lutes and flutes and concertinas,
Serpents, shawms and ocarinas.

The sun is shining, there are miles
Of peeling skin and healing smiles.
Also water which is doing
What it ought to, fro- and to-ing.

But can the band the bandstand stand?
Or can the bandstand stand the band?
The sand, the sand, it cannot stand
The strain of bandstand and a band!

Now swallowed up are band and stand
And smiling faces black and tanned.
The sand was quick and they were slow.
You hear them playing on below.

C. Day Lewis

Cornet Solo

Thirty years ago lying awake,
Lying awake
In London at night when childhood barred me
From livelier pastimes, I'd hear a street-band break
Into old favourites – 'The Ash Grove', 'Killarney'
Or 'Angels Guard Thee'.

That was the music for such an hour –
A deciduous hour
Of leaf-wan drizzle, of solitude
And gaslight bronzing the gloom like an autumn flower –
The time and music for a boy imbrued
With the pensive mood.

I could have lain for hours together,
Sweet hours together,
Listening to the cornet's cry
Down wet streets gleaming like patent leather
Where beauties jaunted in cabs to their revelry,
Jewelled and spry.

Plaintive its melody rose or waned
Like an autumn wind
Blowing the rain on beds of aster,
On man's last bed: mournful and proud it complained
As a woman who dreams of the charms that graced her,
In young days graced her.

Strange how those yearning airs could sweeten
And still enlighten
The hours when solitude gave me her breast.
Strange they could tell a mere child how hearts may beat in
The self-same tune for the once-possessed
And the unpossessed.

Last night, when I heard a cornet's strain,
It seemed a refrain
Wafted from thirty years back – so remote an
Echo it bore: but I felt again
The prophetic mood of a child, too long forgotten,
Too lightly forgotten.

Wolfgang Borchert

Lots and Lots of Snow

From *The Man Outside*

Snow hung in the branches. The machine-gunner sang. He stood in a Russian forest, far forward, on guard. He sang Christmas carols although it was already the beginning of February. But that was because the snow lay yards high. Snow between the black tree-trunks. Snow on the black-green twigs. Left hanging in the branches, blown on to bushes like cotton-wool and caked on to black tree-trunks. Lots and lots of snow. And the machine-gunner sang Christmas carols, although it was already February.

Now and then you must let fly a few shots. Otherwise the thing freezes up. Just hold it straight out into the darkness. So it doesn't freeze up. Take a shot at those bushes there. Yes, those, then you'll know if there's anyone sitting in them. It reassures you. Every quarter of an hour you can safely let fly a burst. It reassures you. Otherwise the thing freezes up. And then it's not so silent, if one fires now and then. The man he'd relieved had said that. And also: You must pull your balaclava back off your ears. Regimental order. On guard, you must push your balaclava back off your ears. Otherwise you hear nothing. That's an order. But you don't hear anything anyway. Everything's silent. Not a squeak. For weeks now. Not a squeak. Well, I'm off. Fire every now and then. It reassures you.

That's what he said. Then he stood there alone. He pulled the balaclava back off his ears and the cold clutched at them with sharp fingers. He stood there alone. And snow hung in the branches. Stuck on the blue-black tree-trunks. Heaped up over the bushes. Piled up high, drifting, and sinking in hollows. Lots and lots of snow.

And the snow in which he was standing made danger so quiet. So far off. And it could be standing right behind one. It silenced it. And the snow in which he was standing, standing alone in the night, standing alone for the first time, it made the nearness of the others so quiet. It made them so far away. It silenced them, for it made everything so quiet that the blood grew loud in one's ears, grew so loud that one couldn't escape it. So silent the snow.

Then there was a sigh. On the left. In front. Then on the right. Then left again. And behind, suddenly. The machine-gunner held his breath. There, again. A sigh. The rushing in his ears grew enormous. Then it sighed again. He tore his coat-collar open. His fingers tugged, trembled. They tore his coat-collar open, so that it didn't cover his ear.

There. A sigh. The sweat came out cold from under his helmet and froze on his forehead. Froze there. There were forty-two degrees of frost. From under his helmet the sweat came out and froze. A sigh. Behind. And on the right. Far in front. Then here. There. There too.

The machine-gunner stood in the Russian forest. Snow hung in the branches. And the blood rushed loud in his ears. And the sweat froze on his forehead. And the sweat came out from under his helmet. For it was sighing. Something. Or someone. The snow concealed it. So the sweat froze on his forehead. For fear was big in his ears. For it was sighing.

Then he sang. He sang loud, so as not to hear the fear any more. Nor the sighs any more. And so that the sweat wouldn't freeze any more. He sang. And he no longer heard the fear. Christmas carols he sang, and he no longer heard the sighs. He sang loud Christmas carols in the Russian forest. For snow hung in the blue-black branches in the Russian forest. Lots of snow.

And then a branch broke suddenly. And the machine-gunner was silent. And whirled round. And tore out his pistol. Then with great bounds the sergeant came towards him through the snow.

Now I shall be shot, thought the machine-gunner. I've been singing on guard. And now I'll be shot. There's the sergeant already. And how he's running! I've been singing on guard and now they'll come and shoot me.

And he held the pistol firmly in his hand.

Then the sergeant was there. And held on to him. And looked round. Shaking. And then gasped:

My God! Hold me tight, man. My God! My God!

And then he laughed. His hands shook. And yet he laughed: I'm hearing Christmas carols. Christmas carols in this damned Russian forest. Christmas carols. Isn't it February? Sure it's February now. But I hear Christmas carols. It's because of this terrible silence. Christmas carols! God in heaven! Just hold me tight, man. Be quiet a minute. There! No. Now it's gone. Don't laugh, said the sergeant and gasped again and held the machine-gunner tight, don't laugh, man. But it's because of the silence. Weeks of this silence. Not a squeak! Nothing! So after a while you hear Christmas carols. Although it's long since been February. But it comes from the snow. There's so much here. Don't laugh, man. It drives you mad, I tell you. You've only been here two days. But we've been sitting in it here for weeks now. Not a squeak! Nothing. It drives you mad. Everything always silent. Not a squeak! For weeks. Then gradually you start hearing Christmas carols. Don't laugh. Only when I saw you they suddenly stopped. My God. It drives you mad. This everlasting silence. Everlasting!

The sergeant gasped again. And laughed. And held him tight. And the machine-gunner held him tight, too. Then they both laughed. In the Russian forest. In February.

Sometimes a branch bent under the snow. And then between the blue-black twigs it slid to the ground. And sighed as it did so. Quite softly. Sometimes in front. On the left. Then here. There, too.

It sighed everywhere. For snow hung in the branches. Lots and lots of snow.

Translated by David Porter

Sunday Music

Igor Stravinsky

Of Church Music

From *Conversations with Igor Stravinsky*

Whether or not the Church was the wisest patron – though I think it was; we commit fewer musical sins in church – it was rich in musical forms. How much poorer we are without the sacred musical services, without the Masses, the Passions, the round-the-calendar cantatas of the Protestants, the motets and Sacred Concerts, the Vespers and so many others. These are not merely defunct forms but parts of the musical spirit in disuse.

The Church knew what the Psalmist knew: music praises God. Music is as well or better able to praise Him than the building of the church and all its decoration; it is the Church's greatest ornament. Glory, glory, glory; the music of Orlando Lassus's motet praises God, and this particular 'glory' does not exist in secular music. And not only glory, though I think of it first because the glory of the Laudate, the joy of the Doxology, are all but extinct, but prayer and penitence and many others cannot be secularized. The spirit disappears with the form. I am not comparing 'emotional range' or 'variety' in sacred and secular music. The music of the nineteenth and twentieth centuries – it is all secular – is 'expressively' and 'emotionally' beyond anything in the music of the earlier centuries: the *Angst* in *Lulu*, for instance (gory, gory, gory), or the tension, the perpetuation of the moment of epitasis, in Schoenberg's music. I say, simply, that without the Church, 'left to our own devices', we are poorer by many musical forms.

When I call the nineteenth century 'secular' I mean by it to distinguish between religious religious music and secular religious music. The latter is inspired by humanity in general, by art, by *Übermensch*, by goodness, and by goodness knows what. Religious music without religion is almost always vulgar. It can also be dull. There is dull church music from Hucbald to Haydn, but not vulgar church music. (Of course there is vulgar church music now, but it is not really of or for the church.) I hope, too, that my sacred music is a protest against the Platonic tradition, which has been the Church's tradition through Plotinus and Erigena, of music as anti-moral. Of course Lucifer had music. Ezekiel refers to his 'tabrets and pipes' and Isaiah to the 'noise of his viols'. But Lucifer took his music with him from Paradise, and even in Hell, as Bosch shows, music is able to represent Paradise and become the 'bride of the cosmos'.

'It has been corrupted by musicians,' is the Church's answer, the Church whose musical history is a series of attacks against polyphony, the true musical expression of Western Christendom, until music retires from it in the eighteenth century or confounds it with the theatre. The corrupting musicians Bosch means are probably Josquin and Ockeghem, the corrupting artefacts the polyphonic marvels of Josquin, Ockeghem, Compère, Brumel.

George Herbert

Church Music

Sweetest of sweets, I thank you: when displeasure
    Did through my body wound my mind,
You took me thence; and in your house of
    pleasure
    A dainty lodging me assign'd.

Now I in you without a body move,
    Rising and falling with your wings:
We both together sweetly live and love,
    Yet say sometimes, *God help poor kings.*

Comfort, I'll die; for if you post from me,
    Sure I shall do so, and much more:
But if I travel in your company,
    You know the way to heaven's door.

Amy Clampitt

Sunday Music

The Baroque sewing machine of Georg Friedrich
going back, going back to stitch back together
scraps of a scheme that's outmoded, all
those lopsidedly overblown expectations
now severely in need of revision, re
the nature of things, or more precisely
(back a stitch, back a stitch) the
nature of going forward.

No longer footpath-perpendicular, a monody
tootled on antelope bone, no longer
wheelbarrow heave-ho, the nature of going
forward is not perspective, not stairways,
not, as for the muse of Josquin or Gesualdo,
sostenuto, a leaning together
in memory of, things held onto
fusing and converging,

nor is it any longer an orbit, tonality's
fox-and-goose footprints going round
and round in the snow, the centripetal
force of the dominant. The nature of next
is not what we seem to be hearing
or imagine we feel: is not dance,
is not melody, not elegy,
is not even chemistry,

not Mozart leaching out seraphs
from a sieve of misfortune. The nature
of next is not fugue or rondo, not footpath
or wheelbarrow track, not steamships'
bass vibrations, but less and less
knowing what to expect, it's
the rate of historical
change going faster

and faster: it's noise, it's droids' stone-
deaf intergalactic twitter, it's get ready
to disconnect! – no matter how filled
our heads are with backed-up old
tunes, with polyphony, with basso
profundo fioritura, with this Concerto
Grosso's delectable (back a stitch,
back a stitch) Allegro.

Robert Minhinnick

Sunday Morning

I choose back lanes for the pace they will impose,
    An old perspective half forgotten
Surprising me now as the world slows
With these things the broad road lacked:
    Carboys of vitriol stacked in a garage,
Orange hooks of honeysuckle gripping a wall.

Here a church window becomes an arch of light
    And the pitching of a hymn a brief
Infusion of the air. Voices, and low
Indistinguishable words, the organ's bass
    The foundation for a ritual
I trespass in, that suddenly

Intensifies the day. On the other side
    I picture them: the ranked devout
Pulling the ribbons from the black prayerbooks
And each with his or her accustomed doubt
    Submitting to a poetry
Triumphant as the church's muscular brass.

Thus Sunday morning: a gleaning
    Of its strange wisdoms. The certainty
Of hymns comes with me through a different town
Of derelict courts and gardens, a stable
    Where a vizored man beats sparks from a wheel,
An old man splitting marble in a mason's yard.

The creamy splinters falling into my mind
    Like the heavy fragments of hymns,
Then walking on, much further, this morning being Sunday.

Herbert Williams

The Castle Choir

'And now, *Caersalem.*' Fingers gloved
Against the itch of love flick through
The hymnbooks. Throats are cleared. And then
The harmonies surge out across the bay.
It is the Castle Choir, replete
With righteousness and love of minor keys.
They sing here every Sunday in the summer,
And the tourists stop, their fancy
Tickled by the natives' curious ways.

I used to hate the sound of them.
They made me feel like death. Those hymns,
Admonishing the hedonistic prom.
So we hurried past, derisive
Boyos with an eye for grosser curves
Than those the educated baton traced.

They crucified the sun, those dismal hymns,
And yet they had a relevance.
It wasn't long ago, but then the Welsh
Still had a Sunday. Now
The beaches are transistorized, and joy
Is straining on a less attentive leash.

And Pantycelyn's proud reproaches sound
Like distant music in our alien ears.

D.H. Lawrence

Piano

Softly, in the dusk, a woman is singing to me;
Taking me back down the vista of years, till I see
A child sitting under the piano, in the boom of the tingling
     strings
And pressing the small, poised feet of a mother who smiles as
     she sings.

In spite of myself, the insidious mastery of song
Betrays me back, till the heart of me weeps to belong
To the old Sunday evenings at home, with winter outside
And hymns in the cosy parlour, the tinkling piano our
     guide.

So now it is vain for the singer to burst into clamour
With the great black piano appassionato. The glamour
Of childish days is upon me, my manhood is cast
Down in the flood of remembrance, I weep like a child for
     the past.

David Wright

The Musician

In the south aisle of the abbey at Hexham
I turned to make a remark on its Roman
Tomb; but she did not hear me, for the organ
Was playing in the loft above the rood-screen,
Laying down tones of bronze and gold, a burden
Of praise-notes, fingerings of a musician
There at the keys, a boy, his master by him,
Whose invisible sound absorbed my saying.

Music inaudible to me, barbarian,
But legible. I read in my companion
Its elation written in her elation.
'He is so young he can be only learning,
You would not have expected to hear such playing.
It's like a return to civilization.'
Unable to hear, able to imagine
Chords pondering decline, and then upwelling

There in that deliberate enclave of stone,
I remembered music was its tradition;
Its builder, Acca, taught by one Maban
To sing; who may have been the god of song,
Mabon the god of music and the young;
That another bishop of this church, St John,
Taught here a dumb man speech, says Bede; became
Patron and intercessor of deaf men.

Jean-Jacques Rousseau
Voices in Church
From *Confessions*

A kind of music far superior, in my opinion, to that of operas, and which in all Italy has not its equal, nor perhaps in the whole world, is that of the *scuole*. The *scuole* are houses of charity, established for the education of young girls without fortune, to whom the Republic afterwards gives a portion either at marriage or on entering the cloister. Amongst the talents cultivated in these young girls music is in the first rank. Every Sunday at the church of each of the four *scuole*, during vespers, motets or anthems, with full choruses, accompanied by a great orchestra, and composed and directed by the best masters in Italy, are sung in the galleries by girls only, not one of whom is more than twenty years of age. I cannot conceive of anything so pleasing and affecting as this music: the richness of the art, the exquisite taste of the vocal parts, the excellence of the voices, the correctness of the execution, everything in these delightful concerts, combines to produce an impression which is certainly not in the fashion, but against which I am convinced no heart is secure. Carrio and I never failed to be present at these vespers of the *mendicanti*, and we were not alone. The church was always full of the lovers of the art, and even the actors of the opera came there to form their taste with these excellent models. What vexed me was the iron grating which suffered nothing to escape but sounds, and concealed from me the angels of which they were worthy. I talked of nothing else. One day I spoke of it at Le Blond's. 'If you are so keen,' said he, 'to see those little girls, it will be an easy matter to satisfy your wishes. I am one of the administrators of the house, I will take you to tea with them.' I did not let him rest until he had fulfilled his promise. On entering the saloon which contained these beauties I so much longed to see, I felt a trembling of love which I had never before experienced. M. le Blond presented to me one after another these celebrated female singers whose names and voices were all that I knew. Come, Sophia – she was horrible. Come, Cattina – she had but one eye. Come, Bettina – smallpox had entirely disfigured her. Scarcely one of them was without some striking defect. Le Blond laughed at my surprise; however, two or three of them appeared tolerable; these never sang but in the choruses; I was almost in despair. During tea we endeavoured to entertain them, and they soon became animated: ugliness does not exclude the graces, and I found they possessed them. I said to myself, 'They cannot sing in this manner without intelligence and sensibility, they must have both': my manner of seeing them thus changed to such a degree that I left the house almost in love with each of these ugly faces. I had scarcely courage enough to return to vespers. But after having seen the girls, the danger was lessened. I still found their singing delightful; and their voices so much embellished their persons, that, in spite of my eyes, I obstinately continued to think them beautiful.

Translated by Joan Abse

Musical Instruments

Pablo Casals

Of All Instruments

From *Joys and Sorrows*

From infancy I was surrounded by music. You might say music was for me an ocean in which I swam like a little fish. Music was inside me and all about me; it was the air I breathed from the time I could walk. To hear my father play the piano was an ecstasy for me. When I was two or three, I would sit on the floor beside him as he played, and I would press my head against the piano in order to absorb the sound more completely. I could sing in tune before I could speak clearly; notes were as familiar to me as words. My father used to have my little brother Artur and me stand behind the piano – we were too small to see over the top of it – and he would stand in front of the piano with his back to it. Reaching behind him and spreading out the fingers of both hands, he would strike chords at random on the piano. 'Now what notes did I play?' he would say. And we would have to name all the notes in the dissonant chords he had played. Then he would do it again, and again. Artur was two years younger than I was – he died at five from spinal meningitis. He was a lovely little boy, and he had a sharper ear for music than mine.

I began playing the piano when I was four years old. I must say I am glad I learned to play the piano at the very beginning. For me it is the best of all instruments – yes, despite my love of the cello. On a piano you can play anything that has been written. Violinists, for example, have a big repertory and many do not have or take the time to learn what composers have written for other instruments or for the orchestra as a whole; and so, in that sense, many are not complete musicians. With the piano it is a different matter; the instrument encompasses everything. That is why everyone who wants to devote his life to music should know how to play the piano, whether or not he prefers another instrument. I can say that I became a good pianist – although I am afraid that I no longer am. I have no technique now. But every morning of course I still play the piano.

It was my father who taught me to play the piano and gave me my first lessons in composition. It was he who taught me how to sing. I was five when I became a second soprano in the church choir. It was a momentous event in my life – to actually be a member of the choir and to sing while my father played the organ! I was paid for every service; my fee amounted to the sum of ten cents; and so one might say that this was my first professional job as a musician. It was for me a very serious duty, and I felt responsible not only for my own singing but for the singing of the other boys as well. I was the youngest member of the choir, but I would say, 'Watch it, now! Be careful with that note.' It would seem I already had aspirations to be a conductor.

In those days, bands of itinerant musicians wandered from village to village, eking out a meager existence on whatever money the villagers could spare them. They played in the streets and at village dances. They often dressed in bizarre costumes, and performed on a weird variety of instruments, often of their own contriving. I always greeted their arrival with great excitement. One day a group of three such musicians came to Vendrell; they called themselves Los Tres Bemoles, or The Three Flats. I made my way to the front of the crowd that had gathered in the plaza to hear them, and I crouched there on the cobblestones completely enthralled, enchanted by the appearance of the players – they were dressed as clowns – and I listened spellbound to every note they played. I was especially fascinated by their instruments. They had mandolins, bells, guitars, and even instruments made out of kitchen utensils like teapots, cups and glasses – I think these instruments must surely have been the forerunners of some of the curious contraptions that are played in jazz orchestras today. One man played on a broom handle that was strung something like a cello – though I had never seen or even heard of a cello at that time. For some reason – possibly I had some sort of prescience! – that broom-handle instrument fascinated me most of all. I couldn't take my eyes off it. It sounded wonderful to me. When I went home, I told my father breathlessly about it. He laughed, but I talked so passionately about it that he said, 'All right, Pablo, I'll make you an instrument like it.' And he did – though I must say it was a considerable improvement on the broom handle and sounded much better. He fashioned it out of a gourd, with a single string. I suppose you might say that this instrument was my first cello. I still have it at San Salvador. I have kept it in a glass case, like a real museum treasure.

On that homemade contrivance I learned to play many of the songs my father wrote, as well as popular melodies that reached our village from the outer world. Years later, when I was visiting the nearby ancient monastery of Santes Creus, I met an old innkeeper who said that he remembered hearing me play that strange instrument one night, when I was a boy of nine, in the cloisters of the monastery. And I too remembered that night – when I played in the moonlight and the music echoed among the shadows and against the crumbling white monastery walls . . .

Sometimes I awakened in the morning to the sound of folk songs, the villagers – fishermen and men who worked in the vineyards – singing as they went to work. Sometimes in the evening there were dances in the plaza and sometimes festivals at which the *gralla* was played. The *gralla* is a reed instrument which, I think, is probably of Moorish origin – it resembles an oboe and has a very strident sound. Every day I would hear my father playing the piano or the organ. There were his songs and church music and compositions of the masters. He took me to all the services at the church – the Gregorian chant, the chorals and the organ voluntaries became part of my daily life. And then, too, there were always the wonderful sounds of nature, the sound of the sea, the sound of the wind moving through the trees, the delicate singing of the birds, the infinitely varied melody of the human voice, not only in song but in speech. What a wealth of music! It sustained and nourished me.

I was curious about all instruments, and I wanted to play them all. By the time I was seven I was playing the violin, and I played a solo at a concert in Vendrell at the age of eight. I longed especially to play the organ. But my father said I could not touch the instrument until my feet could reach the pedals. How I waited for that day! I was never very tall, so the day took somewhat longer to arrive than it would have for another child. In fact, it seemed to me an interminable time. I kept on trying, sitting at the stool alone in the church and stretching out my feet, but – alas! – that did not help me grow any more quickly. The great moment finally came when I was nine. I hurried to my father and told him, 'Father, I can touch the pedals!' He said, 'Let me see.' I reached out my feet and they touched – barely, but they touched. My father said, 'All right, now you can play the organ.' It was a lovely old instrument, made at the same time as the one that Bach used in Leipzig. It is still in the church in Vendrell.

Before long I had learned to play the organ well enough so that I sometimes took my father's place when he was ill or busy with some other work. Once when I had finished playing and was leaving the church, a friend of my father's who was a shoemaker came up to me and said, 'How magnificently your father played today!' At that time, shoemakers in our village worked in the streets, sitting on stools. This man had been sitting outside the church and listening while he worked. I told the shoemaker that my father was not well, and that I was the one who had been playing. At first he would not believe me, but I assured him it was so. He summoned his wife and told her with great excitement, 'That was not Carlos at the organ. You will not believe me, but it was Pablito!' The shoemaker and his wife put their arms around me and kissed me; then they took me into their house and gave me biscuits and wine.

I see no particular merit in the fact that I was an artist at the age of eleven. I was born with an ability, with music in me, that is all. No special credit was due me. The only credit we can claim is for the use we make of the talent we are given. That is why I urge young musicians: 'Don't be vain because you happen to have talent. You are not responsible for that; it was not of your doing. What you do with your talent is what matters. You must cherish this gift. Do not demean or waste what you have been given. Work – work constantly and nourish it.'

Of course the gift to be cherished most of all is that of life itself. One's work should be a salute to life.

When I was eleven years old, I heard the cello played for the first time. That was the beginning of a long and cherished companionship! A trio had come to play at a concert in Vendrell – a pianist, a violinist and a cellist. My father took me to the concert. It was held at the small hall of the Catholic Center, with an audience of townspeople, fishermen and peasants, who, as always for such an occasion, were dressed in their Sunday clothes. The cellist was Josep García, a teacher at the Municipal School of Music in Barcelona; he was a handsome man with a high forehead and a handlebar mustache; and his figure somehow seemed fitted to his instrument. When I saw his cello I was fascinated by it – I had never seen one before. From the moment I heard the first notes I was overwhelmed. I felt as if I could not breathe. There was something so tender, beautiful and human – yes, so very human – about the sound. I had never heard such a beautiful sound before. A radiance filled me. When the first composition was ended, I told my father, 'Father, that is the most wonderful instrument I have ever heard. That is what I want to play.'

After the concert I kept talking to my father about the cello, pleading with him to get me one. From that time, more than eighty years ago, I was wedded to the instrument.

Elizabeth Barrett Browning

A Musical Instrument

What was he doing, the great god Pan,
    Down in the reeds by the river?
Spreading ruin and scattering ban,
Splashing and paddling with hoofs of a goat,
And breaking the golden lilies afloat
    With the dragon-fly on the river.

He tore out a reed, the great god Pan,
    From the deep cool bed of the river;
The limpid water turbidly ran,
And the broken lilies a-dying lay,
And the dragon-fly had fled away,
    Ere he brought it out of the river.

High on the shore sat the great god Pan
    While turbidly flowed the river;
And hacked and hewed as a great god can,
With his hard bleak steel at the patient reed,
Till there was not a sign of the leaf indeed
    To prove it fresh from the river.

He cut it short, did the great god Pan
    (How tall it stood in the river!),
Then drew the pith, like the heart of a man,
Steadily from the outside ring,
And notched the poor dry empty thing
    In holes, as he sat by the river.

'This is the way,' laughed the great god Pan
    (Laughed while he sat by the river),
'The only way, since gods began
To make a sweet music, they could succeed.'
Then, dropping his mouth to a hole in the
    reed,
    He blew in power by the river.

Sweet, sweet, sweet, O Pan!
    Piercing sweet by the river!
Blinding sweet, O great god Pan!
The sun on the hill forgot to die
And the lilies revived, and the dragon-fly
    Came back to dream on the river.

Yet half a beast is the great god Pan,
    To laugh as he sits by the river,
Making a poet out of a man;
The true gods sigh for the cost and pain
For the reed which grows nevermore again
    As a reed with the reeds in the river.

John Scott

Ode on Hearing the Drum

I hate that drum's discordant sound,
Parading round, and round, and round:
To thoughtless youth it pleasure yields,
And lures from cities and from fields,
To sell their liberty for charms
Of tawdry lace, and glittering arms;
And when ambition's voice commands,
To march, and fight, and fall, in foreign lands.

I hate that drum's discordant sound,
Parading round, and round, and round:
To me it talks of ravaged plains,
And burning towns, and ruined swains,
And mangled limbs, and dying groans,
And widows' tears, and orphans' moans;
And all that misery's hand bestows,
To fill the catalogue of human woes.

Thomas Hardy

A Duettist to her Pianoforte

Song of Silence

(E.L.H. – H.C.H.)

Since every sound moves memories,
How can I play you
Just as I might if you raised no scene,
By your ivory rows, of a form between
My vision and your time-worn sheen,
As when each day you
Answered our fingers with ecstasy?
So it's hushed, hushed, hushed, you are for me!

And as I am doomed to counterchord
Her notes no more
In those old things I used to know,
In a fashion, when we practised so,
''Good-night! – Good-bye!' to your pleated show
Of silk, now hoar,
Each nodding hammer, and pedal and key,
For dead, dead, dead, you are to me!

I fain would second her, strike to her stroke,
As when she was by,
Aye, even from the ancient clamorous 'Fall
Of Paris,' or 'Battle of Prague' withal,
To the 'Roving Minstrels,' or 'Elfin Call'
Sung soft as a sigh:
But upping ghosts press achefully,
And mute, mute, mute, you are for me!

Should I fling your polyphones, plaints, and quavers
Afresh on the air,
Too quick would the small white shapes be here
Of the fellow twain of hands so dear;
And a black-tressed profile, and pale smooth ear;
– Then how shall I bear
Such heavily-haunted harmony?
Nay: hushed, hushed, hushed, you are for me!

Alfred Brendel

From *Coping with Pianos*

'There are no bad pianos, only bad pianists.' An impressive statement, one that looks round for applause. A statement that will at once ring true to the layman and make him feel initiated as well as amused. A statement addressed perhaps to some revered virtuoso who did not refuse to play at a private party – Busoni would have left the house right away – and who, in spite of the detestable instrument, managed to hold his audience spellbound.

It is a statement to confound any pianist. Admittedly, many a piano will sound less awful under the hands of an expert than under those of an amateur; but does that make it a good piano? To 'carry the day' on a badly regulated, unequally registered, faultily voiced, dull or noisy instrument implies as often as not that one has violated the music for which one is responsible, that control and refinement have been pushed aside, that the 'personal approach' has been greatly exaggerated and a dubious sort of mystique has taken over, far removed from the effect the piece should legitimately produce.

How often does the player find a piano he can rely on, a piano which will do justice to the exactness of his vision? Is it to be wondered at that many of his performances remain compromises? After all, he should not have to struggle with the instrument, or impose his will tyrannically upon it, any more than the instrument should turn into a fetish, an object of idolization that dominates him. On the contrary, the player should make friends with the piano and assure himself of its services – especially when Pianism with a capital P is to be transcended. He should give the instrument its due by showing how capable it is of transforming itself.

A piano is not a mass-produced article. Every instrument, even from the same renowned maker, presents the pianist with a new experience. What shapes his reaction is not only the 'individuality' of a particular instrument, but also the materials used in it and the processes of manufacture – in other words, the difference in quality between one instrument and another. Enviously he watches the cellist dragging his own cello around; his only consolation is that the adjustment problems of organists and harpsichordists exceed his own. What energy is sometimes needed to 'listen into' a particular piano, and what pertinacity to make it amenable to a certain piece of music! The pianist will find that the instrument readily responds to some pieces, but balks at others. He may, unexpectedly, be reminded of the piano he used in his youth, or on which he studied a certain piece:

intention and execution suddenly coalesce once more; something of the joy and concentration of his early strivings comes back to him; old, crumpled fingerings regain their pristine smoothness – it is a homecoming into the lower reaches of memory.

Once in a while a piano will surprise the player by demonstrating to him the nature of the instrument on which a composer conceived a particular work: a piano with a singing tone, a tender treble, gentle bass, and a harp-like, whispering soft pedal will bring Liszt's *Bénédiction* to life, and the lower middle range of a Bösendorfer will remove Schubert's accompaniment figures to their proper distance. A Pleyel upright amidst velvet draperies, cushions, carpets and plush furnishings might perhaps reveal the sense of Chopin's pedal markings. Pianos and rooms are generally interdependent: anyone who has ever travelled with a piano knows that the same Steinway or Bösendorfer not only sounds different in different halls, but also seems to react differently in its mechanism. Indeed, the resistance of the key, over and above the measurable mechanical aspect, is a psychological factor. The characteristics of a concert hall – its greater or lesser resonance, brightness, clarity, and spaciousness of sound – are reflected in the player's technical approach and have an influence on his sense of well-being. There are halls that coarsen or deaden the sound; others absorb one's pedalling like blotting-paper or, conversely, require constant non-legato playing. Thus (to return to Chopin's pedal signs) there can be no universally valid pedalling instructions – these exist only in the imagination of some piano teachers. Excepted, of course, are pedal markings which determine the colour of entire sections, indicate pedal points, or ask for some kind of pedalling which is not self-evident; most of Beethoven's infrequent pedal markings belong in these categories.

Much will depend on the previous concert: are the new hall and instrument reassuringly similar, or will the pianist have to readjust himself? If the latter, his aural and technical reorientation before the concert will have the additional aim of ridding his memory as far as possible of all recently acquired habits of listening and playing. However, the pianist's attempts to adapt himself to instrument and hall are beset by a multitude of difficulties.

In the first place, the full hall during the concert sometimes sounds completely different from the empty one during the rehearsal. The halls of the Vienna Musikverein, for instance, famous for their acoustics, overflow in a welter of sound when empty. (The only time that Viennese orchestral musicians can hear one another at all clearly is during the performance.)

Moreover, the sound reaching the public in the auditorium only rarely corresponds to that heard on the platform. In extreme cases, the player may know perfectly well what is happening on stage, but not at all what is coming across. He must then try to translate his musical intentions into a presumed sound which he himself can control only indirectly. This acoustic equivalent of reading the tea-leaves can at times lead even the most experienced pianist astray. Unless he has sat in the hall himself as a member of the audience and knows exactly what the sound is like from there, the player will have to rely on the advice of musical friends. At recording sessions, the sound of test tapes through the speakers in the playback room will tell him whether and in what proportions he will have to split his musical personality.

Another problem is that, on the rare occasions when he has the luxury of choice, the pianist cannot often compare the available pianos side by side in the hall. He has to go to the storage room of the hall or hiring firm, or encounter each instrument in a different location. The divergent acoustics can widely mislead him in his choice.

Lastly, there is no denying the fact that we pianists do not always 'function like clockwork'. I am referring not only to the changing lubrication level of our physical apparatus, which at times enables us to throw off with the grace of an acrobat what at other times weighs upon us like a ton of bricks; I am referring also to the quality of our hearing, which may vary under the influence of tiredness or freshness, anxiety or repose.

There are some pianists fatalistic enough to assail the platform blissfully unaware. However, they are as rare as albinos. In spite of all the obstacles, the experience gained at the rehearsal will be useful at the performance, even though, as might happen, the pianist may well have to revise his impressions yet again. At any rate, he has over-hauled the instrument with the help of the tuner. He has positioned the piano correctly, not too close to the edge of the platform, the keyboard exactly in the centre of the hall. He has removed the music stand, tried and rejected three piano stools (the fourth, at last, did not creak or wobble), arranged the lighting so that no shadow falling on the keys should disturb his concentration, and located an old upright on which to warm up briefly before facing the audience. He has also, with luck, almost at the back of his mind, recalled the whole programme he is to play. Now he may sleep through the afternoon.

John Heath-Stubbs

The Watchman's Flute

Through the Nigerian night the Tuareg watchman,
Ferociously armed with sword, dagger and whip,
Intermittently blows his flute – a piece of piping
Bored with five holes: to pass the time –

To ward off tedium, and perhaps
Lurking malignant ghosts that always throng
This ambient, African darkness:

Infinite rhythmical variations
On a simple tetrachord, with a recurrent pedal point –
Libyan music, antique – as Orpheus
Cajoled the powers of Hell, made them disgorge
Eurydice – to him she was love
(Her jurisdiction be wide).

Those deliquescent forms shrink back
To hollow pits of non-entity:
Music implies an order – light,
Particles in regular motion,
The first articulate Word.

May my lips likewise
Mould such melodious mouthfuls still, amid
The European, the twentieth-century tediums:
We too are haunted, we are in the dark.

D.J. Enright

The Noodle-Vendor's Flute

In a real city, from a real house,
At midnight by the ticking clocks,
In winter by the crackling roads:
Hearing the noodle-vendor's flute,
Two single fragile falling notes . . .
But what can this small sing-song say,
Under the noise of war?
The flute itself a counterfeit
(Siberian wind can freeze the lips),
Merely a rubber bulb and metal horn
(Hard to ride a cycle, watch for manholes
And late drunks, and play a flute together).
Just squeeze between gloved fingers,
And the note of mild hope sounds:
Release, the indrawn sigh of mild despair . . .
A poignant signal, like the cooee
Of some diffident soul locked out,
Less than appropriate to cooling macaroni.
Two wooden boxes slung across the wheel,
A rider in his middle age, trundling
This gross contraption on a dismal road,
Red eyes and nose and breathless rubber horn.
Yet still the pathos of that double tune
Defies its provenance, and can warm
The bitter night.

Sleepless, we turn and sleep.
Or sickness dwindles to some local limb.
Bought love for one long moment gives itself.
Or there a witch assures a frightened child
She bears no personal grudge.
And I, like other listeners,
See my stupid sadness as a common thing.
And being common,
Therefore something rare indeed.
The puffing vendor, surer than a trumpet,
Tells us we are not alone.
Each night that same frail midnight tune
Squeezed from a bogus flute,
Under the noise of war, after war's noise,
It mourns the fallen, every night,
It celebrates survival –
In real cities, real houses, real time.

Federico García Lorca

The Guitar

The lament
of the guitar begins.
The glasses of the dawn
are broken.
The lament
of the guitar begins.
It is useless
to hush it.
It is impossible
to hush it.
Monotonously weeping
as the water weeps,
as the wind weeps
over the snowfall.
It is impossible
to hush it.
Weeping for things
far away.
Sands of the warm South
seeking white camelias.
It weeps, like an arrow without a target,
evening without morning,
and the first bird dead
upon the branch.
Oh guitar!
Heart pierced through
with five swords.

Translated by G. L. Gili and Stephen Spender

John Fuller

Concerto for Double Bass

He is a drunk leaning companionably
Around a lamp post or doing up
With intermittent concentration
Another drunk's coat.

He is a polite but devoted Valentino,
Cheek to cheek, forgetting the next step.
He is feeling the pulse of the fat lady
Or cutting her in half.

But close your eyes and it is sunset
At the edge of the world. It is the language
Of dolphins, the growth of tree-roots,
The heart-beat slowing down.

Music Lessons

Clarence Day

The Noblest Instrument

From *Life with Father*

Father had been away, reorganizing some old upstate railroad. He returned in an executive mood and proceeded to shake up our home. In spite of my failure as a singer, he was still bound to have us taught music. We boys were summoned before him and informed that we must at once learn to play on something. We might not appreciate it now, he said, but we should later on. 'You, Clarence, will learn the violin. George, you the piano. Julian – well, Julian is too young yet. But you older boys must have lessons.'

I was appalled at this order. At the age of ten it seemed a disaster to lose any more of my freedom. The days were already too short for our games after school; and now here was a chunk to come out of playtime three days every week. A chunk every day, we found afterward, because we had to practice.

George sat at the piano in the parlor, and faithfully learned to pound out his exercises. He had all the luck. He was not an inspired player, but at least he had some ear for music. He also had the advantage of playing on a good robust instrument, which he didn't have to be careful not to drop, and was in no danger of breaking. Furthermore, he did not have to tune it. A piano had some good points.

But I had to go through a blacker and more gruesome experience. It was bad enough to have to come in from the street and the sunlight and go down into our dark little basement where I took my lessons. But that was only the opening chill of the struggle that followed.

The whole thing was uncanny. The violin itself was a queer, fragile, cigar-boxy thing, that had to be handled most gingerly. Nothing sturdy about it. Why, a fellow was liable to crack it putting it into its case. And then my teacher, he was queer too. He had a queer pickled smell.

I dare say he wasn't queer at all really, but he seemed so to me, because he was different from the people I generally met. He was probably worth a dozen of some of them, but I didn't know it. He was one of the violins in the Philharmonic, and an excellent player; a grave, middle-aged little man – who was obliged to give lessons.

He wore a black, wrinkled frock coat, and a discolored gold watch-chain. He had small, black-rimmed glasses; not tortoise-shell, but thin rims of metal. His violin was dark, rich, and polished, and would do anything for him.

Mine was balky and awkward, brand new, and of a light, common color.

The violin is intended for persons with a passion for music. I wasn't that kind of person. I liked to hear a band play a tune that we could march up and down to, but try as I would, I could seldom whistle such a tune afterward. My teacher didn't know this. He greeted me as a possible genius.

He taught me how to hold the contraption, tucked under my chin. I learned how to move my fingers here and there on its handle or stem. I learned how to draw the bow across the strings, and thus produce sounds . . .

Does a mother recall the first cry of her baby, I wonder? I still remember the strange cry at birth of that new violin.

My teacher, Herr M., looked as though he had suddenly taken a large glass of vinegar. He sucked in his breath. His lips were drawn back from his teeth, and his eyes tightly shut. Of course, he hadn't expected my notes to be sweet at the start; but still, there was something unearthly about that first cry. He snatched the violin from me, examined it, readjusted its pegs, and comforted it gently, by drawing his own bow across it. It was only a new and not especially fine violin, but the sounds it made for him were more natural – they were classifiable sounds. They were not richly musical, but at least they had been heard before on this earth.

He handed the instrument back to me with careful directions. I tucked it up under my chin again and grasped the end tight. I held my bow exactly as ordered. I looked up at him, waiting.

'Now,' he said, nervously.

I slowly raised the bow, drew it downward. . . .

This time there were *two* dreadful cries in our little front basement. One came from my new violin and one from the heart of Herr M.

Herr M. presently came to, and smiled bravely at me, and said if I wanted to rest a moment he would permit it. He seemed to think I might wish to lie down awhile and recover. I didn't feel any need of lying down. All I wanted was to get through the lesson. But Herr M. was shaken. He was by no means ready to let me proceed. He looked around desperately, saw the music book, and said he would now show me that. We sat down side by side on the window-seat, with the book in his lap, while he pointed out the notes to me with his finger, and told me their names.

After a bit, when he felt better, he took up his own violin, and instructed me to watch him and note how he handled the strings. And then at last, he nerved himself to let me take my violin up again. 'Softly, my child, softly,' he begged me, and stood facing the wall . . .

We got through the afternoon somehow, but it was a ghastly experience. Part of the time he was maddened by the mistakes I kept making, and part of the time he was plain wretched. He covered his eyes. He seemed ill. He looked often at his watch, even shook it as though it had stopped; but he stayed the full hour.

That was Wednesday. What struggles he had with himself before Friday, when my second lesson was due, I can only dimly imagine, and of course I never even gave them a thought at the time. He came back to recommence teaching me, but he had changed – he had hardened. Instead of being cross, he was stern; and instead of sad, bitter. He wasn't unkind to me, but we were no longer companions. He talked to himself, under his breath; and sometimes he took bits of paper, and did little sums on them, gloomily, and then tore them up.

During my third lesson I saw the tears come to his eyes. He went up to Father and said he was sorry but he honestly felt sure I'd never be able to play.

Father didn't like this at all. He said he felt sure I would. He dismissed Herr M. briefly – the poor man came stumbling back down in two minutes. In that short space of time he had gallantly gone upstairs in a glow, resolved upon sacrificing his earnings for the sake of telling the truth. He returned with his earnings still running, but with the look of a lost soul about him, as though he felt that his nerves and his sanity were doomed to destruction. He was low in his mind, and he talked to himself more than ever. Sometimes he spoke harshly of America, sometimes of fate.

But he no longer struggled. He accepted this thing as his destiny. He regarded me as an unfortunate something outside the human species, whom he must simply try to labor with as well as he could. It was a grotesque, indeed a hellish experience, but he felt he must bear it.

He wasn't the only one – he was at least not alone in his sufferings. Mother, though expecting the worst, had tried to be hopeful about it, but at the end of a week or two I heard her and Margaret talking it over. I was slaughtering a scale in the front basement, when Mother came down and stood outside the door in the kitchen hall and whispered, 'Oh, Margaret!'

I watched them. Margaret was baking a cake. She screwed up her face, raised her arms, and brought them down with hands clenched.

'I don't know what we shall do, Margaret.'

'The poor little feller,' Margaret whispered. 'He can't make the thing go.'

This made me indignant. They were making me look like a lubber. I wished to feel always that I could make anything go . . .

I now began to feel a determination to master this thing. History shows us many examples of the misplaced determinations of men – they are one of the darkest aspects of human life, they spread so much needless pain: but I knew little history. And I viewed what little I did know romantically – I should have seen in such episodes their heroism, not their futility. Any role that seemed heroic attracted me, no matter how senseless.

Not that I saw any chance for heroism in our front basement, of course. You had to have a battlefield or something. I saw only that I was appearing ridiculous. But that stung my pride. I hadn't wanted to learn anything whatever about fiddles or music, but since I was in for it, I'd do it, and show them I could. A boy will often put in enormous amounts of his time trying to prove he isn't as ridiculous as he thinks people think him.

Meanwhile Herr M. and I had discovered that I was nearsighted. On account of the violin's being an instrument that sticks out in front of one, I couldn't stand close enough to the music book to see the notes clearly. He didn't at first realize that I often made mistakes from that cause. When he and I finally comprehended that I had this defect, he had a sudden new hope that this might have been the whole trouble, and that when it was corrected I might play like a human being at last.

Neither of us ventured to take up this matter with Father. We knew that it would have been hard to convince him that my eyes were not perfect, I being a son of his and presumably made in his image; and we knew that he immediately would have felt we were trying to make trouble for him, and would have shown an amount of resentment which it was best to avoid. So Herr M. instead lent me his glasses. These did fairly well. They turned the dim grayness of the notes into a queer bright distortion, but the main thing was they did make them brighter, so that I now saw more of them. How well I remember those little glasses. Poor, dingy old things. Herr M. was nervous about lending them to me; he feared that I'd drop them. It would have been safer if they had been spectacles: but no, they were pince-nez; and I had to learn to balance them across my nose as well as I could. I couldn't wear them up near my eyes because my nose was too thin there; I had to put them about half-way down where there was enough flesh to hold them. I also had to tilt my head back, for the music stand was a little too tall for me. Herr M. sometimes mounted me on a stool, warning me not to step off. Then when I was all set, and when he without his glasses was blind, I would smash my way into the scales again.

All during the long winter months I worked away at this job. I gave no thought, of course, to the family. But they did to me. Our house was heated by a furnace, which had big warm air pipes; these ran up through the walls with wide outlets into each room, and sound traveled easily and ringingly through their roomy, tin passages. My violin could be heard in every part of the house. No one could settle down to anything while I was practicing. If visitors came they soon left. Mother couldn't even sing to the baby. She would wait, watching the clock, until my long hour of scale-work was over, and then come downstairs and shriek at me that my time was up. She would find me sawing away with my forehead wet, and my hair wet and stringy, and even my clothes slowly getting damp from my exertions. She would feel my collar, which was done for, and say I must change it. 'Oh, Mother! Please!' – for I was in a hurry now to run out and play. But she wasn't being fussy about my collar, I can see, looking back; she was using it merely as a barometer or gauge of my pores. She thought I had better dry myself before going out in the snow.

It was a hard winter for Mother. I believe she also had fears for the baby. She sometimes pleaded with Father; but no one could ever tell Father anything. He continued to stand like a rock against stopping my lessons.

Schopenhauer, in his rules for debating, shows how to win a weak case by insidiously transferring an argument from its right field, and discussing it instead from some irrelevant but impregnable angle. Father knew nothing of Schopenhauer, and was never insidious, but, nevertheless, he had certain natural gifts for debate. In the first place his voice was powerful and stormy, and he let it out at full strength, and kept on letting it out with a vigor that stunned his opponents. As a second gift, he was convinced at all times that his opponents were wrong. Hence, even if they did win a point or two, it did them no good, for he dragged the issue to some other ground then, where he and Truth could prevail. When Mother said it surely was plain enough that I had no ear, what was his reply? Why, he said that the violin was the noblest instrument invented by man. Having silenced her with this solid premise he declared that it followed that any boy was lucky to be given the privilege of learning to play it. No boy should expect to learn it immediately. It required persistence. Everything, he had found, required persistence. The motto was, Never give up.

All his life, he declared, he had persevered in spite of discouragement, and he meant to keep on persevering, and he meant me to, too. He said that none of us realized what he had had to go through. If he had been the kind that gave up at the very first obstacle, where would he have been now – where would any of the family have been? The answer was, apparently, that we'd either have been in a very bad way, poking round for crusts in the gutter, or else nonexistent. We might have never even been born if Father had not persevered.

Placed beside this record of Father's vast trials overcome, the little difficulty of my learning to play the violin seemed a trifle. I faithfully spurred myself on again, to work at the puzzle. Even my teacher seemed impressed with these views on persistence. Though older than Father, he had certainly not made as much money, and he bowed to the experience of a practical man who was a success. If he, Herr M., had been a success he would not have had to teach boys; and sitting in this black pit in which his need of money had placed him, he saw more than ever that he must learn the ways of this world. He listened with all his heart, as to a god, when Father shook his forefinger, and told him how to climb to the heights where financial rewards were achieved. The idea he got was that perseverance was sure to lead to great wealth.

Consequently our front basement continued to be the home of lost causes.

Of course, I kept begging Herr M. to let me learn just one tune. Even though I seldom would whistle them, still I liked tunes; and I knew that, in my hours of practicing, a tune would be a comfort. That is, for myself. Here again I never gave a thought to the effect upon others.

Herr M., after many misgivings, to which I respectfully listened – though they were not spoken to me, they were muttered to himself, pessimistically – hunted through a worn old book of selections, and after much doubtful fumbling chose as simple a thing as he could find for me – for me and the neighbors.

It was spring now, and windows were open. That tune became famous.

What would the musician who had tenderly composed this air, years before, have felt if he had foreseen what an end it would have, on Madison Avenue; and how, before death, it would be execrated by that once peaceful neighborhood. I engraved it on their hearts; not in its true form but in my own eerie versions. It was the only tune I knew. Consequently I played and replayed it.

Even horrors when repeated grow old and lose part of their sting. But those I produced were, unluckily, never the same. To be sure, this tune kept its general structure the same, even in my sweating hands. There was always the place where I climbed unsteadily up to its peak, and that difficult spot where it wavered, or staggered, and stuck; and then a sudden jerk of resumption – I came out strong on that. Every afternoon when I got to that difficult spot, the neighbors dropped whatever they were doing to wait for that jerk, shrinking from the moment, and yet feverishly impatient for it to come.

But what made the tune and their anguish so different each day? I'll explain. The strings of a violin are wound at the end around pegs, and each peg must be screwed in and tightened till the string sounds just right. Herr M. left my violin properly tuned when he went. But suppose a string broke, or that somehow I jarred a peg loose. Its string then became slack and soundless. I had to re-tighten it. Not having an ear, I was highly uncertain about this.

Our neighbors never knew at what degree of tautness I'd put such a string. I didn't myself. I just screwed her up tight enough to make a strong reliable sound. Neither they nor I could tell which string would thus appear in a new role each day, nor foresee the profound trans-formations this would produce in that tune.

All that spring this unhappy and ill-destined melody floated out through my window, and writhed in the air for one hour daily, in sunshine or storm. All that spring our neighbors and I daily toiled to its peak, and staggered over its hump, so to speak, and fell wailing through space.

Things now began to be said to Mother which drove her to act. She explained to Father that the end had come at last. Absolutely. 'This awful nightmare cannot go on,' she said.

Father pooh-poohed her.

She cried. She told him what it was doing to her. He said that she was excited, and that her descriptions of the sounds I made were exaggerated and hysterical – must be. She was always too vehement, he shouted. She must learn to be calm.

'But you're downtown, *you* don't have to hear it!'

Father remained wholly skeptical.

She endeavored to shame him. She told him what awful things the neighbors were saying about him, because of the noise I was making, for which he was responsible.

He couldn't be made to look at it that way. If there really were any unpleasantness then I was responsible. He had provided me with a good teacher and a good violin – so he reasoned. In short, he had done his best, and no father could have done more. If I made hideous sounds after all that, the fault must be mine. He said that Mother should be stricter with me, if necessary, and make me try harder.

This was the last straw. I couldn't try harder. When Mother told me his verdict I said nothing, but my body rebelled. Self-discipline had its limits – and I wanted to be out: it was spring. I skimped my hours of practice when I heard the fellows playing outside. I came home late for lessons – even forgot them. Little by little they stopped.

Father was outraged. His final argument, I remember, was that my violin had cost twenty-five dollars; if I didn't learn it the money would be wasted, and he couldn't afford it. But it was put to him that my younger brother, Julian, could learn it instead, later on. Then summer came, anyhow, and we went for three months to the seashore;

In the autumn little Julian was led away one afternoon, and imprisoned in the front basement in my place. I don't remember how long they kept him down there, but it was several years. He had an ear, however, and I believe he learned to play fairly well. This would have made a happy ending for Herr M. after all; but it was some other teacher, a younger man, who was engaged to teach Julian. Father said Herr M. was a failure.

Alastair Reid

A Lesson in Music

Play the tune again: but this time
with more regard for the movement at the source of it
and less attention to time. Time falls
curiously in the course of it.

Play the tune again: not watching
your fingering, but forgetting, letting flow
the sound till it surrounds you. Do not count
or even think. Let go.

Play the tune again: but try to be
nobody, nothing, as though the pace
of the sound were your heart beating, as though
the music were your face.

Play the tune again. It should be easier
to think less every time of the notes, of the measure.
It is all an arrangement of silence. Be silent, and then
play it for your pleasure.

Play the tune again; and this time, when it ends,
do not ask me what I think. Feel what is happening
strangely in the room as the sound glooms over
you, me, everything.

Now,
play the tune again.

Yehudi Menuhin

Learning the Violin

From *Unfinished Journey*

With my newly purchased instrument in hand, I was first trotted off to a neighborhood teacher whose reputation depended on a sign board, 'Violin Lessons,' hung over the entrance to his ramshackle house. Up the dark stairs we went, Imma and I, only to be driven down again by the dust and decay, the old man's winy breath and the tobacco fumes, at the top. If there was a lesson or two before we beat our retreat, they have left no trace in my memory. Our second approach was to Louis Persinger, possibly less in recognition of my original request than because, having seen the worst, Imma could be satisfied only with the best. Cantor Rinder duly sang my praises, but Persinger had heard that song sung in all its variations by doting friends and parents and had grown deaf to it. Four-year-old beginners offered no rewards to his full and busy life. Between worst and best the compromise, where I then came to rest, was the studio of the local Svengali, Sigmund Anker, who, with the techniques of a drill sergeant, transformed boys and girls into virtuosi by the batch.

Anker's business in life was to groom the young to brilliant performance of Sarasate and Tchaikovsky, and as far as I can gather from dim memories of those distant days, he had neither capacity nor ambition for anything more subtle. He knew nothing of style, the classics, chamber music; more fundamentally, he knew nothing of the process of violin playing, or if he did, lacked the skill to pass his knowledge on. Not that he was alone in his darkness, for violin teaching was altogether a hit-and-miss activity then, as indeed it still too largely is. Anker's method was to set up a target – correct intonation, full round tone, or whatever – and whip his pupils toward it by unexplained command. The result was that one taught or failed to teach oneself, as one had earlier learned to walk and talk mainly by self-instruction; but violin playing being more complex than such inbuilt human skills, an illumination beyond what one's own nerves and muscles could supply would have been gratefully received.

At the outset merely holding the violin, at arm's length, very tightly, lest it fall (or recoil), seemed problem enough; where did one find a second pair of arms to play it? I was invited to fly; I answered by hanging on for dear life. Where the left hand, in the 'golden mean' position, should form spirals round the neck of the instrument (as the right hand does around the bow), mine pinioned it between thumb and the base of my first finger. Where the digits should arch softly over the fingerboard, each muscularly independent of the others, mine – all but the smallest, which drooped behind – cleaved to one another like three parade ponies, moving *en masse* from one positional rung to another up the chromatic ladder as if they found safety in numbers. Where the violin should lie on the collarbone, secured there by the head's natural but delicate weight, I clamped it tight. Where the right hand (and by extension the wrist, elbow, arm, scapula) and the bow function rather as the wheel and axis of a gyroscope, the former rotating in order to keep the latter on a true course, I sawed a straight line and, on every downstroke, swerved or 'turned the corner' (to make matters worse, the bow was too long for me). At crucial points where sound should have vibrated freely, it was hopelessly grounded. These abominations were so many symptoms of my ignorance of the violin's nature, an ignorance which clearly was not going to be corrected by the explanations of a third party, but only by personal exploration. The gyres, the pendular swings, the waves required by an instrument that itself forms one continuous curve, I had to teach myself, and could do so the more easily perhaps for inhabiting my own absolute space, for lacking the linear perspective that relates people to one another, for feeling in circles.

After six months I had made remarkably little progress. Mr. Anker would bode the worst, having expected the best, Imma would report his diminishing hopes, Aba would fall silent, and I felt like a terminal case bandied by future pallbearers. Then, for no reason I could explain, the violin began to lose its foreignness, my grip relaxed, my body discovered the freedom to forget itself, and I could enjoy what I was doing. I was at last launched. At this distance what I recall most clearly is my conquest of vibrato. To teach vibrato, Anker would shout, 'Vibrate! Vibrate!' with never a clue given as to how to do it. Indeed I would have obeyed him if I could. I longed to achieve vibrato, for what use was a violin to a little boy of Russian-Jewish background who could not bring a note to throbbing life? As with my struggle to roll an *r*, the problem was not to imagine the sound so much as to produce it; but vibrato proved a more elusive skill. I had already left Anker's tutelage and was perhaps six or seven years old when, lo and behold, one bright day my muscles had solved the puzzle. By such strokes of illumination, the solution proving as mysterious as the problem and leaving one almost as blind as before, most violinists learned their craft. (The quest to perfect vibrato was to last for many years yet. Even when I was regularly performing in public as a boy, my vibrato was never very fast, and it wasn't until, as an adult, I undertook to unpick the mechanics of the operation and put them together again that I really began to satisfy myself.)

Once a year at the Fairmont Hotel, Anker's budding virtuosi gave a concert, half display, half competition, to their friends and relations. My turn came in November 1921, when I played a little piece called 'Remembrance' and was placed second, to my slight chagrin. I have not the world's best memory for names, but I recall my successful rival to this day, a girl of twelve called Sarah Kreindler, whose performance of Sarasate's 'Gypsy Airs' justly merited first place. My early champion, Reuben Rinder, was in the audience and gave me a book, perhaps a prize for doing well, more probably a consolation prize for not having done better. This first public appearance was a milestone in more ways than one: it marked the end of the Sigmund Anker era. Either because Imma had concluded he had no more to offer me or, quite possibly, because I hadn't managed to play better than Sarah Kreindler, she contacted Louis Persinger again. What extra persuasions were used, I have no idea, but this time he agreed to take me on.

Fleur Adcock

Piano Concerto in E Flat Major

In her 1930s bob or even, perhaps,
if she saw something quainter as her fashion,
long thick hair in a plait, the music student
showed her composition to her tutor;
and she aroused, or this enhanced, his passion.

He quoted from it in his new concerto,
offering back to her as homage
those several bars of hers the pianist plays
in the second movement: part of what she dreamed
re-translated, marked more with his image.

But the seven steady notes of the main theme
are his alone. Did the romance go well?
Whether he married her's recorded somewhere
in books. The wistful strings, the determined
percussion, the English cadences, don't tell.

Katherine Mansfield

The Singing Lesson

With despair – cold, sharp despair – buried deep in her heart like a
wicked knife, Miss Meadows, in cap and gown and carrying a little
baton, trod the cold corridors that led to the music hall. Girls of all
ages, rosy from the air, and bubbling over with that gleeful excitement
that comes from running to school on a fine autumn morning,
hurried, skipped, fluttered by; from the hollow classrooms came a
quick drumming of voices; a bell rang; a voice like a bird cried,
'Muriel.' And then there came from the staircase a tremendous
knock-knock-knocking. Someone had dropped her dumbbells.

The Science Mistress stopped Miss Meadows.

'Good mor-ning,' she cried, in her sweet, affected drawl. 'Isn't it
cold? It might be win-ter.'

Miss Meadows, hugging the knife, stared in hatred at the Science
Mistress. Everything about her was sweet, pale, like honey. You
would not have been surprised to see a bee caught in the tangles of that
yellow hair.

'It is rather sharp,' said Miss Meadows, grimly.

The other smiled her sugary smile.

'You look fro-zen,' said she. Her blue eyes opened wide; there came
a mocking light in them. (Had she noticed anything?)

'Oh, not quite as bad as that,' said Miss Meadows, and she gave the
Science Mistress, in exchange for her smile, a quick grimace and
passed on . . .

Forms Four, Five, and Six were assembled in the music hall. The noise
was deafening. On the platform, by the piano, stood Mary Beazley, Miss
Meadows' favourite, who played accompaniments. She was turning the
music stool. When she saw Miss Meadows she gave a loud, warning 'Sh-
sh! girls!' and Miss Meadows, her hands thrust in her sleeves, the baton
under her arm, strode down the centre aisle, mounted the steps, turned
sharply, seized the brass music stand, planted it in front of her, and gave
two sharp taps with her baton for silence.

'Silence, please! Immediately!' and, looking at nobody, her glance
swept over that sea of coloured flannel blouses, with bobbing pink
faces and hands, quivering butterfly hair-bows, and music-books
outspread. She knew perfectly well what they were thinking. 'Meady
is in a wax.' Well, let them think it! Her eyelids quivered; she tossed
her head, defying them. What could the thoughts of those creatures
matter to someone who stood there bleeding to death, pierced to the
heart, to the heart, by such a letter –

. . . 'I feel more and more strongly that our marriage would be a mistake. Not that I do not love you. I love you as much as it is possible for me to love any woman, but, truth to tell, I have come to the conclusion that I am not a marrying man, and the idea of settling down fills me with nothing but – ' and the word 'disgust' was scratched out lightly and 'regret' written over the top.

Basil! Miss Meadows stalked over to the piano. And Mary Beazley, who was waiting for this moment, bent forward; her curls fell over her cheeks while she breathed, 'Good morning, Miss Meadows,' and she motioned towards rather than handed to her mistress a beautiful yellow chrysanthemum. This little ritual of the flower had been gone through for ages and ages, quite a term and a half. It was as much part of the lesson as opening the piano. But this morning, instead of taking it up, instead of tucking it into her belt while she leant over Mary and said, 'Thank you, Mary. How very nice! Turn to page thirty-two,' what was Mary's horror when Miss Meadows totally ignored the chrysanthemum, made no reply to her greeting, but said in a voice of ice, 'Page fourteen, please, and mark the accents well.'

Staggering moment! Mary blushed until the tears stood in her eyes, but Miss Meadows was gone back to the music stand; her voice rang through the music hall.

'Page fourteen. We will begin with page fourteen. "A Lament". Now, girls, you ought to know it by this time. We shall take it all together; not in parts, all together. And without expression. Sing it, though, quite simply, beating time with the left hand.'

She raised the baton; she tapped the music stand twice. Down came Mary on the opening chord; down came all those left hands, beating the air, and in chimed those young, mournful voices:

> Fast! Ah, too Fast Fade the Ro-o-ses of Pleasure;
> Soon Autumn yields unto Wi-i-nter Drear.
> Fleetly! Ah, Fleetly Mu-u-sic's Gay Measure
> Passes away from the Listening Ear.

Good Heavens, what could be more tragic than that lament! Every note was a sigh, a sob, a groan of awful mournfulness. Miss Meadows lifted her arms in the wide gown and began conducting with both hands. '. . . I feel more and more strongly that our marriage would be a mistake . . .' she beat. And the voices cried: *Fleetly! Ah, Fleetly.* What could have possessed him to write such a letter! What could have led up to it! It came out of nothing. His last letter had been all about a fumed-oak bookcase he had bought for 'our' books, and a 'natty little hall-stand' he had seen, 'a very neat affair with a carved owl on a bracket, holding three hat-brushes in its claws'. How she had smiled at that! So like a man to think one needed three hat-brushes! *From the Listening Ear*, sang the voices.

'Once again,' said Miss Meadows. 'But this time in parts. Still without expression.' *Fast! Ah, too Fast.* With the gloom of the contraltos added, one could scarcely help shuddering. *Fade the Roses of Pleasure.* Last time he had come to see her, Basil had worn a rose in his buttonhole. How handsome he had looked in that bright blue suit, with that dark red rose! And he knew it, too. He couldn't help knowing it. First he stroked his hair, then his moustache; his teeth gleamed when he smiled.

'The headmaster's wife keeps on asking me to dinner. It's a perfect nuisance. I never get an evening to myself in that place.'

'But can't you refuse?'

'Oh, well, it doesn't do for a man in my position to be unpopular.'

Music's Gay Measure, wailed the voices. The willow trees, outside the high, narrow windows, waved in the wind. They had lost half their leaves. The tiny ones that clung wriggled like fishes caught on a line. '. . . I am not a marrying man . . .' The voices were silent; the piano waited.

'Quite good,' said Miss Meadows, but still in such a strange, stony tone that the younger girls began to feel positively frightened. 'But now that we know it, we shall take it with expression. As much expression as you can put into it. Think of the words, girls. Use your imaginations. *Fast! Ah, too Fast*,' cried Miss Meadows. 'That ought to break out – a loud, strong *forte* – a lament. And then in the second line, *Winter Drear*, make that *drear* sound as if a cold wind were blowing through it. *Dre-ear!*' said she so awfully that Mary Beazley, on the music stool, wriggled her spine. 'The third line should be one crescendo. *Fleetly! Ah, Fleetly Music's Gay Measure.* Breaking on the first word of the last line, *Passes.* And then on the word, *Away,* you must begin to die . . . to fade . . . until *The Listening Ear* is nothing more than a faint whisper . . . You can slow down as much as you like almost on the last line. Now, please.'

Again the two light taps; she lifted her arms again. *Fast! Ah, too Fast.* '. . . and the idea of settling down fills me with nothing but disgust – ' Disgust was what he had written. That was as good as to say their engagement was definitely broken off. Broken off! Their engagement! People had been surprised enough that she had got engaged. The Science Mistress would not believe it at first. But nobody had been as surprised as she. She was thirty. Basil was twenty-five. It had been a miracle, simply a miracle, to hear him say, as they walked home from church that very dark night, 'You know, somehow or other, I've got fond of you.' And he had taken hold of the end of her ostrich feather boa. *Passes away from the Listening Ear.*

'Repeat! Repeat!' said Miss Meadows. 'More expression, girls! Once more!'

Fast! Ah, too Fast. The older girls were crimson; some of the younger ones began to cry. Big spots of rain blew against the windows, and one could hear the willows whispering, '. . . not that I do not love you . . .'

'But, my darling, if you love me,' thought Miss Meadows, 'I don't mind how much it is. Love me as little as you like.' But she knew he didn't love her. Not to have cared enough to scratch out that word 'disgust', so that she couldn't read it! *Soon Autumn yields unto Winter Drear.* She would have to leave the school, too. She could never face the Science Mistress or the girls after it got known. She would have to disappear somewhere. *Passes away.* The voices began to die, to fade, to whisper . . . to vanish . . .

Suddenly the door opened. A little girl in blue walked fussily up the aisle, hanging her head, biting her lips, and twisting the silver bangle on her red little wrist. She came up the steps and stood before Miss Meadows.

'Well, Monica, what is it?'

'Oh, if you please, Miss Meadows,' said the little girl, gasping, 'Miss Wyatt wants to see you in the mistresses' room.'

'Very well,' said Miss Meadows. And she called to the girls, 'I shall put you on your honour to talk quietly while I am away.' But they were too subdued to do anything else. Most of them were blowing their noses.

The corridors were silent and cold; they echoed to Miss Meadows' steps. The head mistress sat at her desk. For a moment she did not look up. She was as usual disentangling her eyeglasses, which had got caught in her lace tie. 'Sit down, Miss Meadows,' she said very kindly. And then she picked up a pink envelope from the blotting-pad. 'I sent for you just now because this telegram has come for you.'

'A telegram for me, Miss Wyatt?'

Basil! He had committed suicide, decided Miss Meadows. Her hand flew out, but Miss Wyatt held the telegram back a moment. 'I hope it's not bad news,' she said, no more than kindly. And Miss Meadows tore it open.

'Pay no attention to letter must have been mad bought hat-stand to-day Basil,' she read. She couldn't take her eyes off the telegram.

'I do hope it's nothing very serious,' said Miss Wyatt, leaning forward.

'Oh, no, thank you, Miss Wyatt,' blushed Miss Meadows. 'It's nothing bad at all. It's' – and she gave an apologetic little laugh –

'it's from my *fiancé* saying that . . . saying that – ' There was a pause.

'I *see*,' said Miss Wyatt. And another pause. Then – 'You've fifteen minutes more of your class, Miss Meadows, haven't you?'

'Yes, Miss Wyatt.' She got up. She half ran towards the door.

'Oh, just one minute, Miss Meadows,' said Miss Wyatt. 'I must say I don't approve of my teachers having telegrams sent to them in school hours, unless in case of very bad news, such as death,' explained Miss Wyatt, 'or a very serious accident, or something to that effect. Good news, Miss Meadows, will always keep, you know.'

On the wings of hope, of love, of joy, Miss Meadows sped back to the music hall, up the aisle, up the steps, over to the piano.

'Page thirty-two, Mary,' she said, 'page thirty-two,' and, picking up the yellow chrysanthemum, she held it to her lips to hide her smile. Then she turned to the girls, rapped with her baton: 'Page thirty-two, girls. Page thirty-two.'

> We come here To-day with Flowers o'erladen,
> With Baskets of Fruit and Ribbons to boot,
> To-oo Congratulate. . . .

'Stop! Stop!' cried Miss Meadows. 'This is awful. This is dreadful.' And she beamed at her girls. 'What's the matter with you all? Think, girls, think of what you're singing. Use your imaginations. *With Flowers o'erladen. Baskets of Fruit and Ribbons to boot.* And *Congratulate.*' Miss Meadows broke off. 'Don't look so doleful, girls. It ought to sound warm, joyful, eager. *Congratulate.* Once more. Quickly. All together. Now then!'

And this time Miss Meadows' voice sounded over all the other voices – full, deep, glowing with expression.

For St Cecilia's Day

John Dryden

A Song for St Cecilia's Day

From harmony, from heavenly harmony
　　This universal frame began:
　　When Nature underneath a heap
　　　Of jarring atoms lay,
　　And could not heave her head,
The tuneful voice was heard from high:
　　　'Arise, ye more than dead.'
Then cold, and hot, and moist, and dry,
　　In order to their stations leap,
　　　And Music's power obey.
From harmony, from heavenly harmony
　　This universal frame began:
　　　From harmony to harmony
Through all the compass of the notes it ran,
The diapason closing full in Man.

What passion cannot Music raise and quell?
　　When Jubal struck the corded shell,
　　His listening brethren stood around,
　　　And, wondering, on their faces fell
　　To worship that celestial sound:
Less than a god they thought there could not
　　dwell
　　　Within the hollow of that shell
　　　That spoke so sweetly and so well.
What passion cannot Music raise and quell?

　　The Trumpet's loud clangour
　　　Excites us to arms,
　　With shrill notes of anger
　　　And mortal alarms.
　　The double double double beat
　　　Of the thundering Drum
　　　Cries: 'Hark! the foes come;
Charge, charge, 'tis too late to retreat.'

　　The soft complaining Flute
　　In dying notes discovers
　　The woes of hopeless lovers,
Whose dirge is whispered by the warbling
　　　Lute.

Sharp Violins proclaim
Their jealous pangs, and desperation,
Fury, frantic indignation,
Depths of pains, and height of passion,
    For the fair, disdainful dame.

    But O! what art can teach,
    What human voice can reach,
        The sacred Organ's praise?
    Notes inspiring holy love,
Notes that wing their heavenly ways
    To mend the choirs above.

Orpheus could lead the savage race;
And trees unrooted left their place,
        Sequacious of the lyre;
But bright Cecilia raised the wonder higher:
When to her organ vocal breath was given,
An angel heard and straight appeared,
        Mistaking earth for heaven.

            Grand Chorus
        As from the power of sacred lays
            The spheres began to move,
        And sung the great Creator's praise
            To all the Blest above;
        So, when the last and dreadful hour
        This crumbling pageant shall devour,
        The Trumpet shall be heard on high,
        The dead shall live, the living die,
        And Music shall untune the sky.

Alexander Pope

Ode on St Cecilia's Day

MDCCVIII

I

Descend, ye Nine! descend and sing;
　The breathing instruments inspire,
Wake into voice each silent string,
　And sweep the sounding lyre!
　　In a sadly-pleasing strain
　　Let the warbling lute complain;
　　　Let the loud trumpet sound,
　　　Till the roofs all around
　　　The shrill echoes rebound:
While in more lengthen'd notes and slow,
The deep, majestic, solemn organs blow.
　　　Hark! the numbers soft and clear
　　　Gently steal upon the ear;
　　　Now louder, and yet louder rise,
　　　And fill with spreading sounds the skies;
Exulting in triumph now swell the bold notes,
In broken air, trembling, the wild music floats;
　　　Till, by degrees, remote and small,
　　　　The strains decay,
　　　　And melt away,
　　　In a dying, dying fall.

II

By music, minds an equal temper know,
　Nor swell too high, nor sink too low.
If in the breast tumultuous joys arise,
Music her soft, assuasive voice applies;
　Or, when the soul is press'd with cares,
　Exalts her in enlivening airs.
Warriors she fires with animated sounds;
Pours balm into the bleeding lover's wounds:
　　Melancholy lifts her head.
　　Morpheus rouses from his bed,
　　Sloth unfolds her arms and wakes,
　　Listening Envy drops her snakes;
Intestine war no more our passions wage,
And giddy factions hear away their rage.

III

But when our country's cause provokes to arms,
How martial music every bosom warms!
So when the first bold vessel dared the seas,
High on the stern the Thracian raised his strain,
    While Argo saw her kindred trees
      Descend from Pelion to the main.
    Transported demi-gods stood round,
    And men grew heroes at the sound,
      Inflam'd with glory's charms:
Each chief his sevenfold shield display'd,
And half unsheath'd the shining blade,
And seas, and rocks, and skies rebound,
'To arms, to arms, to arms!'

IV

But when through all the infernal bounds,
Which flaming Phlegethon surrounds,
    Love, strong as Death, the Poet led
    To the pale nations of the dead,
    What sounds were heard,
    What scenes appear'd,
      O'er all the dreary coasts!
        Dreadful gleams,
        Dismal screams,
        Fires that glow,
        Shrieks of woe,
        Sullen moans,
        Hollow groans,
    And cries of tortured ghosts!
But, hark! he strikes the golden lyre:
And see! the tortured ghosts respire.
    See shady forms advance!
    Thy stone, O Sisyphus, stands still,
    Ixion rests upon his wheel,
      And the pale spectres dance!
The Furies sink upon their iron beds,
And snakes uncurl'd hang listening round their heads.

V

'By the streams that ever flow,
By the fragrant winds that blow
    O'er the Elysian flowers;
By those happy souls who dwell
In yellow meads of Asphodel,
    Or Amaranthine bowers;
By the hero's armed shades,
Glittering through the gloomy glades;
By the youths that died for love,
Wandering in the myrtle grove,
Restore, restore Eurydice to life:
O take the husband, or return the wife!'
    He sung, and hell consented
        To hear the Poet's prayer:
    Stern Proserpine relented,
        And gave him back the fair.
        Thus song could prevail
        O'er death, and o'er hell,
A conquest how hard and how glorious:
        Though fate had fast bound her
        With Styx nine times round her,
Yet music and love were victorious.

VI

But soon, too soon, the lover turns his eyes:
Again she falls, again she dies, she dies!
How wilt thou now the fatal sisters move?
No crime was thine, if 'tis no crime to love.
    Now under hanging mountains,
    Beside the falls of fountains,
    Or where Hebrus wanders,
    Rolling in meanders,
        All alone,
        Unheard, unknown,
        He makes his moan;
        And calls her ghost,
For ever, ever, ever lost!
Now with Furies surrounded,
Despairing, confounded,
He trembles, he glows,

Amidst Rhodope's snows:
See, wild as the winds, o'er the desert he flies;
Hark! Haemus resounds with the Bacchanals' cries –
                            Ah see, he dies!

Yet ev'n in death Eurydice he sung,
Eurydice still trembled on his tongue,
        Eurydice the woods,
        Eurydice the floods,
Eurydice the rocks, and hollow mountains rung.

VII

Music the fiercest grief can charm,
And fate's severest rage disarm:
    Music can soften pain to ease.
    And make despair and madness please:
    Our joys below it can improve,
    And antedate the bliss above.
This the divine Cecilia found,
And to her Maker's praise confined the sound.
When the full organ joins the tuneful quire,
    Th' immortal powers incline their ear;
Borne on the swelling notes our souls aspire,
While solemn airs improve the sacred fire;
    And Angels lean from heaven to hear.
Of Orpheus now no more let Poets tell,
    To bright Cecilia greater power is given;
His numbers raised a shade from hell,
    Hers lift the soul to heaven.

W.H. Auden

From *Song for St Cecilia's Day*

In a garden shady this holy lady
With reverent cadence and subtle psalm,
Like a black swan as death came on
Poured forth her song in perfect calm:
And by ocean's margin this innocent virgin
Constructed an organ to enlarge her prayer,
And notes tremendous from her great engine
Thundered out on the Roman air.

Blonde Aphrodite rose up excited,
Moved to delight by the melody,
White as an orchid she rode quite naked
In an oyster shell on top of the sea;
At sounds so entrancing the angels dancing
Came out of their trance into time again,
And around the wicked in Hell's abysses
The huge flame flickered and eased their pain.

Blessed Cecilia, appear in visions
To all musicians, appear and inspire:
Translated Daughter, come down and startle
Composing mortals with immortal fire.

Notes and
Acknowledgements

Dannie Abse's 'Three Street Musicians' is taken from his *Collected Poems* (Hutchinson, 1977).

Fleur Adcock was born in New Zealand in 1934 and has lived and worked in England since 1963. 'Piano Concerto in E Flat Major' comes from her *Selected Poems* (Oxford University Press, 1983).

Sholom Aleichem is the pseudonym of Solomon Rabinowitz, a Yiddish humorous writer who was born in the Ukraine in 1859, and died in New York in 1916. He wrote in Yiddish, Hebrew and Russian. 'The Fiddle' appeared in a collection *The Old Country* translated by Frances and Julius Butwin (Crown Publishers, Inc., 1946).

W.H. Auden (1907 – 73) was a major British poet. He was a great opera lover and, indeed, wrote several libretti in collaboration with Chester Kallman, among them Stravinsky's *The Rake's Progress*. 'The Composer' is to be found with many other memorable and exciting pieces in his *Collected Poems* (Faber and Faber, 1976). Both this poem and the extract from 'Song for St. Cecilia's Day' are reprinted by permission of Faber and Faber.

Ludwig van Beethoven was born in Bonn in 1770, and died in Vienna in 1827. Deafness began to afflict him before he was thirty. By 1819 he was totally deaf but many of his greatest masterpieces were composed during this period. 'The Heiligenstadt Testament' was written for his brothers in 1802. It is here translated by Michael Hamburger and comes from *Beethoven, Letters, Journals, Conversations* edited by him (Thames and Hudson, 1951).

Gottfried Benn (1886 – 1956) was born near West Berlin. Benn became a doctor as well as a poet. He is still a controversial figure, for at one time he had Nazi sympathies. His 'Chopin' is taken from *Primal Vision* (Marion Boyars, 1976).

Hector Berlioz was born near Grenoble in 1803, and died in Paris in 1869. Berlioz' *Mémoires*, from which two extracts have been chosen, engaged him intermittently and in various forms for many years and were not finally published until 1870, the year after his death. They make compulsive and rewarding reading.

Wolfgang Borchert was born in Hamburg 1921, and died in Basle in 1947. A private in the German army invading Russia, Borchert was wounded in 1942. Subsequently he spent six months in solitary confinement for views expressed in letters. In 1944 he served on the Russian front again and was again imprisoned. 'Lots and Lots of Snow' comes from *The Man Outside*, a collection published in Germany in 1947 and in Britain (by Hutchinson) in 1952.

Alfred Brendel was born in 1931. A pianist of great international renown he now lives in London. 'Coping with Pianos' comes from his *Musical Thoughts and Afterthoughts* (Robson Books, 1976).

Elizabeth Barrett Browning (1806 – 61) might well have become the first British woman Poet Laureate when Wordsworth died in 1850 had Tennyson not been available!

Robert Browning (1812 – 89) wrote a number of poems about music among them 'Abt Vogler', 'Master Hugues of Saxe-Gotha' and 'A Toccata of Galuppi's' which we have included here.

Elias Canetti was born in Bulgaria in 1905. He moved to England when he was six and later lived in Vienna, Switzerland, France, Germany and England again. 'The Orchestral Conductor' is a section from his book *Crowds and Power* (Gollancz, 1962). Canetti was awarded the Nobel Prize for Literature in 1981.

Thomas Carlyle was born in Ecclefechan, Scotland, in 1795, and died in London in 1881. The essay 'Opera' was first published in the magazine, *The Keepsake*, in 1852, Carlyle humorously proposing it to the editor as 'a bit of an Excerpt from that singular *Conspectus of England*, lately written, not yet printed, by Professor Ezechiel Peasemeal, a distinguished American friend of mine'.

Pablo Casals was born in Catalonia in 1876, and died in 1973. A world famous cellist, he was noted also for his opposition to the Franco régime in Spain. The piece here comes from *Joys and Sorrows* (Macdonald, 1970).

Amy Clampitt is an American whose poem 'Sunday Music' is taken from her first book of poems *The Kingfisher* and which is reprinted by permission of Faber and Faber Ltd.

S.T. Coleridge (1772 – 1834) was a celebrated English poet, essayist and literary critic.

Iain Crichton Smith is a Scots poet, born 1928. His *Selected Poems* were published (by Gollancz) in 1970.

Roald Dahl was born in 1916 at Cardiff, South Wales, of Norwegian parentage. He began writing short stores in 1942 when he was an assistant air attaché in Washington. 'Edward the Conqueror' first appeared in his collection *Kiss Kiss* and subsequently in *The Best of Roald Dahl* (Michael Joseph and Penguin Books).

Clarence Day (1874 – 1935) is best known for his humorous, autobiographical sketches. *Life with Father*, from which 'The Noblest Instrument' comes, was the most successful. When *Life with Father* was dramatized in 1939 it had over 3,000 performances.

Cecil Day Lewis (1904 – 72) was born in Ireland of Anglo-Irish parentage. He was named Poet Laureate in 1968. He worked for many years as literary adviser for his publisher Chatto and Windus. 'Cornet Solo' is taken from *Collected Poems* (Hogarth Press 1954) with permission from the Executors of the Estate of C. Day Lewis and Jonathan Cape Ltd.

John Dryden (1631 – 1700) was an English poet and dramatist. His 'A Song for St Cecilia's Day' rather makes nonsense of Matthew Arnold's remark: 'Dryden and Pope are not classics of our poetry, they are classics of our prose.'

Ralph Ellison was born in 1914. A black American writer, he is famed for his extraordinary novel, *The Invisible Man*, published in 1952. 'Living with Music' comes from a collection of autobiographical essays *Shadow and Act* (Random House, 1964). Acknowledgements are also owed to William Morris (U.K.) Ltd.

D.J. Enright was born in 1920 in Leamington, England. His *Collected Poems* in a revised and enlarged edition has recently been published by Oxford University Press. Acknowledgements are also owed to Watson, Little Ltd.

John Fuller, English poet and novelist, was born in 1937. His *Selected Poems 1954 – 1982* was published (by Secker and Warburg) in 1985.

Valerie Gillies was born in Canada in 1948, grew up in Scotland and lived for a time in India. She is at present domiciled in Scotland again. 'The Piano Tuner' is taken from *Each Bright Eye* (Canongate, 1977).

Tito Gobbi was a great opera singer who made his debut in Rome in 1938. 'Remembering Callas' comes from *My Life* (Doubleday, 1980). He died in 1984.

Giles Gordon was born in Edinburgh in 1940. He has written several novels and collections of short stories and worked as publisher, literary agent and theatre critic. 'Maestro' comes from *The Illusionist* (Harvester Press, 1978).

Michael Hamburger, poet and translator, was born in Berlin in 1924 and emigrated to England in 1933. His *Collected Poems* was published in 1984 by Carcanet and he was awarded the European Translation Prize in May 1985.

Thomas Hardy (1840 – 1928) wrote *Under the Greenwood Tree*, from which an extract here is chosen, in 1872 and drew on the experiences of his father and grandfather as members of a local church choir. Hardy wrote a number of poems on musical themes. In his youth he himself was an ardent fiddle player.

John Heath-Stubbs was born in London in 1918. His *Collected Poems* was published (by Carcanet) in 1988.

Heinrich Heine (1797 – 1856) was born in Dusseldorf and died in Paris. This tale concerning Paganini is the most celebrated of his collection *Florentine Nights*, published in 1837.

George Herbert (1593 – 1633) was one of the most revered British poets of the seventeenth century and was also an enthusiastic musician. He described the singing at Salisbury Cathedral as 'Heaven upon earth'.

Charles Lamb (1775 – 1834): it was said of him that 'no better purifier of Taste ever lived than Charles Lamb'. Would music-lovers agree?

Philip Larkin was born in Coventry in 1922, and died in 1985. Currently he is one of Britain's most popular poets. A volume of essays, *Required Writing*, 1983, included a selection of jazz-record reviews written for the *Daily Telegraph* between 1960 and 1968. The extract 'The Pleasure of Jazz' is taken from *Required Writing* and the poem 'Broadcast' from *Whitsun Weddings* both published by Faber and Faber and reprinted here with their permission.

D.H. Lawrence (1885 – 1930). His fame as a novelist tends to overshadow the fact that he is one of the major British poets of the twentieth century.

Bernard Levin, born in 1928, is a writer and broadcaster noted for his incisive comment on politics, the arts and other human activities. 'The Year of the Missing Lemon Juice' comes from *Conducted Tour* (Jonathan Cape, 1981).

Federico García Lorca (1898 – 1936) was a Spanish poet and dramatist born in Andalusia and murdered by the Nationalists soon after the outbreak of the Civil War. 'The Guitar' was translated by G.L. Gili and Stephen Spender and published in *Selected Poems* (Hogarth Press, 1943).

Louis MacNeice (1907 – 63) was born in Belfast. MacNeice worked for the BBC for many years. 'Street Scene' is reprinted by permission of Faber and Faber Ltd from *The Collected Poems of Louis MacNeice*.

Thomas Mann was born in Lübeck in 1875, and died in Switzerland in 1955. 'The Infant Prodigy' is taken from his collection *Stories of a Lifetime*. Mann was awarded the Nobel Prize for Literature in 1929.

Katherine Mansfield was born in Wellington, New Zealand, in 1888, and died in Fontainebleau in 1923. After being educated in London, 1903 – 6, she studied music in New Zealand for two years but soon returned to London and devoted herself to writing. 'The Singing Lesson' first appeared in *The Garden Party and Other Stories* in 1922.

Felix Mendelssohn was born in Hamburg in 1809, and died in Leipzig in 1847. 'Mendelssohn at Buckingham Palace' derives from a letter Mendelssohn wrote to his mother on 19 July 1842 while on a visit to England. An earlier visit to Scotland had resulted in his *Hebrides* overture and Scottish Symphony (No. 3).

Yehudi Menuhin is a celebrated violinist born in America in 1916 of Russian – Jewish parentage. *Unfinished Journey*, from which the extract here derives, was published (by Macdonald and Jane's) in 1976.

William Meredith is an American poet, born in 1919 in New York. 'About Opera' is taken from *Earth Walk, New and Selected Poems* (Knopf, 1970).

James Miller is an early eighteenth-century poet. 'Italian Opera' comes from *Harlequin-Horace* or *The Art of Modern Poetry*, 1731.

John Milton (1608 – 74). It may be of interest to observe that Milton's father (also John Milton) was a composer of music.

Robert Minhinnick, born in 1952, is one of the best of the younger poets now living and working in Wales. 'Sunday Morning' is taken from *Life Sentences* (Poetry Wales Press 1983)

Frank O'Connor is the pseudonym of Michael Francis O'Donovan who was born in Cork, Ireland, 1903, and died in 1966. He is best known for his short stories about Ireland. 'The Cornet Player Who Betrayed Ireland' was published by Poolbeg Press and is reprinted by permission of A.D. Peters & Co. Ltd.

John Ormond was born in 1923 in South Wales. His *Selected Poems* was published (by Poetry Wales Press) in 1987. He has made many distinguished television films for BBC (Wales).

Niccolò Paganini was born in Genoa in 1782, and died in Nice in 1840. A virtuoso violinist, he introduced revolutionary technical innovations into violin-playing. The letter published here was written (from notes given to him by Paganini) by F.J. Fétis, Chapel Master to the King of the Belgians and Director of the Royal Conservatoire. It was published in the Belgian *Revue Musicale* and in Paris in 1831.

Alexander Pope (1688 – 1744) claimed that his *Essay on Criticism* which made him famous was written when he was only twelve years old. Because of his acidulous wit and invective he was called the Wicked Wasp of Twickenham.

Peter Porter, an Australian poet now living in Britain, has written many notable poems about music. The poem is taken from *Three Poems for Music* which he included in his *Collected Poems* (Oxford University Press, 1983).

Marcel Proust (1871 – 1922). Music is an important, if subsidiary, ingredient of Proust's vast novel, *Remembrance of Things Past*. The passage chosen comes from the second part of *Swann's Way*. The composer Vinteuil discussed in the piece is said to be based on the French composer Saint-Saëns.

Alastair Reid, a Scots poet who has often lived abroad, is a regular contributor to the *New Yorker*. 'A Lesson in Music' has been taken from *Weathering* (Canongate, 1978).

Anne Ridler was born in Rugby in 1912. She was at one time secretary to T.S. Eliot. Her books have been published by Faber and Faber in Britain and her *Selected Poems* by Macmillan in New York. 'Beecham Concert' comes from the volume *Some Time After and is reprinted by permission of Faber and Faber Ltd.*

Rainer Maria Rilke is the most celebrated of twentieth-century poets writing in German. He died in 1926. 'To Music' was written in Munich on 11 – 12 January 1918.

Jeremy Robson is the author of several books of poems, including *In Focus*, published by Allison and Busby, from which 'Words to a Conductor' is taken.

Jean-Jacques Rousseau was born in Geneva in 1712, and died in Paris in 1778. The extract 'Rousseau in Church' comes from Book 7 of his famous autobiographical work, *The Confessions*. In his early years Rousseau both taught music and was a music copyist. He also wrote the musical articles for Diderot's *Encyclopaedia*.

Gjertrud Schnackenberg, one of the most appealing of young American poets, was born in Tacoma, Washington, in 1953. Her poem 'The Living Room' is taken from a sequence of poems about people who lived in 19 Hadley Street at different times in different centuries. It is published in *Portraits and Elegies* (Hutchinson, 1987).

Delmore Schwartz (1913 – 66) was an American poet born in Brooklyn, New York. His *Selected Poems: Summer Knowledge* (New Directions), from which 'Vivaldi' is taken, won the Bollingen Poetry Prize for 1959. But seven years later he was living alone, neglected and disconsolate in a Times Square hotel when he suffered a fatal heart attack. Acknowledgements are owed to Laurence Pollinger Ltd.

John Scott (1730 – 83) was born in Southwark of Quaker stock. He became a friend to many London notables including Dr Johnson.

William Shakespeare (1564 – 1616). The lines quoted here come from *The Merchant of Venice*, Act V, Scene 1 and are spoken by Lorenzo.

George Bernard Shaw (1856 – 1950). 'How I Became a Music Critic' is part of a preface Shaw wrote in June 1935 to *London Music in 1888 – 9 as heard by Corno di*

Bassetto. Love Among the Artists, a chapter of which is published here, was written in 1881. While he was writing it Shaw suffered an attack of smallpox. Both extracts are to be found in the *Collected Works* (Constable). Acknowledgements are also owed to the Society of Authors on behalf of the Estate of Bernard Shaw.

John Smith was born in 1924, in England. His *Selected Poems* were published (by Robson Books) in 1982.

Louis Spohr was born in Brunswick in 1784, and died in Cassel in 1859. Spohr enjoyed a great reputation in his day both as composer and violinist. Among his works were fifteen violin concertos, thirty-four string quartets, nine symphonies and ten operas. His autobiography from which this extract is taken was published in Britain over a hundred years ago.

Wallace Stevens (1879–1955) was one of the major American poets of this century. For many years he wrote poetry 'on the side' while industriously working for the Hartford Accident and Indemnity Company. 'Mozart 1935' is reprinted by permission of Faber and Faber Ltd from *The Collected Poems of Wallace Stevens*.

Igor Stravinsky was born in Oranienbaum, near St Petersburg in 1882, and died in New York in 1971. Stravinsky's many conversations with his friend and admirer Robert Craft, recorded and published by the latter, provide insight into his views on the nature and purpose of music. *Conversations with Igor Stravinsky* from which the extract here derives, was published by Faber and Faber in 1959 and is reprinted here with their permission.

Gwyn Thomas (1913–81) was born in the Rhondda Valley, South Wales, the youngest of twelve children of a miner. He wrote short stories, novels and plays. *Gazooka*, a passage from which is published here, was published (by Gollancz) in 1957.

Leo Tolstoy (1828–1910). This extract on Wagner's opera is drawn from Chapter 13 of Tolstoy's lengthy essay *What is Art?* which first appeared in 1898 and encapsulated his views on the purpose, the quality and the necessity of art.

Ivan Turgenev (1818–83) was a Russian novelist and short story writer. 'The Singers' comes from his group of stories *A Sportsman's Sketches*, written between 1847 and 1851.

Mark Twain is the pseudonym of Samuel Clemens who was born in 1835, and died in 1910. Apart from his fiction and essays, Twain produced splendid humorous travel writings. 'At the Shrine of St Wagner, a part of which is quoted here, is to be found in the *Collected Works*, published in 1929.

Richard Wagner was born in Leipzig in 1813, and died in Venice in 1883. 'A Pilgrimage to Beethoven', the tale of an imaginary visit to the composer who died when Wagner was only fourteen, first appeared in serialized form in the *Gazette Musicale* (Paris) during November–December 1840.

Eudora Welty was born in 1909. An American writer from the Mississippi region, she is renowned for her short stories. 'Powerhouse' comes from her collection *A Curtain of Green*. Acknowledgements are owed to Marion Boyars Ltd.

Herbert Williams is a Welshman, born in 1932. He is a BBC producer and has had published several volumes of poetry.

William Wordsworth (1770–1850). Wordsworth indicated in a note that the poem, 'Power of Music' was 'taken from life'.

David Wright was born in Johannesburg, South Africa, in 1920. He was educated at the Northampton School for the Deaf and at Oxford. He has written a number of telling poems in which he refers to his deafness, 'The Musician' being but one. It comes from *To the Gods the Shades* (Carcanet, 1976).

Paul Zimmer is an American, born in 1934 in Ohio. At present he is the Director of the University of Iowa Press. 'The Duke Ellington Dream' comes from *The Ancient Wars* (Slow Loris Press, Pittsburgh, 1981).